Bones of the Ancestors

Bones of the Ancestors

The Ambum Stone: From the New Guinea Highlands to the Antiquities Market to Australia

BRIAN EGLOFF

ALTAMIRA PRESS

A division of
ROWMAN & LITTLEFIELD PUBLISHERS, INC.
Lanham • New York • Toronto • Plymouth, UK

ALTAMIRA PRESS

A division of Rowman & Littlefield Publishers, Inc.
A wholly owned subsidiary of The Rowman & Littlefield Publishing Group, Inc.
4501 Forbes Boulevard, Suite 200, Lanham, MD 20706
www.altamirapress.com

Estover Road, Plymouth PL6 7PY, United Kingdom

British Library Cataloguing in Publication Information Available

Library of Congress Cataloging-in-Publication Data

Egloff, Brian.
Bones of the ancestors : the Ambum Stone : from the New Guinea highlands to the antiquities market to Australia / Brian Egloff.
p. cm.
Includes bibliographical references and index.
ISBN-13: 978-0-7591-1159-2 (cloth : alk. paper)
ISBN-10: 0-7591-1159-6 (cloth : alk. paper)
ISBN-13: 978-0-7591-1160-8 (pbk. : alk. paper)
ISBN-10: 0-7591-1160-X (pbk. : alk. paper)
1. Enga (Papua New Guinean people)—Antiquities—Collection and preservation. 2. Ambum Stone. 3. Enga (Papua New Guinean people)—Claims. 4. Enga (Papua New Guinean people)—Ethnic identity. 5. Papua New Guinea—Antiquities—Collection and preservation. 6. Figurines, Prehistoric—Social aspects—Case studies. 7. Cultural property—Protection—Social aspects—Case studies. 8. Cultural property—Protection—Political aspects—Case studies. 9. Ethnicity—Political aspects—Case studies. I. Title.

DU740.42.E35 2008
995.6'3—dc22

2007031220

Printed in the United States of America

∞™ The paper used in this publication meets the minimum requirements of American National Standard for Information Sciences—Permanence of Paper for Printed Library Materials, ANSI/NISO Z39.48-1992.

Contents

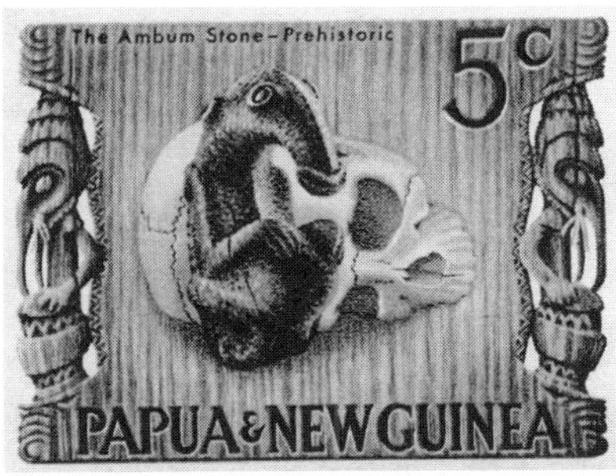

Acknowledgments

GRATITUDE: "A STATE OF GRATEFULNESS"[1]

It is said that one can see further by standing upon the shoulders of giants. As this account of the Ambum Stone spans the world and many decades, centuries, and millennia, it was imperative to obtain information through the goodwill of numerous strangers, colleagues, friends, and family, as well as adversaries. All are owed my thanks, but, as one must, I assume responsibility for my own expressions and foibles. Personalities and agents that have contributed in one way or another are listed, but I must acknowledge those individuals that have clearly gone well and truly out of their way to foster our understanding of the Ambum Stone.

Acknowledgment must be given to Polly Wiessner, who has studied the social archaeology of the Ambum Stone, as well as the Kendi brothers, who spoke openly with Polly in 2001 about their taking of a stone in 1962. Akii Tumu assisted Polly in her fieldwork and was instrumental in locating and introducing her to the Kendi brothers. Fellow academic travelers such as Chris Ballard, Ralph Bulmer, Robin Hide, Hartmut Holzknecht, Roy Mackay, Mervyn Meggitt, Jim Specht, Glenn Summerhayes, Norm Wilson, and Paul Wholt gave me their time and shared their ideas. In particular, I must acknowledge *Samting Bilong Tumbuna: The Collection, Documentation and Preservation of the Material Cultural Heritage of Papua New Guinea* by Barry Craig. This superb doctoral thesis supplied me with considerable information that was not available from any other source. Life experiences in Papua New Guinea were shared with me by Beverly Lawrence, John Coleman, Denys Faithful, Chris Vass, Father Joe Verwilt, Christina Wright, Roy Mackay, and Bishop Doug Young. Staff of the National Gallery of Australia has provided me with the incentive to undertake research into the story of the Ambum Stone. In particular, Wally Caruana, Brian Kennedy, Robyn Maxwell, and John Santolin have made generous contributions. Ian Farrington is to be thanked for providing me with a copy of the report that discusses the restitution of the Paracas textile held by the Australian National Gallery.

"Ears bashed to bits" is the only way to describe the invidious position of Bill Gammage, Jack Golson, Beata Tworek Matuszkiewicz, Juliet Ramsay, and Pamela Swadling. They also read and discussed with me parts of the story. Graeme Ward devoted many hours to a detailed editorial review of the draft of the manuscript.

Albert Speer provided me with information on the Papua New Guinea medical service, and Michelle Buxton spoke to me about her father, Keith Buxton, a former medical assistant at Wabag. Tony Corp assisted me with identifying material in the National Archives of Australia relating to the collecting activities of the commonwealth Art Advisory Board in Papua New Guinea.

Unqualified gratitude must be expressed to two individuals. First, to Pamela Swadling, who assisted throughout the investigation and in the closing moments brought to my attention valuable research notes of the late Graeme Pretty, then curator of archaeology, at the South Australian Museum that in turn led me to focus on carved stone artifacts from Wabag that had been acquired in 1965 by the Queensland Museum. Information at the Queensland Museum provides clues to the most likely scenario for the transfer of the Ambum Stone from the highlands of New Guinea to Queensland and then on to Goldman in London. A decade later the Ambum Stone was added to the collections of the then Australian National Gallery. And second, my thanks to Philip Goldman, who is unique in the world of art dealers, for in the 1950s he studied social anthropology under Phyllis Kaberry (1910–1977) at the University College, London. He also had a mission during the 1960s and 1970s to ensure that the art of New Guinea was recognized as being on a par with that of Africa and Pre-Columbian America. Philip shared with me on the phone many hours of his time, numerous e-mails, as well as the documentary information on the Ambum Stone that he had acquired. It was he who confirmed the tentative link provided by Pamela Swadling to the government officer who apparently transferred the stone from Papua New Guinea.

Paul Brennan provided photographs of prehistoric carved stones and an image of the only example of an Ambum-like stone in the possession of an Enga villager, and Geoff Hope assisted me with the map of Papua New Guinea.

Douglas Newton, who died while the story was being written, will not be forgotten, and although the book is dedicated to the spirit of the Ambum Stone, the tale really embodies much about what Douglas sought in a public gallery. As Curator of the Museum of Primitive Art in New York, he was intellectually involved with the art of New Guinea. In the 1970s, Douglas assisted the Papua New Guinea Museum and Art Gallery in its transition into a mainstream institution. In the same decade he provided sage advice to the Australian National Gallery. In the last months of his life he shared his thoughts with me, written in one instance on one of those postcards that we all have left over from past holidays. Douglas has my gratitude for sharing moments of his life with me.

Burra Valley,
April 2007

NOTE

1. Definitions are derived from the *Oxford Shorter English Dictionary* and *Macquarie Encyclopedic Dictionary*.

ONE

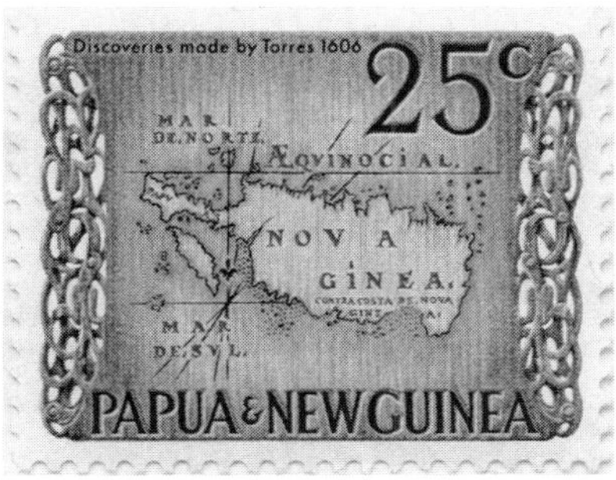

From Samting Bilong Tumbuna to Treasure

From the remote and troubled Ambum Valley of Papua New Guinea, a carved stone artifact no larger than a dinner plate was featured on the "New National Heritage Stamp Issue" of 1970. Now a treasure of the National Gallery of Australia, this artifact deserves a detailed history. For the Enga of the Highlands of Papua New Guinea these stones are the "bones of the ancestors" or *samting bilong tumbuna*: the New Guinea pidgin expression for possessions of the ancestors.[1] During the all-important cult ceremonies the stones are imbued with strong powers to ward off danger and promote prosperity and fertility. But the Enga did not carve the stone, as is implied by the term *samting bilong tumbuna*. The enigmatic Ambum Stone was carved during prehistoric times.

Archaeologists have no idea as to why the Ambum Stone was carved some 3,500 years ago. Perhaps it functioned in the prehistoric past much the same as it did in more recent times as a religious cult object. It must have been an incredibly difficult task to produce such a masterful work using only stone tools. We do not know what the image was intended to be; there has been speculation that it might have been modeled after a fetal echidna, a bird, or an extinct mega-sized marsupial. Over the years there has been a "romancing of the stone" in each of its three or four cultural manifestations. When it was carved it must have served some purpose, but just what that use might have been we do not know. Then, as an object found thousands of years later by the Enga, the Ambum Stone acquired magical properties when incorporated into their fertility cults. When the villagers believed that the power of the spirit cults had been diminished by the imposition of Australian administration and Western Christianity, and the stones of the ancestors were no longer needed, the sacred Ambum Stone allegedly was taken from the clan ceremonial ground to be purchased and publicized by Europeans. The Ambum Stone then was in the dubious position of being both the national heritage of the Territory of Papua New Guinea and, following its acquisition in 1977, a treasure of the newly constructed Australian National Gallery. For most of the following years it was on display. Unfortunately, twenty-three years after its acquisition by the gallery, the Ambum Stone was broken into three pieces when on loan to the Musée d'Arts Africains, Océaniens, Amérindiens in Marseilles.

Media coverage[2] of the breaking of the stone brought to the fore concerns about how the Ambum Stone came to be in the collections of the National Gallery of Australia, as I knew without a doubt that it was the cultural property of Papua New Guinea. I understood that the Australian gallery had purchased an artifact that, from my perspective most likely, had been exported illegally from Papua New Guinea. Multidisciplinary research over the next seven years would establish that a whole host of adventures had taken place, including, as suggested, the presumed transfer of national cultural property in contravention of ordinances that had been in place as early as 1913 for Papua and 1922 for the Territory of New Guinea. Documents acquired under "freedom of information" from the files of the National Gallery of Australia (previously the Australian National Gallery), fill in the gaps in the convoluted process that led to the Ambum Stone, the national cultural property of Papua New Guinea, becoming a treasure of the National Galley of Australia.

As H. L. Mencken said: "For every complex problem, there is a solution that is simple, neat, and wrong." The actual story of the Ambum Stone is complex, disorderly, and ambiguous.

TAINT: "A TOUCH OF DISCREDIT"

A case-study approach has been chosen as the most economical means to communicate the contentious and complex issue of tainted art: it brings together ethnographic, archaeological, and historical information within the context of museum and gallery practice, and the discipline of cultural heritage management. Generally speaking, discussions of the illicit trade in artifacts are published as a compendium of case studies, each by a different author, in an edited volume or journal monograph: often as conference proceedings.[3] An example is *Illicit Antiquities: The Theft of Culture and the Extinction of Archaeology*, initially a symposium entitled "Illicit Antiquities: Destruction and Response," held at the World Archaeology Congress in Cape Town, South Africa.[4] Other publications are dedicated to particular celebrated cases such as the illicit trade in antiquities from Italy reported by Peter Watson and Cecilia Todeschini in the *Medici Conspiracy*[5] or the Cycladic carved stone figures from island Greece studied by Christopher Chippendale and David W. J. Gill.[6]

Skeletal material has proven to be a particularly emotive issue, and a substantial body of literature has been published on the restitution of human remains.[7] There are also publications detailing legal perspectives of the trade in antiquities and the "ownership" of skeletal material.[8] Publications on antiquities and human remains have been increasing in number over the last two decades, mirroring the increasing frequency of headlines announcing in the popular press the misadventures of museum and gallery, curators and directors.

Not all of the publications are well received: *The Return of Cultural Treasures* by Jeanette Greenfield[9] was reviewed by Anthony Shelton[10] and by John Henry Merryman,[11] with the former stating:

> Greenfield's graphic view of history is pertinent when considering the more rhetorical sections of her text: "The history of the world is the history of an intricate web of universal plunder, of fetishism, and of the cannibalization of cultures." This rhetorical strain works itself through the conclusion that is largely devoted to further examples of successful restitution, with less than one page discussing the case against it, and hardly any mention of the fate of cultural property after restitution. This is not therefore a dispassionate, legalistic examination of the issues of cultural restitution, but a book that aims at a compromise solution in favor of victim states.

One could argue the same one-sided approach is a feature of publications championing the return of skeletal material. In *Collecting the Dead: Archaeology and the Reburial Issue*, Fforde is silent on the issue of what is to be gained by allowing research to be conducted on human skeletal remains, as is Jane Hubert in "A Proper Place for the Dead: A Critical Review of the 'Reburial' Issue."[12]

Who Owns Objects? The Ethics and Politics of Collecting Cultural Artefacts is an exception to the rule in that this collection of essays brings together the opinions of archaeologists, scholars, a life-long collector of considerable renown, dealers, and museum curators in a lively and informal fashion.[13] As this book, published in 2006, is the most recent and dramatic contribution to an evaluation of the licit and illicit trade in artifacts, a review of the articles will add flavor to the closing considerations of the story of the Ambum Stone.

FRESH: "TO MAKE LIVELY"

How can a case study of a single artifact seek to cover in depth and breadth such complex issues? Quite simply, because the investigation of the Ambum Stone has taken more than seven years, and the narrative extends in time through at least 3,500 years; literally spans the globe, with the tempo increasing from the early 1960s, when it was brought to the attention of Western academics, and with a spurt of activity after 2000 when it was shattered. Considerable help with the investigation has come from quite a few sources, particularly from what is known as the "New Guinea mafia"; expatriates that have in common what can only be referred to as a life-defining experience in Papua New Guinea. Just a single example: recently in my morning mail there was an envelope containing a creased photograph of an Enga man holding a carved sacred stone that is very similar to the Ambum Stone. To the best of my knowledge this photograph has never been published and is the only one of its kind. Taken in 1969, or earlier, by the late John Wormersley, the chief botanist of Papua New Guinea, the picture came into the hands of Paul Brennan, a linguist working with the Enga, and was passed on to me by Paul many decades later while this manuscript was in its final draft.

I have a somewhat different perspective from other authors that have written on the illicit traffic in cultural objects, as my interests are not purely academic. From 1972 to 1978, as part of my duties as Curator of Anthropology at the Papua New Guinea National Museum and Art Gallery, I was responsible for the enforcement of the national cultural property export controls. For six years, I went wherever there was evidence of illegal trading and export, amassing informants' testimonies and evidence, drafting reports, seizing collections, laying charges, and appearing in court. At times postcards or letters were received informing on dealers who in one way or another had angered an associate. Once a threatening note was sent to me stating that the people I was trying to apprehend were killers. A few of the more notorious cases, including the illegal export of national cultural property by personnel of the Royal Australian Navy, are mentioned later.

The story of the Ambum Stone provides a detailed and fresh outlook on the vexing issue of "who owns the past." By fresh, I mean that to the present most discussions of restitution turn over the same repetitive ground: the Elgin Marbles with respect to returning national icons;[14] the human remains found at Kennewick as an exemplar of the restitution of burials to native peoples;[15] and, the forced return of archaeological collections from Tasmania as indigenous politics clash with the scientific values of archaeologists.[16] Deep-seated within the archaeological profession, these issues have been discussed in dozens of publications.

Museums and art galleries around the world are being assailed by claims that they have objects in their collections that more correctly belong elsewhere—in their descendent communities

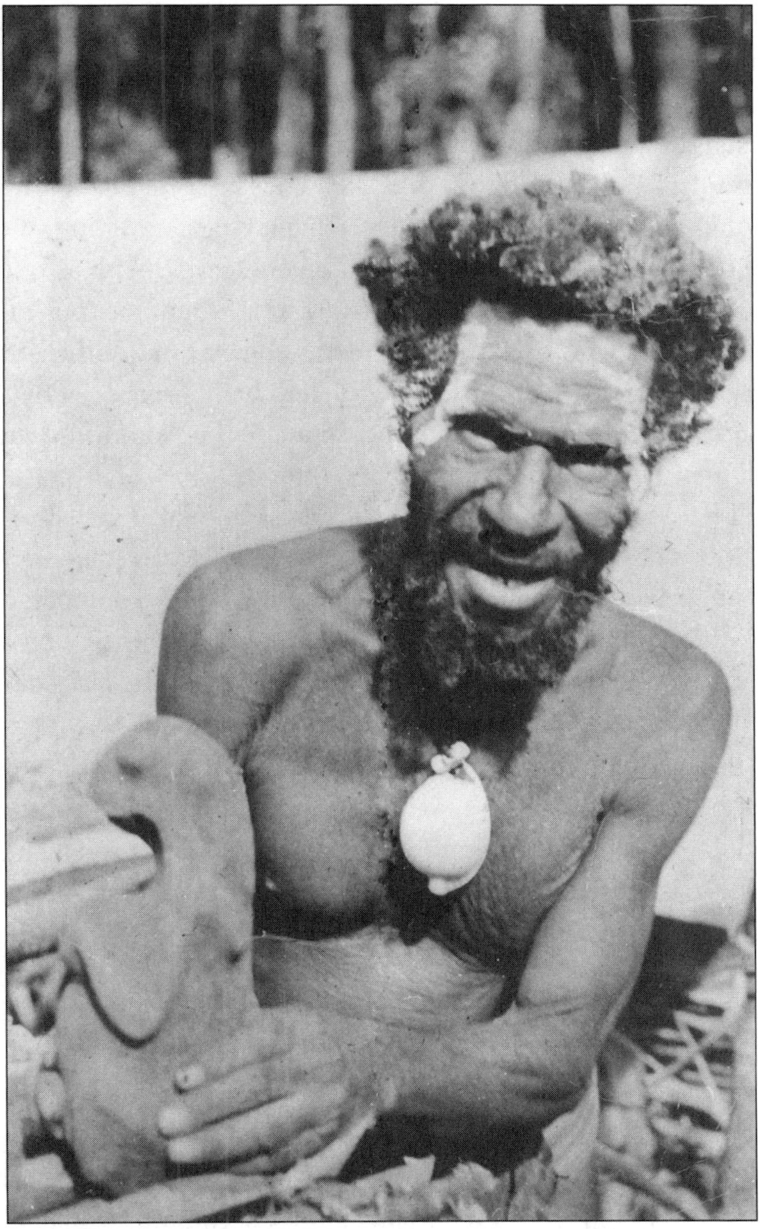

Figure 1.1. Photograph of Kanopato Taneya of clan Lilyano, taken prior to 1969 by John Womersley, chief botanist at Meriamanda, near Wabag. Courtesy of Paul Brennan and Jon Womersley.

or country of origin.[17] These issues will not go away during our lifetime. The story of the Ambum Stone is meant to offer the reader an insightful, practical, and academic basis for understanding the complexities of the international trade in ethnographic and archaeological objects. Clues are offered as to what to look for as positive approaches to managing conflicting values, and the reader is alerted to what to be concerned with as potential negative situations develop. Above all, the emphasis is on the agents: those who have participated in one way or another in the story of the Ambum Stone. I have taken the liberty of listing and describing the participants in the drama of the Ambum Stone in an appendix to this story.

There is a need at this time to place the narrative within its academic context. That will be done as briefly and painlessly as possible. Please bear with me. Depending upon your perspective, the Ambum Stone is both an ethnographic specimen and an archaeological artifact, as well as belonging to the class of cult objects referred to by the Enga of the highlands of New Guinea as "bones of the ancestors." Each academic discipline that manages and studies, collects and curates such things—anthropology, ethnology, archaeology, museology, and cultural heritage management—has a particular interest and a different perspective.

ANTHROPOLOGY: "SCIENCE OF MAN, IN THE BROADEST SENSE"

No single theoretical approach dominates this narrative; as the reader will discover, it is the search for truth and the need to manage difficult and potentially emotive situations that have guided my research. The focus of anthropology is on exploring and documenting the human experience through time and space, with one of its primary goals being to present ways of reflexively looking at ourselves through the study of other peoples' reactions to equivalent situations. Anthropology is an academic discipline that seeks to enlighten, inform, and reflect on current events; it has always dealt in a systematic fashion with the study of cultural values. As a university lecturer teaching applied anthropology, my focus is upon the notions of culture, community, change, and choice as they form and impact upon values. Values shape our responses to the range of challenges that we face every day of our lives in one way or the other as individuals, as societies, and as nations. Choices correctly made during periods of change, as we know from personal experience, are ultimately important but fraught with uncertainties and trauma.

A broad anthropological approach, incorporating the methodologies of two of the subdisciplines of anthropology, ethnography and archaeology, provides the important academic launching pad for the story of the Ambum Stone. Nicholas Thomas explores exchange of cultural materials in contemporary postcolonial societies of the Pacific.[18] Thomas asserts that individuals and societies have fashioned identities through the exchange and possession of objects, be they from the immediate present or from the distant past. Similarities were forged between Western and Melanesian societies by shared histories of colonialism and exchange.[19] We mark our personal value and enhance our collective identity as nations and communities, or as individuals, through the objects that we possess. Westerners may choose to appropriate objects from other peoples to demonstrate our worldliness or our developed sense of aesthetic taste or our economic and political ability to dominate others or as tokens of affection, friendship, and loving. Observing and participating to some degree in the lives of different peoples, and collecting and documenting the cultural materials of a single society, wherever it may be, is referred to as ethnography. When the artifacts studied are products of the past obtained through scientific excavations or chance finds, the field of study is known as archaeology or prehistory. These disciplines are subsets of the larger field of anthropology: the study of human societies as organized groups, or cultures, with customs transmitted through learning.

It might be expedient to do both ethnography and archaeology at the same time. An example of this dual approach is when the anthropologist lives in a village and studies the crafts of the villagers, their means of production and distribution, and the social and economic value of pottery. While at the same time, the archaeologist excavates the remains of the village refuse deposits, or middens, to study the antiquity of pottery making in that location. This is the kind of research that I did into ceramic production in contemporary villages in eastern Papua.[20] I then compared contemporary and historical pottery with the ceramic fragments from prehistoric archaeological deposits in the area. This kind of research is referred to as ethno-archaeology. In applying the information obtained as an ethno-archaeologist in Papua New Guinea to a contemporary situation, the acquisition of artifacts from villagers by museums and art galleries, I am practicing applied anthropology.

As the researcher moves one step further and places this information and the focus of their actions upon management and legislative frameworks, the work enters the field of cultural heritage management. Anthropology offers a broad and holistic view of human societies through cross-cultural comparisons, with the subdiscipline of ethnography being the study of particular societies, and archaeology as the study of the remains of prehistoric and historic societies. Ethno-archaeology combines the study of ethnography and archaeology, often with an emphasis on a historical perspective. There are other subfields of anthropology, each with its own professional associations and annual conferences, such as linguistics, biological anthropology, medical anthropology, and social anthropology, which offer different perspectives of the human condition. Today, rather than have a single individual work in two subdisciplines, we draw together multidisciplinary teams, and in highly contentious situations the research program may need to incorporate a specialist familiar with legal and management requirements.[21]

Applied anthropology is the application of data and theory gained through firsthand observations, usually with small social groups, to contemporary issues. Like the general field of anthropology, one of its strengths is an ability to compare similar institutions in different societies. There is a field of anthropology termed "practicing anthropology," which works outside academic agendas and theory construction to deliver a relatively immediate solution to the problems of small-scale societies. Cultural heritage management, also referred to as cultural resource management, incorporates the expertise of many disciplines (anthropology, archaeology, history, architecture, town planning, engineering, and others) and is about identifying and documenting, and more importantly safeguarding, significant objects and places. It is necessary to maintain administrative systems to conserve the things and places that our society values. Depending upon the type of heritage that we are managing, particular kinds of expertise will be incorporated into the program. An indigenous rock-art site might involve anthropologists, art specialists, linguists, and archaeologists along with, and perhaps under the direction of, the elders of the indigenous community. Cultural heritage managers are often called upon to assist in the implementation of government polices with respect to both cultural and natural resources with an aim to either rehabilitate it, relocate it out of danger, exploit it for tourism, or demolish it.

ARCHAEOLOGY: "ANCIENT PERIOD"

Archaeology is inherently a destructive process, and archaeologists know that they should be as conservation aware as is possible. This is one of the reasons why archaeologists are so troubled when they see prehistoric sites destroyed by looters. Archaeological heritage conservation and management may seem to be relatively straightforward, and one would expect that there is a universal agreement on the fundamentals of the process. However, it is apparent that archaeology in many instances is a tool that is used, or in all too many instances misused, to achieve a variety of goals, and conservation of the resource may not always be of paramount importance. Various agendas, such as political nation building, tourism enhancement, and period-specific reconstructions are well known to specialists familiar with the recent application of heritage management to archaeology. The empowerment of other stakeholders within certain contexts is hotly debated within archaeology, while embraced in other disciplines. Instances of minority or special-interest groups enhancing their position within mainstream society through the exercising of control over the archaeological record, perhaps with negative impacts on its conservation, also are found.

Pillaging of Cycladic tombs to acquire carved stone sculptures is an example of a prehistoric culture where our information is far from perfect. Chippendale and Gill discuss the intellectual consequences of the archaeological manifestation of an entire culture being destroyed.[22] Collaborative research by the two archaeologists is one of the few detailed studies of the illicit trade in one particular kind of prehistoric art object. Material and intellectual consequences of the illicit trade in artifacts are stressed in their research outcomes. Streamlined thin forms crafted from the pure white marble of the Greek island group of Cyclades are highly sought after by collectors and investors. When exhibited, the sculptures are generally displayed standing in an upright position supported by a display stand. The figures date from the Late Neolithic and Early Bronze Age circa 3300 to 2000 BCE, before the Middle Bronze Age "Minoan civilization" arose in Crete. Cycladic figures are mortuary goods added to burial tombs and were meant to be placed lying down, not standing up. As "modernist-looking," they are sought as high-status decorative art objects, perhaps in part because the figures are reminiscent of the work of modern sculptors such as Jean Arp or Constantin Brancussi.[23] Illegal excavation, or looting, leaves behind a trail of pillaged tombs with materials torn from their context. When the looted (or fake) objects are brought forward by auction houses, the paucity of information, or—just as worrying—the misinformation, accompanying the Cycladic figures means that as individual objects they do little to advance our understanding of their cultural context. Chippendale and Gill state that

> there must have been much looting in the Cycladic cemeteries to provide the present corpus of several hundred marble figures; we estimate that some 85% of the funerary record of the early Bronze Age Cyclades may have been lost through pursuit of the figures.
>
> Our calculations suggested that perhaps some 10,000 graves had been looted in pursuit of the Cycladic marble figures.[24]

The "Neocycladic harpist," a celebrated white marble figure playing a harp in the collection of the Metropolitan Museum of Art in New York, had for many years been considered by experts in the field, based upon stylistic evaluations, as one of the best of its kind. Like nearly all of the Cycladic figures it had no known provenance. Publications cited by Craxton and Warren, dating to as recent as 2002, assert that the figure is genuine and "the best preserved of its type."[25] On stylistic grounds the authenticity was questioned, with the harp being considered as too large relative to the size of the figure, that the shape of the harp was wrong, and that the harpist's hands were not correctly placed to pluck the stings.[26] In addition, there is a persuasive argument that the harpist had been carved in the early 1940s by a Greek sculptor who was asked by a presumably reputable art dealer to make a copy of a harp-playing figure. He provided a lime-encrusted patina for the Cycladic figure by immersing it in lime-rich stream waters. There is no indication that the self-taught artist, who made bas-reliefs of himself and his wife for their tomb, knew that a dealer would be passing off the sculpture as genuine.

Excavations on the island of Keros under the direction of Colin Renfrew have considerably broadened our knowledge of the ritual use of Cycladic figures. Recovery by archaeologists of fragments—that do not fit together—of marble bowls and figurines is interpreted as being representative of a place where ritual objects had been brought after they had been purposefully destroyed. The figurines could have come from sanctuaries throughout the Cycladies and at a particular point of time in the ritual cycle were ritually smashed and then brought to Keros to be deposited at a shrine.[27]

Looting and copying of high-value artworks also applies to the Apulian vases from southern Italy that feature in *The Medici Conspiracy* by Watson and Todeschini. The best place to seek a relatively intact object is not in a prehistoric rubbish dump but in the burial tombs of upper-class individuals. Scores if not hundreds of tombs must have been looted to unearth prized objects like the large and finely decorated ceramic vessels of Apulia. Fakers are active in the antiquities market, hoping to add their wares undetected to the stream of looted artifacts, as is emphasized by Chippendale and Gill:

> A colleague in the Italian *carabinieri* specialised unit for fine art and antiquities reports that seizures of illicitly excavated classical antiquities in southern Italy typically include both genuine and faked pieces, which enter the supply chain to the marketplace together.[28]

It makes perfectly good sense when you think about it, and like the Cycladic figures and the vases of Apulia, the Ambum Stone no doubt has its own imitators.

Chippendale and Gill conclude that there is a substantial problem, but none of the scenarios that they explore seems to offer a solution. It is all but impossible to confine objects to their country of origin: emphasizing national patrimony does not give due attention to the loss of information; a freeze on the trade does not seem to have any "special merit"; and the actions of governments and museums do not offer immediate hope.[29]

Cultural heritage management seeks to manage conflicting values in such a way that the least angst is caused to the concerned parties. Conflicts over ownership of highly prized objects recur in different guises through time, with each generation seeking new terms and conditions. I wish that the story of the Ambum Stone had a readily apparent outcome, but it does not. That is why it is such an appropriate and powerful vehicle for studying the nature of the trade in artifacts and the institutional approach to transactions involving objects. If you learn nothing else by reading this book, you will discover that every meaningful conflict in cultural values is likely to be more complex than could ever have been imagined at the outset.

Box 1.1

FREEDOM OF INFORMATION

The story of the Ambum Stone is unique in that the core data comprises approximately 120 documents obtained under the Freedom of Information Act, 1982, from a public art gallery. In Australia, for a fee, a member of the public can request information held in the files of national government agencies. The institution, in this instance the National Gallery of Australia, has to provide that information. To the best of my knowledge this kind of information has not previously been used to research the illicit trade in artifacts.

INSTRUMENT: "FORMAL LEGAL DOCUMENT"

Laws regulating the transfer and ownership of cultural objects are not new. For more than one hundred years the trade in artifacts has been controlled by national statutes. In the twenty-first century, antiquities and artifact laws are varied and may or may not be more stringently enforced than they were in the past with respect to the internal transfer of ownership, acquisition, export, or import of cultural property. Just how active is the policing of national cultural property laws will depend upon priorities that are given to enforcement and the capacity of the nation-state to dedicate resources to what can be a time-consuming and expensive activity. The challenge can be multiplied many times over in a nation-state like Papua New Guinea where the police force has difficulty dealing with domestic disputes and tribal conflicts and where there are extensive and easily violated coastlines, remote islands, and poor internal communications. In such circumstances it is not surprising that any institution would have difficulty in ensuring that national cultural property legislation is adequately enforced.

What has brought about the recent increased interest in cultural property? There are at least three distinct factors adding to the pressure on collecting institutions. First, there are many countries that have suffered under colonialism or during international wars. "Donor" countries and indigenous peoples have had their cultural heritage expropriated under circumstances over which they had little control. Second, there has been a concerted effort to put to right some of the errors of the past. A particular example is the wholesale misappropriation of cultural belongings during the holocaust associated with the Second World War. In trying to do so, it has become apparent that Western legislative frameworks were not at all suited to deal with historical injustices. It proved necessary to invoke international charters and conventions. International instruments rely upon the goodwill of participants and are not strictly enforceable; they require a "political will" that is often lacking.

A third aspect of the increased interest in proper management of cultural property is the growing assertiveness of indigenous peoples that had been suppressed and whose heritages continue to be marginalized by settler societies like those of Australia, Brazil, Canada, New Zealand, and the United States of America. Indigenous peoples are seeking restitution of their properties that were acquired by often devious means when there was a marked imbalance in the power structure. Forums providing indigenous representatives with a place to raise issues of restitution have been provided by UNESCO. An example of international concern is expressed by the United Nations Declaration on the Rights of Indigenous Peoples.[30]

International best practice instruments, guidelines, charters, or conventions and their effectiveness are of concern. Do they work, and if so in what instances? Following the First World War, the League of Nations sought to establish standards for heritage conservation of archaeological sites and materials and for museum objects, taking into account that there can be a fine line between an archaeological or ethnographic specimen and a work of art. The first international instrument to deal with archaeological excavations was the Cairo Act of 1937, drafted following a meeting convened by the government of Egypt and the International Museums Office.[31]

War overtook implementation of international standards. Although promptly pursued following the cessation of hostilities, it was not until the 1950s that the United Nations Education and Scientific Organization (UNESCO) resumed the momentum of the 1930s. Foremost in the collective memory of the family of nations was the wholesale appropriation and destruction of cultural property during the war. It is well known that like earlier invaders, the armies of Britain, Germany, Italy, Japan, Russia, and the United States all took opportunities afforded by the confusion attending hostilities to appropriate things that belonged to other people. Convention for the Protection of National Collections of Art and History of 1954, The Hague Convention, out-

Box 1.2

LEAGUE OF NATIONS

The League of Nations was the first international organization to seek to regulate archaeological excavations and to control the illicit trade in artifacts. Recommendations adopted in 1932 recognized the needs of local communities:

> Believing that the best guarantee for the preservation of monuments and works of art is to be found in the respect and attachment towards them felt by the peoples themselves.[1]

1 International Principals Governing Archaeological Excavations, Preliminary Report, UNESCO/CUA/68, Paris, 8 August 1955, 5.

laws the destruction and illegal acquisition of cultural property during times of war but is widely flouted, particularly during ethnic hostilities such as those of the 1990s in the Balkans. Other instruments have been promulgated such as the UNESCO Convention on the Means of Prohibiting and Preventing the Illicit Import, Export and Transfer of Ownership of Cultural Property, adopted in 1970; the yet to be ratified UNESCO 2001 Convention on the Protection of the Underwater Cultural Heritage; and the recently adopted UNESCO Convention for the Safeguarding of the Intangible Heritage, 2003. International heritage interests have been furthered in diverse ways with archaeological monuments, for better or for worse, being inscribed on the UNESCO World Heritage list.

The International Institute for the Unification of Private Law, UNIDROIT, was established in 1926 by the League of Nations and gains strength today as an independent intergovernmental organization with a membership drawn from most major countries including the United States. UNIDROIT has adopted the Convention on Stolen or Illegally Exported Cultural Objects (Rome 1995), the thrust of which is the restitution of stolen objects and the return of cultural objects removed from countries that have laws regulating the export of cultural objects. The effectiveness of this instrument has yet to be tested.

GAZE: "STEADY OR INTENT LOOK"

A more complete historical perspective of the processes of settlement and colonization of Papua New Guinea has emerged over the past two decades. When anthropology developed in the nineteenth and twentieth centuries, it sought to study peoples untouched by Western societies. By the 1950s, anthropologists had run out of "untouched societies"—the Native American family was described as comprising a "mother, father, offspring, and an anthropologist." In fact, no society has ever existed in true isolation—we just chose to act as if they had.[32] One of the foremost anthropologists of the last century, Bronislaw Malinowski, sought to look at the structure of society by closely associating himself with the "native"; his research on the Trobriand Islands of eastern Papua[33] is presented without a historical perspective—the impact of European contact was not a feature of his research. Subsequent studies noted that by the middle of the nineteenth century, well before the arrival of Malinowski in 1915, Trobriand Islanders had been contacted by European explorers and American seafaring whalers.[34] At the time that Malinowski undertook his research, government administration, plantation, and trading enterprises and Christian missionaries were well established in eastern Papua.

Anthropologists, historians, archaeologists, and geographers have begun to take a closer look at the process of colonization from the perspective of the individuals who had been colonized. Research shifted from studies of the Western experience to that of the studied society, and how the at times markedly different accounts compared with each other. When anthropologists studied the process of colonization through the eyes of the colonized, they found—not surprisingly—that there was a discrepancy between the records of peaceful pacification by government patrols and the statements of villagers who recalled the atrocities that had been committed during those encounters. A more human, more individual picture of the impact of contact with Western societies on indigenous peoples came to be documented.

The last great expeditions of exploration where Western explorers met with the previously unexplored took place in the mountain valleys of central New Guinea in the 1930s.[35] Fifty years later researchers interviewed both the explorers and the explored. Diaries, reports, legers, photographs, cine films[36] and audio recordings mark the legacy of the explorers while the villagers have memories of the encounters mapped on their territorial landscape. Government patrol reports tend to play down conflicts with villagers as pacification was intended by the administration, under the mandate of the League of Nations and later the United Nations, to be a peaceful process. But when speaking to the explored, the statements of the villagers mention rape, armed conflict, intimidation, misadventure, and the misappropriation of goods. Individualizing the accounts of change in the lives of indigenous communities has had a profound impact on the readers of ethnographies and has flowed over into the public arena. A notable example is that of Ongka, a "big man" of the Kawelka of the highlands of Papua New Guinea, immediately to the east of the Enga.[37] Andrew Strathern, an anthropologist, worked for decades with Ongka and formed a close relationship with him. Generations of anthropology students have read about Ongka, his four wives, and nine children. Central to Ongka's life are his preparations for the "last big *moka*." The *moka* is a ceremonial exchange system, similar in some but not all respects to the *tee* of the Enga, where goods are gathered through a complex network of reciprocity and then given away to bind individuals and clans to one another. But because Ongka has no inherited power, he must carry out a complex series of negotiations across a vast mountainous landscape to convince his trade partners that they should contribute valuables to the *moka*. Kawelka gain prestige by what they give away not by what they have. "Big men," or managers, reinforce their external trade links with partners in distant places.[38] Enthralled students watch on the classroom audiovisual display as Ongka negotiates his way between the traditional trade and exchange systems of the highlands and the introduced economic and political systems of British origin.[39] The human dimension is so well displayed that one cannot help but feel an affinity with Ongka.

CONNOISSEUR AND PHILANTHROPIST: "JUDGE OF ART AND FRIEND OF MAN"

Notable objects cross over a somewhat mystical aesthetic threshold and are regarded by connoisseurs as "art" and are bought and sold by commercial galleries. Directors and curators of public galleries deal with objects from both the past and the present that are regarded as having a particular aesthetic value. Often, this elusive quality, if combined with rarity, results in a high economic value. Within this complex equation there are tensions: Whose values have precedence? Is the piece authentic? Is it stolen property? Has it been tainted through myriad illegal actions? Matters spiral out of control when a collection of hundreds of objects is purchased or deeded to an institution. How can a curator possibly investigate, as is required by professional ethics, the provenance and ownership trail of every item? The Jolika collection,[40] donated to the de Young Museum in San Francisco by John Friede, has come under the scrutiny of anthropologists who have questioned how items listed as national cultural property in Papua New Guinea came to be in the collection, and how so many fine pieces of ethnographic art could have received the requisite export permits. We will return to the Jolika collection and these questions later.

REMAINS: "THAT WHICH IS LEFT OF A PERSON WHEN LIFE IS EXTINCT"

Strictly speaking, this book does not deal with human remains and burials. But that is not to say that skeletal material is not important in coming to terms with the complexities of the return and restitution process or that human remains do not have anything to contribute to our understanding of collecting, expropriation and the wider debate of who owns the past. Human remains most certainly are important and can prompt emotive issues, particularly if they are known individuals. For more than half a century, Western institutions have had to deal with the ire of peoples whose ancestral remains they have held, particularly if those peoples have not had control over how the remains are curated. Until 1947 the remains of Truganini, who died in 1876, were on display in the public museum in Hobart, Tasmania. Outrage at the insensitivity of the display of the remains of such a revered public figure brought about the removal of her skeleton from the public gaze. It was not until 1975, with considerable pressure being exerted by members of the Aboriginal community, that Truganini's remains were cremated and the ashes scattered at sea.[41]

Joe Watkins in his discussion of the Pawnee and Salina Burial Pit describes a site in Kansas where the remains of 146 people were on exhibit from the 1930s to the 1980s.[42] In 1984, an income of $20,000 was made by the exhibitors. Members of the Pawnee, Wichita, and affiliated tribes lobbied to have the site purchased and the remains reburied. In 1989, the site was purchased from the owners for $90,000 and a statute was enacted by the state legislature making it illegal to excavate unmarked graves. Over recent decades display of human remains has become unacceptable where descendents actively assert their rights to the proper treatment of the remains of their ancestors.

Cressida Fforde's *Collecting the Dead: Archaeology and the Reburial Issue* not only is an insightful and detailed account of the complex issues of the restitution of human remains but also offers a synopsis of why scientists and institutions collected human remains and continue to hold them against the demands of descendent societies:

> It is apparent from arguments put forward for their retention, that the great reluctance to repatriate ancient and fossil remains was based not only on the importance placed on them by science but also because they were perceived as simply too old and too anonymous to be viewed as ancestors, for whom living people could feel any connection or responsibility, and thus any legitimate claims over.[43]

How does the restitution of skeletal remains pertain to the Ambum Stone, a carved stone object? Simply put, in the eyes of the Enga villagers that once possessed the stone and used it in their cult ceremonies, it represents "the bones of the ancestors."

VEHICLE: "THAT WHICH SERVES AS A MEANS OF TRANSMISSION"

The Ambum Stone is an ideal vehicle with which to explore the far distant past of the highland cultures of the world's second largest island as well as the more recent colonial heritage of the Enga peoples of Papua New Guinea. It also provides us with a glimpse of the peculiar dilemma that faces individuals and institutions when dealing with circumstances arising from events during the immediate past that intrude into the present.

Certain important matters relating to the transfer and ownership are somewhat murky. The Ambum Stone clearly is valued by two distinct cultures, that of the Enga and that of Western art connoisseurs. The nature of those values is not static but changing. This narrative chronicles the conflicts that arise in situations where different cultures meet and there is an inequality of understanding and power between the colonizer and the colonized. A mixed relationship is highlighted when documenting the interchange that the Papua New Guinea Museum and Art Gallery had during the 1970s with the recently established Australian National Gallery.

Papua New Guineans, aware of the prominence that the Ambum Stone acquired by being featured on a five-cent postage stamp, thought that the artifact was in their national museum. Articles in *The Sydney Morning Herald* on 11 and 12 May 2000 reporting that the Ambum Stone had been broken on the morning of 19 April when on loan from the National Gallery of Australia to Musée d'Arts Africains, Océaniens, Amérindiens in Marseilles came as a shock.[44] Needless to say, the gallery was deeply concerned. The press reported incorrectly "that it had been broken before the gallery acquired it in 1977."[45] A report prepared in 1975 by the senior research officer, Alan R. Dodge, records "condition excellent" with no reference to repairs or restorations.[46] In August 2000, yet again the press sought to sensationalize the unfortunate breaking of the stone as the *Canberra Times* elaborated on the tragedy taking the opportunity to present the gallery in an unfavorable light claiming that it had a "Eurocentric emphasis that some gallery scholars find unacceptable." The recent appointment by the gallery of a curator of Pacific art indicates that even if that view was once present, and I highly doubt that it ever was given the presence of the Ambum Stone and other non-European masterpieces in the collections including one of the largest assemblages of Indonesian textiles in the world, the assertion does not have currency today.

FUROR: "A RAGE, CRAZE"

The national and international furor prompted by the breaking of the Ambum Stone led to questions being asked of the National Gallery of Australia by a Senate Committee. Questions focused upon procedural matters and the loans policy of the gallery. At that time, I was still concerned that the Ambum Stone had been acquired by the gallery, and suggested in a letter to the editor of the *Canberra Times* that its transfer from the Territory of Papua New Guinea in the early 1960s was of concern to me and that when purchasing the Ambum Stone in 1977 and subsequently, the National Gallery of Australia would have been well served by conducting investigations into its social context and provenance. Art editor of the *Canberra Times* Helen Musa asked me to air my concerns with curators at the National Gallery of Australia. I then withdrew the letter from publication following discussions with Robyn Maxwell and Wally Caruana of the National Gallery of Australia because I considered that, as an academic, it was my responsibility to add to the understanding of the case, not simply to repeat unsubstantiated rumors.

On 21 September 2000, the *Canberra Times* published an article, presumably based upon information supplied by the National Gallery of Australia and the letter that I had withdrawn from publication, stating that Egloff was concerned with the amount of information known about the stone prior to its acquisition by the Australian National Gallery in 1977 and was worried that there might be no further advance on the understanding of the details of the provenance and the transfer of the Ambum Stone. The article stated that the object was a national treasure of Papua New Guinea and that "In the 1970s, Michael Somare, then President of the Board of Trustees at the National Museum of Papua New Guinea, declined to purchase the Stone." The article went on to allege that "Mr Caruana and curator of Asian Art, Dr Robyn Maxwell, disputed yesterday Dr Egloff's charges, saying that he had got the sequence of events wrong. Dr Maxwell said that Australian legislation for cultural heritage agreements post-dated the gallery's acquisition of the stone. Mr Caruana and Dr Maxwell denied this was the Australian Elgin Marbles case. The gallery's founding director James Mollison had in fact written to the now Sir Michael Somare offering the museum in New Guinea first option on the stone. The museum's director subsequently wrote back to Mr Mollison suggesting that the gallery proceed with the purchase."

I emphasize that my letter to the editor was withdrawn and to the best of my knowledge was not published. One hundred twenty-two documents acquired from the files of the National Gallery of Australia under "freedom of information" provide a fascinating account of the interaction among the Australian National Gallery, the gallery owner Philip Goldman, and the Papua New Guinea Public Museum and Art Gallery during the years leading up to the purchase of the Ambum Stone in 1977. It also chronicles a lost opportunity by myself and others to explore in a more timely fashion the movement of the Amubm Stone from its presumed original location in a village ceremonial ground to the international art market. What defies the common perception of artifact dealers as being highly secretive is the publication in 1965 by Philip Goldman of all of the details that he had at that time regarding the provenance of the stone. The description of its provenance lie unverified by either the Papua New Guinea Public Museum and Art Gallery or the Australian National Gallery until some thirty five years after the publication of the article in 1965. The Australian National Gallery to its credit was proactive in seeking from the Papua New Guinea Museum expressions of interest in the purchase of the Ambum Stone, which was not a common practice in the 1970s.

A salient characteristic of the sacred ritual stones of the Enga is that they are feminine and believed to wander in search of mischief! Barry Craig, who for many years conducted ethnographic research in the highlands of Papua New Guinea, once stayed in a government residence where a sacred object was stored. A few years later after he had returned to South Australia, he telephoned the residence and asked after the whereabouts of the stone. He dialed his old number and made contact with the occupant, who told Craig that the stone, although locked away in a cupboard, had "wandered" and caused them so much distress that they got rid of it.[47]

Research in the 1990s by Polly Wiessner, an anthropologist from the University of Utah, and Akii Tumu, curator of the Enga Cultural Center, detailed the cultural context of Enga cult objects, including the provenance of prehistoric carved stone objects that are found by villagers and incorporated into their cult activities. Inquiries undertaken by Wiessner and myself during 2001, with the assistance of university academics and colleagues and present and former residents of Papua New Guinea, suggests the identity of the owners of the Ambum Stone and the particulars of its removal, transfer, and sale, and reinforce the view that there is little evidence that the stone was acquired in the Territory of Papua New Guinea through permissible means or exported with the required permit of the authorities.

Complex issues are resurfacing; there is urgency in that many of the people who were involved in the events of the 1960s and 1970s are now aging. It is my conviction that a record should be made now of the circumstances of the removal of the Ambum Stone. Was there an innocent mistake in the past? An improper purchase of the artifact by the owner of a trade store in Wabag? An illegitimate transfer of a carved stone object both within and from the Territory of Papua New Guinea? A "romancing of the stone" that has been seized upon as the truth because it is convenient?

Ethical requirements for institutions that collect paintings and artifacts have been explicitly articulated in recent decades and have been both supported and opposed by collecting institutions. More importantly, there has been a shift in emphasis, from condoning a passive role by the acquiring institution to one requiring active involvement in ascertaining the correctness of title, particularly with respect to artifacts whose origins could be tainted by a holocaust. A challenge facing the narrator of this story is how to let the truth be known without it becoming a matter that would serve to frustrate a positive outcome.

ART: "APPLICATION OF SKILL TO OBJECTS OF TASTE"

Carved from stone and said to be in the shape of a fetal echidna, the Ambum Stone has over the past three or more millennia been charged with a supernatural force that is both haunting and forceful. For some of the characters in this narrative, at times it has been central to their existence. The stone came into my life in the 1970s, when I was delegated with the responsibility of enforcing the national cultural property legislation of Papua New Guinea. It came like a wraith, surfacing, disappearing in the mists of time, to reappear and smash into my being thirty years later. But we are getting ahead of ourselves. Let us put into context the highlands, the Enga people, and the carved stone. Then we will track the wandering Ambum Stone and the lives of the people that affected its journey from the highlands of Papua New Guinea, perhaps going directly to England, or maybe it went via

Australia, to Switzerland, where its sale was finalized to the Australian National Gallery, then to France, where it was broken and returned in a semirepaired condition to Australia!

In June 2002, I discussed the Ambum Stone research with Robyn Maxwell and Charlotte Galloway, respectively curator and assistant curator of Asian art, and indicated that important information was emerging about the social context of the stone. This discussion was followed by a letter to the curators, dated 20 June 2002, that stated that the key findings of the Ambum Stone inquiry were to be presented in a paper jointly authored by Polly Wiessner and myself at the "Papua New Guinea Then and Now Symposium" at the University of Sydney.

SYNOPSIS: "GENERAL VIEW OF SOMETHING"

This writing of the story of the Ambum Stone is intended to explore the complexity of issues confronting archaeologists, anthropologists, ethnographers, curators, and museum directors. In Chapter 1, I discuss the nature of the Ambum Stone as an archaeological artifact, with its origins in the distant prehistoric past of the highlands of New Guinea some three thousand or more years ago. The Ambum Stone is presented as a vehicle that conveys the panorama of the past into the colonial period of exploration and pacification, arriving at the contemporary situation of Papua New Guinea. Immediacy is brought into the narrative through the controversy that arose when the artifact was broken in 2000 when on loan to a museum in France. Academic disciplines that contribute to the repatriation of artifacts and human remains are outlined within the context of museums and art galleries. Complex issues of ethics and the acquisition of art objects by collecting institutions are introduced in the closing section of the chapter.

Contested land and mindscapes are the subjects of the second chapter. I provide the reader with a brief history of the island of New Guinea and the development over the past 10,000 years of horticulture, including the relatively recent introduction of the sweet potato and the agricultural revolution that followed. Tribesmen of the highlands are linked through agricultural production systems, trade, and warfare to an economic landscape that has spiritual connotations. Colonization of island New Guinea is brought into focus by discussions of the early explorations of Europeans, the role of the missionaries in the pacification process, and the response of the Enga to introduced religions.

In the third chapter, I consider the conflicting values of indigenous stakeholders, collectors, and academics, within the context of the history of the Ambum Stone. The stone is an artifact of such significance to Papua New Guinea that it was pictured on a postage stamp as "New National Heritage." It's anthropological and ethnographic life as a cult object belonging to the Enga of the western highlands is considered.

Dialogue that has marked the relationship between the National Museum and Art Gallery of Papua New Guinea, on the one hand, and the National Gallery of Australia, on the other, are discussed in chapter 4 within the context of the development of the first two institutions and the legislation that governs the artifact trade in Papua New Guinea and in Australia. The case of a prehistoric Peruvian textile that was acquired by the Australian National Gallery, after being stolen in 1973 from a museum in Peru highlights the need for galleries to take a proactive stance toward documenting within their collections objects with sparse histories. Wholesale destruction of archaeological sites and the consequences for the study of past societies are taken into account in the closing section of the chapter.

"Romancing the Stone," chapter 5, commences in 1962 when the Ambum Stone was taken, then allegedly acquired by a trade store operator in Wabag, an administrative center in the Western Highlands. A short time later, the stone was obtained by Philip Goldman, a London artifact dealer. Goldman published a photograph of the stone and provided, first to the Australian National Gallery and later to me, a map of the presumed "find spot" of the artifact. This enabled Polly Wiessner of the University of Utah to visit the place and determine that the stone had not been found in a cave as had been believed by the National Gallery of Australia but is said to have been taken from the village ceremonial ground; it had been taken by two brothers who openly discussed their actions with Wiessner. Purchase of the stone by the National Gallery of Australia is discussed in the light of information obtained from the gallery files under Freedom of Information.

In chapter 6, "Fitting the Pieces Together," I consider the complexities of the ownership of the Ambum Stone and its link with *Blue Poles*, a major art work by Jackson Pollock, that also was acquired by the National Gallery of Australia. Personalities enter into the equation, particularly those of a former director of the gallery, James Mollison, and the artifact dealer, Philip Goldman, who sold the Ambum Stone to the gallery. Governance of collecting institutions is of major concern, as acquisitions continue to be made and are featured in the popular media.

"Had Enough Romance?" is the title of the concluding chapter. Here the dilemma of who owns cultural objects is discussed, and the best situation for the Ambum Stone is considered in the light of recent events in Papua New Guinea, where a considerable proportion of the stone masterpieces of the National Museum have been stolen.

The epilogue draws together the various threads of the story of the Ambum Stone and looks at them under the light of contemporary views of the illicit trade in artifacts as constituting a kind of ecology. The trail of ownership of the Ambum Stone, as it was finally unravelled after seven years of research, is revealed along with a possible scenario for how to deal with the complexities of the past.

NOTES

1. Fredrich Steinbauer. 1969. *Neo-Melanesian Dictionary*. Kristen Press, Madang, Papua New Guinea, 208.

2. Refer to Kelly Burke and Peter Gotting. 2000. "Artefact Smashed While on Loan." *Sydney Morning Herald*, 11 May, 3; Burke and Gotting. 2000, "Precious Artefact Broken by French Was Already a Bust." *Sydney Morning Herald*, 12 May, 3; and Helen Musa. 2000. "No Blarney Gallery Chief May Be Left Holding the Gnomes." *Canberra Times*, 21 August, C4.

3. Refer to Neil Brodie, Jennifer Doole, and Colin Renfrew (eds.). 2001. *Trade in Illicit Antiquities: The Destruction of the World's Archaeological Heritage*. McDonald Institute Monographs, Cambridge; Elazar Barkan and Ronald Bush (eds.). 2002. *Claiming the Stones, Naming the Bones: Cultural Property and the Negotiation of National and Ethnic Identity*. The Getty Research Institute, Los Angeles; Peter Gathercole and David Lowenthal. 1990/1994. *The Politics of the Past*. Routledge, New York; Barbara T. Hoffman (ed.). 2006. *Art and Cultural Heritage: Law, Policy and Practice*. Cambridge University Press, Cambridge; and Phyllis Mauch Messenger. 1991. *The Ethics of Collecting Cultural Property: Whose Culture? Whose Property?* University of New Mexico Press, Albuquerque.

4. Neil Brodie and Kathryn Walker Tubb (eds.). 2002. *Illicit Antiquities: The Theft of Culture and the Extinction of Archaeology*. Routledge, London.

5. Peter Watson and Cecilia Todeschini. 2006. *The Medici Conspiracy: The Illicit Journey of Looted Antiquities from Italy's*

Tomb Raiders to the World's Greatest Museums. Public Affairs, New York.

6. Christopher Chippendale and David W. J. Gill. 2000. "Material Consequences of Contemporary Classical Collecting." *American Journal of Archaeology* 104: 463–511.

7. Refer to Cressida Fforde. 2004. *Collecting the Dead: Archaeology and the Reburial Issue*. Duckworth, London; and, C. Fforde, J. Hubert, and P. Turnbull (eds.). 2002. *The Dead and Their Possessions*. Routledge, London.

8. Refer to articles in the *International Journal of Cultural Property* and Hoffman, *Art and Cultural Heritage*.

9. Jeanette Greenfield. 1989/1996. *The Return of Cultural Treasures*. Cambridge University Press, Cambridge, 309.

10. Anthony Shelton. 1997. Book review of Jeanette Greenfield, *The Return of Cultural Property [sic]*. In *International Journal of Heritage Studies* 3(2): 126–27.

11. John Henry Merryman. 1998. Book review of Jeanette Greenfield, *The Return of Cultural Treasures*. *International Journal of Cultural Property*, 7(1): 283–84.

12. Refer to Fforde, *Collecting the Dead*; and Jane Hubert. 1989. "A Proper Place for the Dead: A Critical Review of the 'Reburial Issue.'" In Robert Layton (ed.), *Conflict in the Archaeology of Living Traditions*. Routledge, London, 131–66.

13. Eleanor Robson, Luke Treadwell, and Chris Gosden (eds.). 2006. *Who Owns Objects? The Ethics and Politics of Collecting Cultural Artefacts*. Oxbow Books, Oxford.

14. Refer to Isabel McBryde. 1985. Introduction. In Isabel McBryde (ed.), *Who Owns the Past?* Oxford University Press, Oxford, 4–6; David Wilson. 1985. "Return and Restitution: A Museum Perspective." In McBryde (ed.), *Who Owns the Past?* 104–6; Timothy Webb. 2002. "Appropriating the Stones: The 'Elgin Marbles' and English National Taste." In Barkan and Bush (eds.), *Claiming the Stones, Naming the Bones*, 51–96; Anthony Snodgrass. 2004. "The Parthenon Marbles as an Archaeological Issue." In Neil Brodie and

Catherine Hills (eds.), *Material Engagements: Studies in Honour of Colin Renfrew*. McDonald Institute Monographs, Cambridge, 115–24; and, Kate Fitz Gibbon. 2005. "The Elgin Marbles: A Summary." In Kate Fitz Gibbon (ed.), *Who Owns the Past: Cultural Policy, Cultural Property and the Law*. Rutgers University Press, New Brunswick, NJ, and London.

15. Refer to Patty Gerstenblith. 2002. "Cultural Significance and the Kennewick Skeleton: Some Thoughts on the Resolution of Cultural Heritage Disputes." In Barkan and Bush (eds.), *Claiming the Stones, Naming the Bones*, 162–97; Heather J. H. Edgar, Edward A. Jolie, Joseph F. Powell, and Joe E. Watkins. 2007. "Contextual Issues in Paleoindian Repatriation: Spirit Cave Man as a Case Study." *Journal of Social Archaeology* 7(1): 101; and, Laura Jane Smith. 2004. *Archaeological Theory and the Politics of Cultural Heritage*. Routledge, London and New York, 156–73.

16. See Sarah Colley. 2002. *Uncovering Australia: Archaeology, Indigenous People and the Public*. Allen & Unwin, Crows Nest, NSW, 68–71; Hillary du Cros. 2002. *Much More Than Stones and Bones*. Melbourne University Press, Melbourne, 104–16; and Smith, *Archaeological Theory and the Politics of Cultural Heritage*, 187–93.

17. *The Independent*. 2002. "Museums Face New Clamour to Return 'Plunder.'" *Canberra Times*, 1 April, 8.

18. Nicholas Thomas. 1991. *Entangled Objects: Exchange, Material Culture, and Colonialism in the Pacific*. Harvard University Press, Cambridge, MA.

19. Chris Gosden and Chantal Knowles. 2001. *Collecting Colonialism: Material Culture and Colonial Change*. Berg, Oxford and New York, 5.

20. Brian Egloff. 1979. *Recent Prehistory in Papua*. Research School of Pacific Studies, The Australian National University (Terra Australis, 4).

21. Brian Egloff, Nicolas Peterson, and Sue Wesson. 2005. *Biamanga and Gulaga: Aboriginal Cultural Association with Biamanga*

and Gulaga National Parks. Office of the Registrar, Aboriginal Land Rights Act 1983, Surry Hills, New South Wales.

22. Chippendale and Gill, "Material Consequences of Contemporary Classical Collecting."

23. From http://en.wikipedia.org/wiki/Cyclades (accessed on 28 January 2007).

24. Chippendale and Gill, "Material Consequences of Contemporary Classical Collecting," 463, 499.

25. John Craxton and Peter Warren. 2004. "A Neocycladic Harpist?" In Brodie and Hills (eds.), *Material Engagements*, 109–13

26. Peter Watson. 2000. "How Forgeries Corrupt Our Top Museums." *New Statesman* 13(637): 14–15.

27. From www.msnbc.msn.com/id/16418552 (accessed on 9 April 2007).

28. Chippendale and Gill, "Material Consequences of Contemporary Classical Collecting," 495.

29. Chippendale and Gill, "Material Consequences of Contemporary Classical Collecting," 505.

30. Available at http://daccessdds.un.org/doc/UNDOC/LTD/G06/128/65/PDF/G0612865.pdf?OpenElement (accessed on 6 May 2007).

31. International Museums Office. 1940. *Manual on the Technique of Archaeological Excavations*. International Institute of Intellectual Co-operation, Paris.

32. James R. Denbow. 1984. "Prehistoric Herders and Foragers of the Kalahari: The Evidence for 1500 Years of Interaction." In Carmel Schrire (ed.), *Past and Present in Hunter Gatherer Studies*. Academic Press, Orlando, FL, 175–93.

33. Bronislaw Malinowski. 1922. *Argonauts of the Western Pacific*. Routledge, London.

34. Brian Egloff. 1978. "The *Kula* before Malinowski: A Changing Configuration." In J. Specht and J. P. White (eds.), *Trade and Exchange in Melanesia*. Special issue, *Mankind* 11:429–35.

35. For examples of this genre see Bill Gammage. 1998. *The Sky Travellers: Journeys in New Guinea 1938–1939.* The Miegunyah Press of Melbourne University Press, Melbourne; and Edward L. Schiefelin and Robert Crittenden. 1991. *Like People You See in a Dream: First Contact in Six Papua Societies.* Stanford University Press, Stanford, CA.

36. Refer to Bob Connolly and Robin Anderson. 1987. *First Contact: New Guinea's Highlanders Encounter the Outside World.* Penguin Group, New York; and *First Contact*, a film directed by Bob Connolly and Robin Anderson produced in 1983.

37. Andrew Strathern (ed.). 1979. *Ongka: A Self-account by a New Guinea Big-man.* St. Martin's Press, New York.

38. Polly Wiessner. 2002. "Egalitarian Structures and the Institutionalisation of Inequality Among the Enga." *Current Anthropology* 43(2): 233–69.

39. Ernest Vincze, Charlie Nairn, Andrew Strathern, and Pattie Winter. *Ongka's Big Moka.* Video recording. Granada Television International, London.

40. John Friede et al. 2005. *New Guinea Art Masterpieces from the Jolika Collection of Marcia and John Friede* (2 vols.). Fine Arts Museums of San Francisco in Association with 5 Continents Editions, Milan, Italy.

41. Colley, *Uncovering Australia*, 59.

42. Joe Watkins. 2000. *Indigenous Archaeology: American Indian Values and Scientific Practice.* AltaMira Press, Walnut Creek, CA, 105–15.

43. Fforde, *Collecting the Dead*, 155.

44. Alain Nicolas. 2000. *L'art des Papous et des Austronésiens de Nouvelle-Guinée*, Scala, Marseille.

45. Musa. 2000. "No Blarney," C4.

46. Freedom of Information documents provided by the National Gallery of Australia, FOI document 26.

47. Barry Craig, Personal communication.

TWO

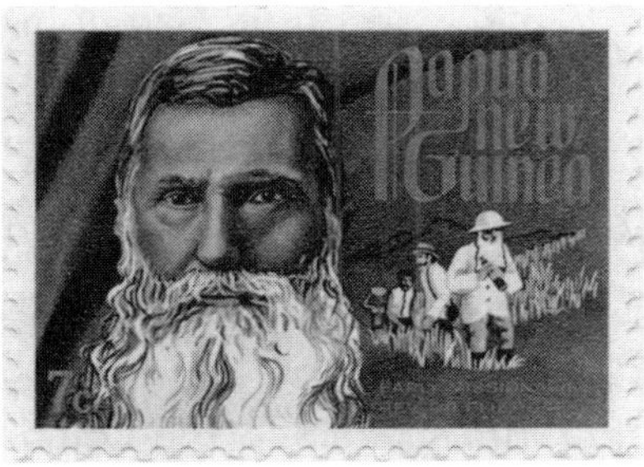

Contested Landscapes and Mindscapes

New Guinea is a relatively recently formed island landscape of lofty mountains, deeply incised valleys, and a coastal plain marked by fetid swamps that take your breath away, or are just as likely to infect you with tropical ulcers, malaria, and dengue fever. Rugged is one of those words that does not do justice to the highlands of New Guinea. Exhilarating is perhaps a better term. For this is a landscape where on a rainy night when you step outside your hut a downpour so intense that it feels akin to being under a waterfall assaults you. Then the next day, the skies are so clear that they seem to open up to eternity, and you feel as if you have been uplifted in body and soul into that clarity.

HISTORY: "RECORD OF PAST EVENTS"

The first European sighting of New Guinea is thought to have been by a Portuguese mariner in 1511. A survey of the north coast was conducted in 1545 by Ynigo Ortis de Retes, who named the island "Nueva Guinea."[1] In 1569 New Guinea, as an island to the north of Terra Australis, was inscribed on the map published by Geradus Mercator.[2] Pamela Swadling has compiled a fascinating account of early contact with the Spice Islands in her *Plumes from Paradise: Trade Cycles in Outer Southeast Asia and Their Impact on New Guinea and Nearby Islands until 1920.*[3] The search for cloves led to contacts with Arab, Indian, and Malay traders, with spices and plumes flowing into the trade networks of ancient Rome and China. In 1828 the Dutch claimed the west of New Guinea following abortive attempts by themselves and the British to foster outposts on the far western tip of the island. The Netherlands government in 1875 adjusted their claim to include all the territory as far to the east as 140°47' east longitude.[4]

A tripartite division of the island came about in the 1880s as Germany sought territory in the Pacific and the Australian colonies became anxious over the fate of New Guinea to their immediate north. The British government had little interest in further colonies in the Pacific and refused a request by Queensland, New South Wales, and South Australia to acquire lands in island New Guinea. The issue was brought to a head when a Queensland resident magistrate was sent from Thursday Island to raise the British flag at Port Moresby. While the claim soon was repudiated by the British parliament,[5] in 1884 the UK government bowed to the inevitable and the Protectorate of British New Guinea was established in 1885. In 1899 the German government reached an agreement with their trading companies in the Pacific islands to administer German New Guinea and assumed direct control of the colony, which came to include the Caroline and Mariana Islands, and Nauru. The extent of the colony was extended in 1906 to include the Marshall Islands to the northeast of Micronesia. Initially, the administration of British New Guinea was undertaken through the government of Queensland with the other Australian colonies contributing to the cost. Shortly after the federation of Australia in 1901, the Papua Act of 1905 transferred governance of the Territory of Papua to the Commonwealth of Australia.

At the outbreak of the First World War in 1914, Australian troops invaded German New Guinea and, as part of the following peace settlement, Australia was awarded the Mandated Territory of New Guinea and Nauru by the League of Nations. The administrative center of Papua was in Port Moresby, and of New Guinea at Rabaul on the eastern extremity of the island of New Britain. Districts with administration centers as well as subdistrict and patrol posts were established. Joint administration of Papua and New Guinea occurred during the Second World War when ANGAU (Australia New Guinea Administrative Unit) was formed. After the close of the war, the Territory of Papua and New Guinea was established with the administration based

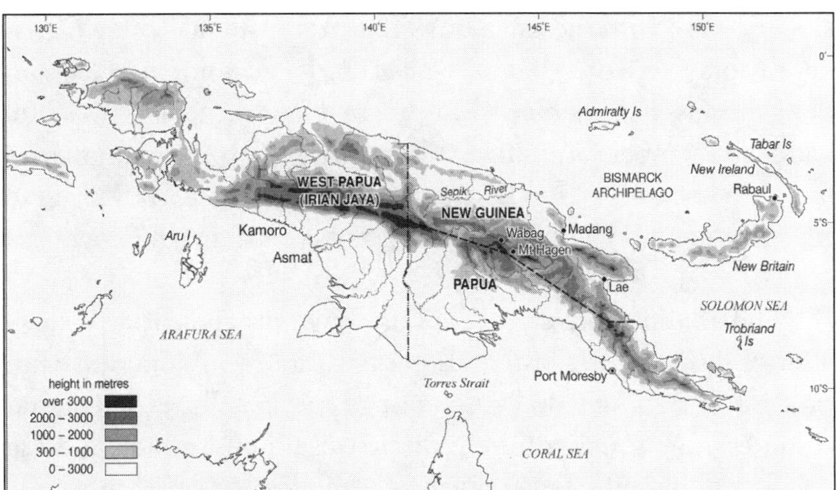

Figure 2.1. Map of Papua New Guinea. Courtesy of Kay Dancey.

at Port Moresby. The highlands were one of the last areas to be brought under the control of the administration. In the 1960s local government authorities were established; this led to self-government of the territory with an elected House of Assembly, followed by independence in 1975. Papua New Guinea, like Australia, is a parliamentary democracy with the head of state being the hereditary monarch, Queen Elizabeth II. Shortly after independence, the districts were designated as provinces, some were renamed, and the administration of the country was partially decentralized.[6]

Some seven hundred languages are spoken in Papua New Guinea, and as such most administrative units include numerous language families. The Enga Province was established in 1971 out of the western-most portion of the Western Highlands Province. Because of their large numbers, Enga speakers overshadow all other language speakers in the Enga Province. The census of 2000 lists the population of the Enga Province, with the highest and most rugged landscape in Papua New Guinea, as 289,299.[7] The Lutheran Church—Missouri Synod—commenced its missionary work with the Enga in 1948 at Yaramanda. Today Christianity plays a considerable social and educational role with the Gutnius (Good News) Lutheran Church having 138,000 baptized members and 204 active pastors. Catholic missionaries from The Society of the Divine Word moved from Mt. Hagen to the Enga area in 1947, and the Dioceses of Mt. Hagen now have 47,549 members.[8]

The administrative center of the Enga Province is at Wabag. The central and eastern portions have more in common with each other than they do with the Enga speakers living at a higher altitude in the rougher terrain to the west. The Ambum and Lai rivers dominate the lower reaches of the landscape as they flow southeastward parallel to each other before merging at Wabag.

From there, the Lai River continues to Wapenamanda, where it turns abruptly northeastward to join the Sau River which, in turn, takes a northwestern direction and joins the Yuat River. In a sluggish and meandering fashion the Yuat crosses the flood plain of the northern coast of New Guinea to flow into the mighty Sepik River. The flow of these highland rivers to the north coast serves to connect the Enga region more firmly with that region of New Guinea than with the south coast.

HORTICULTURE: "CULTIVATION OF A GARDEN"

Early anthropologists and colonial administrators alike appear to have misjudged the Enga and overemphasized the tribesmen's propensity for strife and warfare. Wars serve to uphold the honor of the clan and to resolve conflicts that cannot be dealt with through ritual exchange, debt repayments, or negotiations. To the Enga, what is all-important is status acquired not by aggression in war but by competition through exchange in the *tee* ceremonies. At the highly ritualized *tee*, hundreds of pigs and other valuable luxury commodities such as marine shells, traded into the highlands along complex and ancient routes, entered into the elaborate exchange systems. Today these exchanges feature not only pigs, produced through a massive surplus of agricultural produce, but the national currency, the kina,[9] and occasionally even motor vehicles. The *tee*, like the *moka* of their Melpa neighbors to the east in the Mt. Hagen area, is a system seemingly designed to maintain a tangled web of interdependent indebtedness within a landscape of surplus. Above all, the exchanges serve to reinforce the status of the clan and its leaders.[10]

Elsewhere in the highlands, families have resided in hamlets since European contact, but the Enga continue to live in dispersed rural farmsteads in close proximity to their gardens. Labor-intensive gardens of sweet potato, taro, banana, sugar cane, pandanus, and mixed greens are fenced to exclude marauding domestic sows and wild boars. Casuarina trees dot the cultivated fields, providing both firewood and shade for shelter-seeking plants. Eric Waddell opens his 1972 account of the Enga with, "Central Highlands people live in a profoundly horticultural world."[11] Waddell's research in the 1960s was centered on Wapenamanda, a government administration post linked by road to the major center of the Western Highlands Province, Mt. Hagen. In this locality the Enga prefer to situate their gardens on the natural terraces above the river gorges and below the steep slopes of the Main Range. Characterized by Waddell as mound builders, the Enga are agriculturalists at the very edge of tropical horticulture, experiencing both temperature and altitude limitations and marked population pressures. Waddell explores two conflicting theories, one, that the introduction of the sweet potato brought about a revolution in food production, and the other that looks at the prehistoric data and expresses change as a gradual evolution of systems that had been in place since well before the arrival of the sweet potato.[12]

Excavations by teams led by Jack Golson of The Australian National University, in the broad and fertile Wahgi valley near Mt. Hagen, provide us with some of the earliest evidence for prehistoric managed agricultural landscapes in the world.[13] Here in the 1930s traces of what appeared to be ditches were detected on the valley floor with the aid of aerial reconnaissance. Excavations demonstrated that these are the remains of what started out as a rather straightforward agricultural drainage system but had been overlaid over many millennia by systems of increasing complexity. The monumental size and extent of the ditches suggest that, in order to maintain them, there would have been a system of authority and group participation. One of the constituents of the ditch infill was ash that came from volcanic eruptions, just what is needed for dating. The ash enabled archaeological dating of the initiation of the drainage system to 9,000 years ago. On a world scale, this date is comparable with those for early agriculture in Central America, Southwest Asia, and the Indian subcontinent.

At the time of Australian colonial contact, the mid-1930s, the valley floor was not cultivated and was considered to be an unsafe "no-man's-land." The highlanders preferred to slash and then burn the fallen vegetation of the mountain slopes and river terraces rather than to cultivate the valley bottoms. Botanists understand that the sweet potato is a relatively recent arrival to the island of New Guinea. Most likely about 300 to 350 years ago tubers were brought from its homeland on the Pacific slopes of South America via the Portuguese in the Moluccas Islands. Arrival of the sweet potato meant that taro no longer was the preferred carbohydrate staple, as in the cool climate of the highlands the sweet potato was a more productive source of starch. In turn, poorly drained valley lands with their millennium-old ditches that regularly had to be cleared of silt, once tailor-made for taro crops, were no longer sought after for agricultural purposes and became wastelands. What once had been an exceptionally valuable resource with a history of up to six to eight thousand years of hard labor with wooden spades and sharp-pointed digging sticks, became, upon the arrival and widespread adoption of the sweet potato as a cultigen, a valueless tangle of plant regrowth.

Piecing together the ideas of Golson, Waddell, and Wiessner, it is possible to reconstruct the sequence of events that changed the tropical highland forest into a productive horticultural landscape. Like Australia, the island of New Guinea was populated by at least 50,000 years ago. By 20,000 to 30,000 years ago

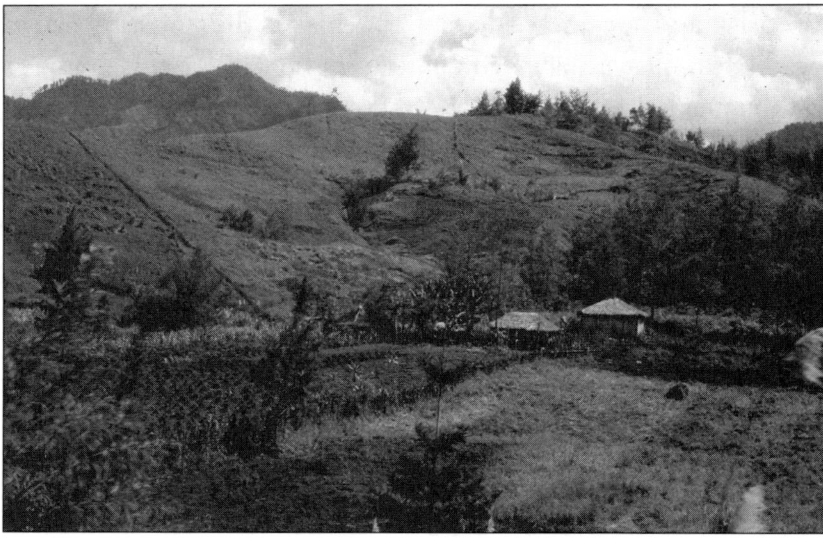

Figure 2.2. Gardens and homes in a highland valley. Photograph by the author.

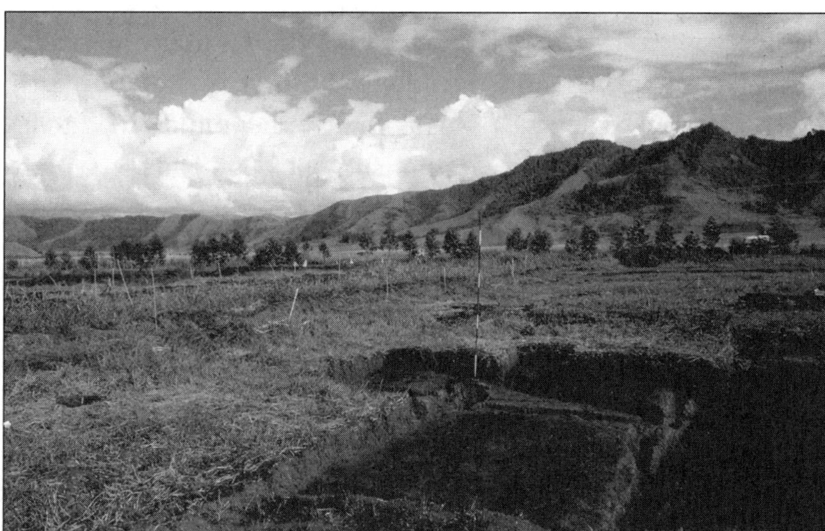

Figure 2.3. Excavations at Kuk Tea Plantation, showing recent stages of prehistoric water-control systems. Photograph by the author.

people had entered the highlands as hunters and gatherers. Collecting usable plant materials, foraging for wild foods, and trapping animals would have been the first human use of the highland landscape. In the process of gathering the readily available primary resources, the new settlers would have intensified the production of the more desirable commodities by tending food plants and nut-bearing trees, developing stone-axe quarries, and maintaining clear of debris the few and highly sought after saltwater soaks. As the forest was used on a more frequent basis, semipermanent hunting-and-gathering shelters would have been built along the most frequently used pathways or where there were resources that took some time to gather and semi-process. By 10,000 years ago there was widespread occupation of the highlands. Shortly thereafter, cultivation of plant foods began as the landscape around what had been the shelters of hunters and gatherers were lightly cleared using ring-barking, slashing and burning to expand horticulture into what, over following millennia, was to become an ever-diminishing forest.

After five or eight or twelve years of cultivation, when the soil of the gardens was exhausted, new plots were semi-cleared with the ashes from recently burnt brush adding to the fertility of the soils. But the old gardens did not readily return to forests: more likely they became patches of grassland, eventually bringing about a local shortage of wood not only for building shelters and fencing gardens, but also for the cooking fires that warm the houses on cold nights. About 7000 BCE the island of New Guinea was separated from Australia when the Torres Strait was flooded. The pig most likely arrived after this separation because it did not enter Australia prior to European colonization. Horticulture would have intensified about 4,000 years ago when cultivars that were not native to the forest were intensely cultivated; these included taro, sugar cane, and banana, all of which require moist but well-drained soils for optimal growth. Now the drainage of damp valley bottoms became a feature of horticulture in some, but definitely not in all, areas of the highlands. Here we see two kinds of gardens develop: the mixed garden and gardens especially cultivated for taro. Digging and maintaining the drainage channels would have required a collective effort beyond that of the extended nuclear family, probably involving closely related family lineages. Expansion of grasslands rather than forest regrowth follows the succession of slash-and-burn horticulture, as it is easier to prepare forestlands for gardening than it is to turn over the thick turf of the anthropogenic grasslands.

According to Bayliss-Smith and Golson,[14] forest regrowth suppresses the taro beetle (*Papuana* spp.) that devastates taro crops (*Colocasia esculenta*). The taro beetle thrives on grassland plants but does not do well in with the forest or swamp wetlands. Also, the beetle does not have a great impact on the sweet potato crop (*Ipomea batatas*). Generally speaking, Papua New Guineans have more than one garden of mixed plants, primarily taro, bananas, and yams, in different stages at any given time. In some locales, the highlanders would most likely have both wetland and dry-land gardens. The wetland gardens would be drained to plant taro, then allowed to flood from time to time and lie fallow to control the beetle population. After some years, the drainage ditches would be cleaned out and the garden replanted in taro and other crops. Digging the ditches and keeping them cleaned out was a labor-intensive task, and the workers would expect a return commensurate with their labor input. Maintaining lengthy drainage ditches would have required some degree of social control if the network was extensive enough to have served several garden plots. For the dry lands, where yams would also have been grown, a garden would be planted in cleared and burned forest lands. This would present to the villager a fertile plot of land that was relatively free of insects. When the plot had lost its fertility and insects were becoming bothersome, the garden would be abandoned and grass would colonize the cleared forestland. Grasslands are difficult to cultivate, and they also have an abundance of the taro beetle. The growth of beetles could be inhibited by the establishment of a forestlike environment of casuarinas, which would also provide the villagers with building materials for houses and fences.

The relationship between the environment, people, crops, and pigs has been the subject of several studies; seminal works are by R. A. Rapport; Bill Clark; Eric Waddell; and, more recently, Paul Sillitoe.[15] Aside from the dog, the pig was the only domesticated animal available to the peoples of Papua New Guinea, although they did maintain cassowary, possum, and other animals taken alive from the forests. What makes the pig such an interesting animal is that it eats the same kind of food as humans and in a similar quantity.[16] If your human population expands, more food production is required. And if pigs as prestige items as well as a source of food during ceremonial times are added to the productivity equation, a considerably greater amount of produce is required. As the garden area is expanded, the forest is diminished and the opportunities to hunt wild pigs are diminished. Until the arrival of Europeans in the highlands, the work of gardening was done with wooden digging sticks; in the wetlands paddle-shaped spades were used to turn the soil and clear the drains, and the stone axe was used to fell brush or to ring-bark trees. Of perhaps equal importance was the use of the axe to make fencing that would exclude wild pigs from the gardens. Gardens would have required an enormous amount of labor. The majority of the day-to-day work was done by women and older girls. Men did the axe work. The rhythm of all would have changed considerably in the 1930s and 1940s when both women and men adopted the newly available steel bush knives and small shovels.

With the introduction of the sweet potato some 300 to 350 years ago, there was an expansion of horticultural activity to what had previously been marginal slopes and forest. The sweet potato is hardy and easily out-produces taro, and a surplus can be used as fodder for pigs. Within 300 years of its introduction it came to dominate the agricultural systems of the highlands. In some places in the highlands the sweet potato is used exclusively as fodder and taro remains the primary crop for human consumption. Watson stresses that:

> pig-keeping implies a different schedule of wants from those of pure cultivation . . . makes rapid adoption of the sweet potato comprehensible, even inevitable.[17]

The highland population expanded through natural reproduction and by immigration from surrounding groups. Forest in close proximity to settlements began to disappear, and soon their resources could only be obtained through trade or travel. As forest products such as the cassowary—required for bride-price in marriage arrangements—and the bird-of-paradise plumes—essential for ceremonial body decorations—became difficult to acquire locally, exchange networks were expanded to places where agriculture had not markedly altered the landscape. Just when pigs began to be a feature of the horticultural life of the highlands is not known, but like taro, the pig most likely came from a Southeast Asian homeland. The Enga came to focus more and more of their productive capacity on converting sweet potatoes into pigs.

As this change occurred there was a need to maintain connections between speakers of a common language, as they spread into a markedly diverse and at times isolating terrain. Within this sequence of landscape change, societal changes were necessary, as increasingly dispersed populations sought to maintain their networks. Interaction networks were driven on the one hand by a surplus and on the other by a need for exotic goods. Stone axe blades were essential, and luxury goods such as marine shells, tree oils, and bird plumes much sought after. Exchange networks developed to fulfill these needs and spread throughout the lands of the Enga speakers, creating ties with far distant dialect groups. In more recent times, ancestral cults developed that acted to reinforce group cohesion as well as promote change and adaptation. Change for highlanders is set within a system where the ability to persuade and negotiate is a mark of status as well as essential in harnessing the productive capabilities of the group. The maintenance of ceremonial exchange systems to moderate aggression and promote the unfettered exchange of goods is of paramount importance.

Revolution and evolution are the two opposing theories for the impacts both of the cultivation of taro as a garden crop in the highlands and the more recent introduction of the sweet potato. Both terms, evolution and revolution, carry emotional baggage and are not particularly well defined. I prefer the term change, to describe the highlanders' conscious and calculated choices based upon how new crops would reinforce or expand their value systems.

PEOPLE: "TO OCCUPY AS INHABITANTS"

Enga women marry into the man's clan, and at the time of the 1979 census, there were 110 females for every 100 males. Some men had more than one wife; a shortage of wives was to some extent compensated for by women marrying at a young age while men married later in life. Eric Waddell writes:

> The primary social and economic unit is normally the elementary or composite family, often with other individuals attached to it. Throughout the succeeding discussion it will be termed the "household." Each is associated with a territory or "residence," comprising one or more houses, and a number of fragmented holdings, referred to as the "farmstead." Male and female members of a household generally occupy separate but adjacent houses. However, the association between household and farmstead is not a strict one for, in the case of polygamous families, individual wives and their children may live some distance apart, producing and consuming much of their food separately. Similarly there are considerable variations in the degree to which the activities and interests of attached members are integrated. Nevertheless all activities are characterized by the fact that ultimate authority in matters of food production, consumption, and distribution and in membership of the household is vested in a single person, the husband or "household head."[18]

Sweet potato gardens are situated on slopes of up to forty-five degrees, where it is difficult to stand, much less to cultivate crops. For the most part the garden plant stock is reproduced vegetatively, requiring each family to have four to five gardens at various stages of maturity at any one time. To grow sweet potatoes, a portion of the vine is planted; with bananas it is a shoot from the base of the stalk that is cut off and replanted; and for taro, a portion of the tuber is put into the new garden. Before the introduction of European axes and shovels, the only tools used were the stone axe and a pointed wooden digging stick that might be paddle-shaped at the other end. One of the more labor-intensive gardening activities is building fences of sharpened wooden stakes. Fences became more important as the Enga shifted from taro, which pigs are not attracted to unless it is cooked, to the cultivation of sweet potatoes that pigs thrive upon. As sweet potato production is at levels of up to ten kilograms per person per day and no one eats that much and it cannot readily be stored, it is converted into pig meat on the hoof. Waddell found that women spent markedly more time in sweet potato cultivation and household work such as cooking, with men involved in land clearing and fencing, house construction, and collecting firewood.[19] He estimated that roughly up to twelve hours each week would have been saved by the use of steel axes, mostly in the men's realm of clearing land, fencing and obtaining materials for house construction.[20]

For the Enga, labor is in short supply and they welcome additions to their work groups. A household of an influential person might consist of three wives, half a dozen children, and an attached widow or spouse of a failed marriage. Adding members to your household is one means of increasing production. Because labor was in short supply, the Enga relied on exchange partners in neighboring clans to finance their exchanges and paid them back at a later date. In the 1960s, influential families might have contributed a dozen or more pigs to the tee,[21] but ten years later in the 1970s they might have given up to two hundred.[22] It is important to emphasize here that 80 or more percent of these pigs were obtained from exchange partners in neighboring clans who had to be repaid.[23] Waddell estimated that as much as two-thirds of the sweet potatoes are fed to pigs. The pig population among highland groups is often said to exceed the human population and traditionally, pigs are almost never consumed for ordinary dietary purposes; they are exchanged and the flesh distributed and then eaten within a ceremonial context.[24] On the other hand, the possession of pigs increases one's status and social standing and gives a "big man" the all-important power to negotiate within a potentially explosive social milieu. As Waddel writes:

> A secondary function of the *tée*, not evident in the festivals themselves, is the economic one of facilitating the distribution

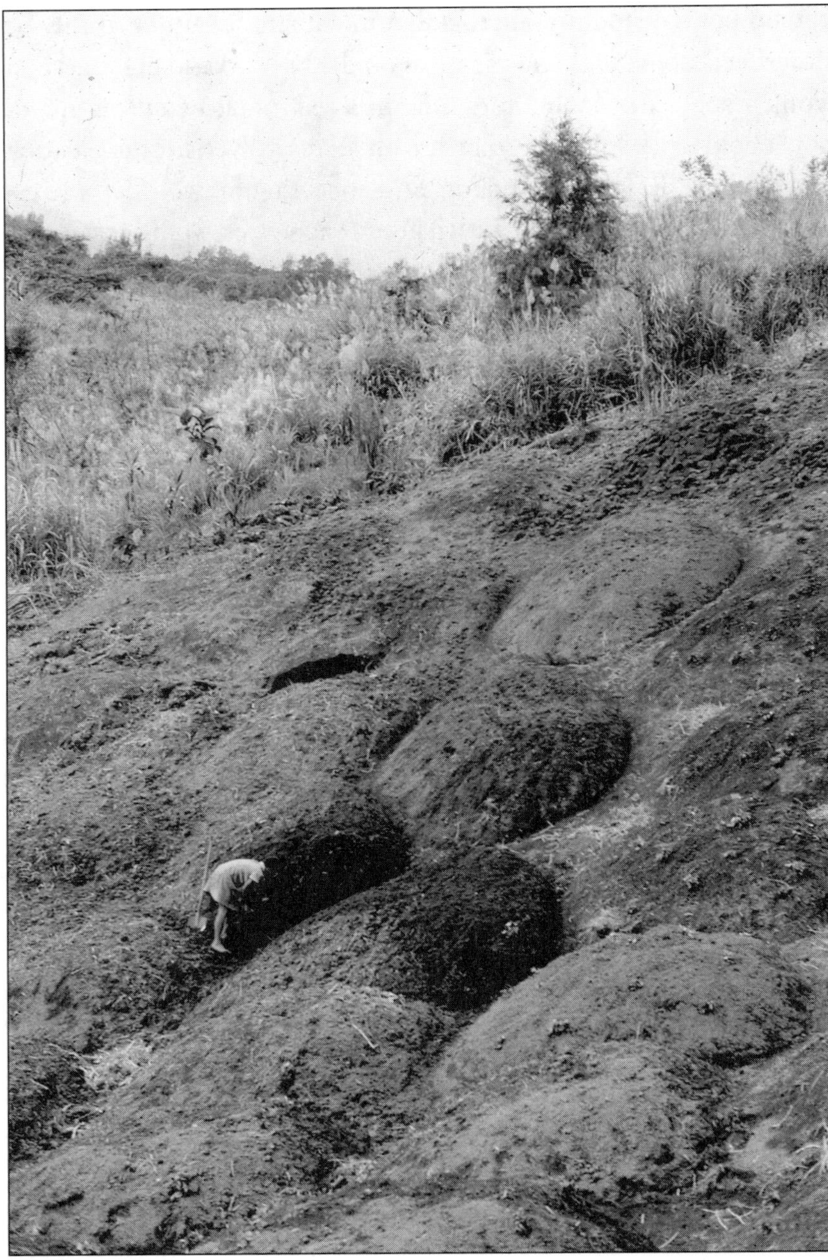

Figure 2.4. Recently cultivated sweet potato garden with composted mounds on a steep slope in the vicinity of Wabag. Photograph by the author.

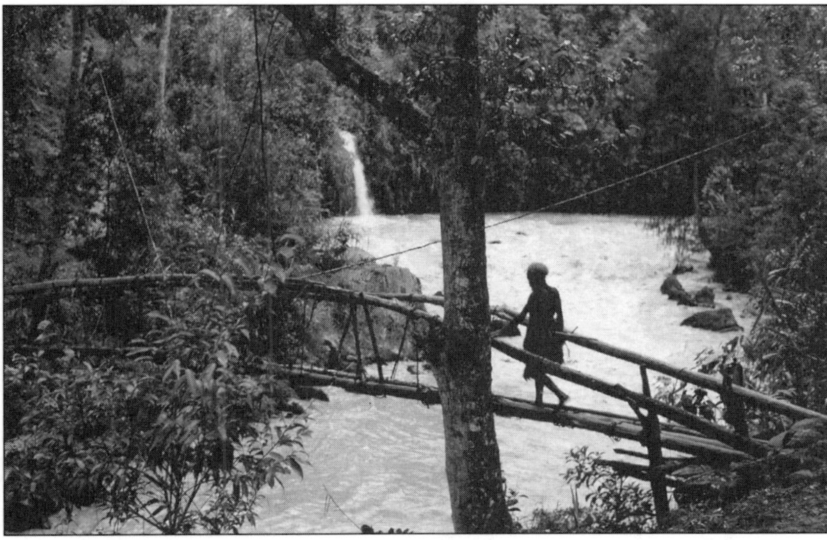

Figure 2.5. Man crossing bridge made of bush materials near Wabag. Photograph by the author.

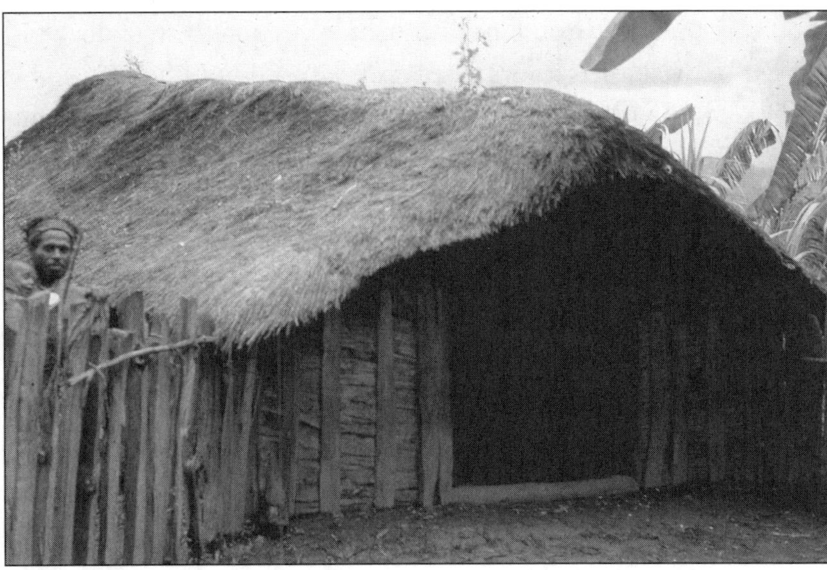

Figure 2.6. Enga man and his house made from locally available materials. Photograph by the author.

> of such locally scarce resources as salt, tree-oil, feathers, shells, cassowaries, drums, spears, and (traditionally) stone axes, by means of informal exchanges effected through the network of *káita minígi*.[25]

When first viewing Enga from a distance, what strikes your eye is the rugged verdant landscape. As you come closer to the scattered homesteads, the nearby gardens dotted over the landscape come into focus. Then there are the open truckloads of elaborately decorated Enga on their way to *tee* ceremonies, hopefully not to war. Ominously, there might be a few puffs of scattered smoke on the hillsides, and one is told that those are houses that were set on fire during clan fighting. For Meggett, war was a mechanism to expand boundaries.[26] Wiessner questions that war was simply a quest for additional land: it more likely was to keep one's enemies at a distance, as often they had no one to populate any conquered area. War, in her words, more often was to solve problems and maintain equality, balance, and respect between neighbors so that exchange could flow.[27]

Wiessner and Tumu were interested in how the Enga remembered their past as narrated in the oral record of origin traditions and genealogies. The core of their 1985–1988 fieldwork developed into a ten-year study of the precolonial history of the Enga. To reach informants they had to traverse rough terrain intersected by steep, narrow valleys, moving through a patchwork of houses, gardens, groves of casuarina trees, grasslands, ceremonial grounds, local markets, and trade stores; invariably there was one form of ceremonial activity taking place at all times within the study area. Often the team would arrive after a two- to four-hour exhausting hike at the place where there was known to be a person with traditional knowledge, only to find that the elder was absent from the village or in fact had gone to Wabag, where Akii and Polly had just come from. The history of the *tee* (*tée*) ceremony was the initial focus of their research; their finding that the exchange networks were restructured each generation put to rest the notion that these were people whose way of life had not changed for thousands of years. They tried to visit and record the historical traditions of all of the major groups, some 110 tribes, including 18 that were regarded as recent immigrants. The tribes encompass 800 clans.

Day-to-day life focused on the family. When husband and wife come from different clans, the family gains important political alliances for defense and aggression as well maintaining and expanding the position of the family within trade networks. For instance, if you want to be involved in the import salt trade based on the few salt soak springs in the district, you marry into a family that is already part of that exchange system and you do your best to minimize conflict and maximize economic returns. As in our Western world, the economics of trade and the politics of warfare merge one into the other.

Wiessner and Tumu discovered more than they had expected; their *Historical Vines*[28] is one of the great epics of anthropological research in New Guinea. As the genealogies and oral histories unfolded, they found that they were dealing with origin stories that encompassed the settlement of the land, often by mythical ancestors in the form of snakes, spirit people, and marsupials. A substantial part of their research touched upon the cults that had been developed by the Enga to communicate with their ancestors. It is one of these cult rituals that the Ambum Stone was a part of. The changing shape and nature of these rituals is embedded in Enga stories. Also, portrayed often in vivid detail, are the recollections of great wars and the elaboration of the *tee* ceremonial exchange system. Enga talk much of warfare, ritual, exchange, and their origins. They discuss what is important to them, and to some extent what they are uncertain about, as well as those things that they wish to air their views about.

Enga distinguish fictive myth (that is constantly updated by the teller) from historical traditions based upon eyewitness accounts, which are supposed to be transmitted accurately.[29] Oral histories go back in some genealogies eight to twelve generations and the recitation of a single myth can go on for an hour.[30] In the rougher lands to the west there is more emphasis in the myths on hunting and forest activities. Sweet potato is for the most part not a focus of the origin legends, while taro, sugar cane, and pandanus are. Here, taro is the predominant food plant, and the gathering of pandanus nuts is also important.[31] Most Enga are now Christians, but prior to conversion their religion was based upon two kinds of spirit beings: the "sky people" and the "ancestors." They expended considerable effort upon communicating with the ancestors, and ceremonies to propitiate the sky people involved processes of change and control by the male leaders. History matters, and the leaders who have a good command of historical precedence and events can embellish and add to their all-important oratory skills. Historical knowledge "is thus an important source of power and influence for Enga people."[32]

DEMAND: "URGENT REQUIREMENT"

Demand is often taken as a given. It is not a matter of chance that some commodities are more sought after than others! In "The Centre Cannot Hold: Trade Networks and Sacred Geography in the Papua New Guinea Highlands," Ballard questions if whether demand as a driving force has been emphasized sufficiently compared with the generation of a surplus that must be distributed. Studies of the subsistence systems of the highlands of Papua New

Guinea have tended to emphasize production of sweet potatoes whose surplus is converted into pigs.[33] Ballard looks at notions of how groups organize themselves on the landscape to meet their subsistence, exchange, and spiritual needs. He finds an emphasis upon the physical nature of the relationship between people and the landscape and little stress upon the sacred or cosmological values that are embedded in "country." Here reference is to the indigenous Australian term country for the lands to which they as individuals and as members of a group "belong." It is important that emphasis is placed upon the individual belonging to the land rather than the land belonging to the person. Highly spiritualized, the concept of country calls upon ancestral spirits and direct ancestors as well as notions of birth, descent, marriage, and occupation. The ancestral spirits provided unique landforms and valued materials such as stone for axe blades, and ochre for decorative and ritual purposes. Landscape as a spiritual concept is of a similar order in Papua New Guinea, but the cosmological forces governing the social landscape are seldom considered by academics. Ballard, based upon his research with the Huli of the southern highlands, notes that all landscapes are social and that what he is referring to is a landscape of ritual and trade. He quotes the epic study by Ian Hughes of highland New Guinea trade networks:

> The "natural scarcity" or "ecological model" of trade adopted by early studies in Highland New Guinea views trade largely as an adaptive means of redistributing scarce or unevenly distributed resources as part of the process of human adaptation to a number of contrasting environments.[34]

Searching for a considerably broader definition of social landscapes, Ballard recognizes that Hughes is in part correct in stating that trade does redistribute scarce resources, but points out that there are other factors at work in stimulating trade. A concept that the "universe is itself constructed upon a notion of exchange between living humans, and ancestral and non-ancestral spirits" is all pervasive, and

> much of the Huli ritual performance involved the conceptual exchange of pork or pig fat with these spirits in an attempt to maintain the stability of the universe and restore fertility to the ground.[35]

Restoring fertility and appeasing the spirits with pig fat resonates in the Enga cult rituals associated with the "bones of the ancestors." Land, the same as human relationships with the spirits, tends to become depleted and needs to be energized through rituals as a matter of course and much more importantly during periods of hardship or strife. Cult rituals place the highlanders at the center of their universe, with the ritual leaders being strengthened through spiritual connections and thereby able to coordinate production and exchange events over a vast secular and sacred landscape. Concepts of a sacred landscape for the Huli are reinforced through the main trade routes being described as "root of the earth."[36] Rituals not only restore fertility to the earth but also renew the knowledge of the elders that managed the rituals. Renewed or energized knowledge is in turn applied by the leaders to the management of the exchange system, with pigs being the nexus between the cosmology and the earthly landscape of the Huli.[37] Pigs are then the manifestation of the successful management of the relationship between the spirits and the landscape.

SKY PEOPLE: "EUROPEANS"[38]

By one of those odd quirks of fate we have a remarkable record of the first European contact with the highlanders. James Taylor, a government officer, and Mick and Dan Leahy, gold miners from Australia, entered the Central Highlands in the early 1930s; they recorded with photography and motion pictures their arrival and the dismay of the villagers at seeing their first Europeans. Fifty years later their recordings received universal acclaim when incorporated into the film *First Contact* and the book by the same title.[39] Bill Gammage describes the first major expedition by the Papua New Guinea administration into the highlands. It was led by James Lindsay Taylor, John Russell Black, and Callaghan (Pat) Baird Walsh. In 1938, walking westward from its starting point at Mt. Hagen, the patrol went through places known today as Wapenamanda, Wabag, Laiagam, Porgera, Lake Kopiago, Telefomin, and then to the headwaters of the May River and Ambunti on the Sepik River. Concluding in 1939 at Mt. Hagen, this was indeed one of the last great epic journeys of exploration. Perhaps because it happened so close to the entry of Australia into the Second World War, its significance went unrecognized until recently. In *The Sky Travellers* we have an account of that expedition as it passed northwestward up the Ambum River to loop to the west and then return to the base camp at Wabag.

Patrolling in the Highlands was no easy task, as tracks were elusive and the irregular mountainous terrain often called for detours around obstacles that took days if not weeks. Carriers were recruited locally as well as brought with the patrol and paid in small cowrie shells, *girigiri*, at the rate of five per hour. Communications were always a problem. The patrol carried a bulky radio to keep in touch with the post in Mt. Hagen. Due to language difficulties, at times the local guides could only guess where the sky travelers wanted to go. Patrol members were not the first sky people to enter Enga country, as "in February–March of 1934 Ludwig Schmidt and Helmuth Schultz rampaged though Enga's north, kidnapping women and shooting locals." Justice was done and "on 25 March 1936 Schmidt became the only white man hung in the Territory for offences against New Guineans."[40] These early misadventures left a legacy of distrust. However, for the most part the patrol was welcomed.

While they rested and reprovisioned at the recently established patrol post and airstrip at Wabag, the patrol soon wore out its welcome. Remember that this was no elite tightly knit group of well-trained explorers. At any one point in time the patrol could comprise between 200 to 250 men including guides; carriers, both local and recruited from elsewhere; numerous tribesmen along for the jaunt and hint of adventure; servants; interpreters; and accompanying women. But, and this is a big but, there might be less than half a dozen officers and a dozen policemen to manage the patrol as well as deal with an at times restive local population that could assemble thousands of warriors at any moment. And then there were equally large numbers of seemingly innocent onlookers who came to gape and stare at the sky travelers.

More importantly, they ate the same things as pigs and as a group consumed up to two-thirds to a ton of sweet potatoes each day. On the move they had to carry not only their gear but also backup rations and continually search out additional food sources. Gold-lipped pearl shells and metal axes and knives were used to trade for foodstuffs. Clans living around Wabag wanted to maintain a monopoly on the goods of the sky travelers; they tried to keep more distant clans away from the patrol camp in order to secure the profitable position of middlemen. Food in close proximity to the camp rose in price as it became scarce. And, human nature being what it is, the men became restless and sought entertaining diversions from the routine of camp life. The strict rule imposed by the officers was to pay for what you obtained, and the policemen were to enforce this rule. But at times they did not. In fact, on more than one occasion they were the perpetrators of some very nasty crimes. Pat Walsh, who was left to manage the camp at Wabag when the other officers went further afield, found the camp troublesome and difficult to control; raids conducted by the police were kept secret from him. In one instance, four police with thirty-five carriers undertook a pig-hunting raid with disastrous consequences. One of the perpetrators, an armed policeman, was killed and his rifle and ammunition taken. Not only was there an unaccounted firearm but soon an estimated 6,000 Enga gathered around talking of raiding the camp. Some degree of control was achieved when more government officers, including Ian Downs with his golf clubs, and police arrived at the poorly formed airstrip and talks to restore peace got under way with the Enga.

People are not as predictable as we would like, and even after all of the misdeeds that were inflicted on the Enga, there were instances of extraordinary generosity and honesty. When Ian Downs and Pat Walsh returned to Wabag after undertaking further patrols, Ian was welcomed back with a joyous festive dance like a long-lost brother. His camp was in perfect order, the doors to the huts had been boarded up and everything within was kept safe, even the rubbish tip was intact.[41]

FAITH: "CONFIDENCE IN A PERSON OR THING"

Although government patrols had entered the lands of the Enga in the late 1930s, the Second World War interrupted the process of contact, pacification, and development. It was not until 1944 that the then military administration, ANGAU,[42] sought to open trails and establish regular patrols. After the war, patrol officers and assistant district officers administered the area, bringing about a rapid and effective change. Various missionaries augmented the efforts of the civil authorities.

Agricultural practices, as well as the endemic warfare of the Enga, were of concern to administrators and others as they dealt with matters of land ownership. Mervyn Meggitt, an anthropologist then at the University of Sydney, was the first social scientist to work extensively with the Enga. He brings forward a puzzling and alarming historical pattern of warfare that fits well with what we know about the changing significance of the Ambum Stone. Meggitt asserts that, from roughly 1955 until the early 1960s, warfare waned among the Enga as they laid aside their ceremonial practices and looked toward the colonial government to adjudicate their disputes in courts. Thus cult objects such as the Ambum Stone may have lost some of their value, particularly to the younger generation.[43] This was a period of active civil administration, with the building of roads, aid and patrol posts, and the consolidation of a subdistrict center at Wabag. However, conflicts that the administration thought were based in land disputes continued to simmer.

Recent research by Polly Wiessner leads her to conclude that what motivates the Enga is exchange. It supplies the wherewithal necessary for basic needs such as bride wealth, compensation, funeral expenses, and the myriad payments that plague the budgets of all families. For exchange to flow between groups, balance and respect must be established between clans; without these, stronger parties will not keep obligations. Wiessner argues that among other things warfare is a way of solving problems, avenging insult and injury, so that balance is reestablished and exchange can flow. The key here is that Enga place emphasis on the distribution and management of wealth, not accumulation.[44] Land is not in short supply, it is labor that is sought, and for Enga it is a necessity to finance their distributions of wealth through exchange with neighbors.

Within this highly charged atmosphere of exchange and warfare, ritual objects such as the Ambum Stone served to reinforce clan solidarity and to present a unified identity to competitors as well as aggressors.

NOTES

1. Barry Craig. 1996. *Samting belong tumbuna: The Collection, Documentation and Preservation of the Material Cultural Heritage of Papua New Guinea*. Unpublished doctoral thesis, Flinders University of South Australia, 48.

2. Noel Gash and June Whittaker. 1975. *A Pictorial History of New Guinea*. The Jackaranda Press, Milton, Queensland, 9.

3. Pamela Swadling. 1996. *Plumes from Paradise: Trade Cycles in Outer Southeast Asia and Their Impact on New Guinea and Nearby Islands until 1920*. Papua New Guinea National Museum, Boroko, in association with Robert Brown & Associates (Qld.) Pty. Ltd.

4. Gash and Wittaker, *A Pictorial History of New Guinea*, 21 and 57.

5. Gash and Wittaker, *A Pictorial History of New Guinea*, 57.

6. Hilary Rowell. 1998/2002. "A History of PNG Records." In Peter Nagle (ed.), *Papua New Guinea Records 1883–1942*. National Archives of Australia, Appendix 4.

7. From http://en.wikipedia.org/wiki/Papua_New_Guinea (accessed on 30 January 2007).

8. From The Religious Television Association of Papua at www.rtapng.com.pg/genb.htm (accessed on 30 January 2007).

9. In 2005 the kina was valued at approximately 0.40 U.S. dollars.

10. This discussion relies heavily upon correspondence with Polly Wiessner in order to adjust the text to correctly reflect the emphasis that the Enga have on exchange competition versus warfare.

11. Eric Waddell. 1972. *The Mound Builders: Agricultural Practices, Environment, and Society in the Central Highlands of New Guinea*. University of Washington Press, Seattle.

12. For examples, James B. Watson. 1967. "Horticultural Traditions in the Eastern New Guinea Highlands." *Oceania* 38(2): 81; Waddell, *The Mound Builders*, 11; and Paul Sillitoe. 1983. *Roots of the Earth: Crops in the Highlands of Papua New Guinea*. New South Wales University Press Limited, Kensington.

13. Jack Golson. 2000. "A Stone Bowl Fragment from the Early Middle Holocene of the Upper Wahgi Valley, Western Highlands Province, Papua New Guinea." *Australian Archaeologist: Collected Papers in Honour of Jim Allen*. Coombs Academic Publishing, The Australian National University, 231–48.

14. Tim Bayliss-Smith and Jack Golson. 1992. "A Colocasian Revolution in the New Guinea Highlands? Insights from Phase 4 at Kuk." *Archaeology in Oceania* 27: 1–21.

15. Roy A. Rapport. 1968. *Pigs for the Ancestors: Ritual in the Ecology of a New Guinea People*. Yale University, New Haven; W. C. Clark. 1971. *Place and People: An Ecology of a New Guinean Community*. University of California Press, Berkeley; Wadell, *The Mound Builders*; and Paul Sillitoe. 1983. *Roots of the Earth: Crops in the Highlands of Papua New Guinea*. New South Wales University Press Limited, Kensington.

16. Bayliss-Smith and Golson, "A Colocasian Revolution in the New Guinea Highlands?" 16.

17. James B. Watson. 1977. "Pigs, Fodder, and the Jones Effect in Postipomoean New Guinea." *Ethnology* 16: 60.

18. Waddell, *The Mound Builders*, 20–21.

19. Waddell, *The Mound Builders*, Table 25.

20. Waddell, *The Mound Builders*, 112.

21. Daryl K. Feil. 1984. *Ways of Exchange: The Enga Tee of Papua New Guinea*. University of Queensland Press, St. Lucia. Feil has a detailed perspective of the roles played by individual Enga within the tee system.

22. Waddell, *The Mound Builders*, 110–11

23. Polly Wiessner. Personal communication.

24. Waddell, *The Mound Builders*, 62.

25. Waddell, *The Mound Builders*, 108.

26. Refer to Mervyn Meggitt. 1958. "The Enga of the New Guinea Highlands." *Oceania* 28: 253–330; Meggitt. 1967. "Patterns of Leadership among the Mae Enga of New Guinea." *Anthropological Forum* 2: 20–35; and Meggitt. 1977. *Blood Is Their Argument: Warfare among the Mae Enga Tribesmen of the New Guinea Highlands*. Mayfield Publishing Company, Palo Alto, CA.

27. Polly Wiessner. 2002. "The Impact of Egalitarian Institutions on Warfare among the Enga: An Ethnohistorical Perspective." Paper prepared for the project: War and Society from an Archaeological and Social Anthropological Perspective, Seminar on Warfare in the South Pacific: Strategies, Histories and Politics, Moesgaard Museum, University of Aahaus, Denmark.

28. Polly Wiessner and Akii Tumu. 1998. *Historical Vines: Enga Networks of Exchange, Ritual, and Warfare in Papua New Guinea*. Smithsonian Institution Press, Washington, DC, and London; and, Tumu, E. Minion, A. Kayaks, and P. Wiessner. 1989. *A View of Enga Culture*. Kristen Press, Madang, Papua New Guinea.

29. Polly Wiessner. Personal communication.

30. Wiessner and Tumu, *Historical Vines*, 18

31. Wiessner and Tumu, *Historical Vines*, 38–39.

32. Wiessner and Tumu, *Historical Vines*, 25–27

33. Roy A. Rapport, *Pigs for the Ancestors*.

34. Cris Ballard. 1994. "The Centre Cannot Hold: Trade Networks and Sacred Geography in the Papua New Guinea Highlands." *Archaeology in Oceania* 29: 131; and, Ballard. 1995. *Death of a Great Land: Ritual, History and Subsistence Revolution in the Southern Highlands of Papua New Guinea*. Unpublished doctoral thesis. The Australian National University.

35. Ballard, "The Centre Cannot Hold," 133.

36. Ballard, "The Centre Cannot Hold," Figure 5.

37. Ballard, "The Centre Cannot Hold," 146.

38. In the 1930s, when Europeans entered the Ambum Valley in the highlands of Papua New Guinea, they were referred to as "sky

people," a form of supernatural being. See Bill Gammage. 1998. *The Sky Travellers: Journeys in New Guinea 1938–1939*. The Miegunyah Press of Melbourne University Press, Melbourne. On the flyleaf of our household copy of *The Sky Travellers* is the inscription, "Julie thanks for putting up with Brian, Bill 13 August 1998."

39. Refer to Bob Connolly and Robin Anderson. 1987. *First Contact: New Guinea's Highlanders Encounter the Outside World*. Penguin Group, New York; and, Bob Connolly, Robin Anderson, and Richard Oxenburgh. 1984. *First Contact* (video recording). Arundel Productions, Glebe, New South Wales.

40. Gammage, *The Sky Travellers*, 153–54.

41. Gammage, *The Sky Travellers*, 159, 165.

42. Australia New Guinea Administration Unit.

43. Meggitt, *Blood Is Their Argument*, 153.

44. Refer to Wiessner, "The Impact of Egalitarian Institutions on Warfare among the Enga"; and Polly Wiessner. 2002. "Egalitarian Structures and the Institutionalisation of Inequality among the Enga." *Current Anthropology* 43(2): 233–69.

THREE

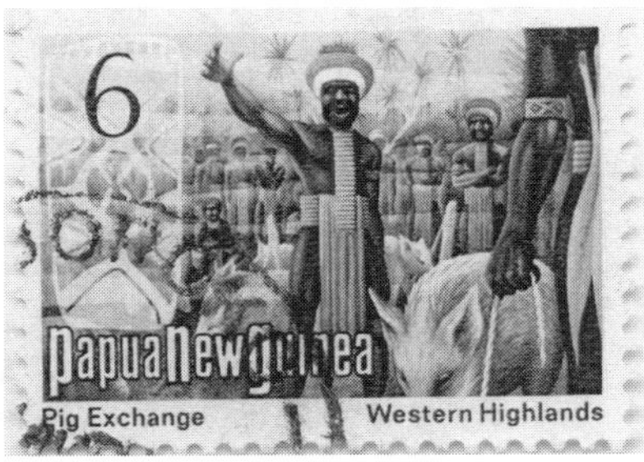

Emotions and Responses

Great works of art, like beautiful and cultured individuals, invariably invoke strong emotions. Exceptional creations can inspire, perplex, and arouse the connoisseur, as well as evoke envy, avarice, and admiration in the collector. Blend these visceral reactions together and a concoction is created that has fueled many a tale of adventure as well as reams of academic papers. All too often, emotions create a desire to possess the beautiful and the unique, seemingly driving collectors beyond all reason to acquire masterpieces, heedless of advice, with little regard for the price, and seemingly oblivious to what the consequences of their actions may be. No matter who we are or what cultures we belong to, objects send us signals. The more awe-inspiring the object is, the more powerful the message will be. At times the messages are all but irresistible and seem to sanction less than correct actions, emitting a force that is virtually a law unto itself.

CHAPTER THREE

COLLECTOR: "ONE WHO COLLECTS SPECIMENS, WORKS OF ART, CURIOSITIES, ETC."

One of the many characteristics that the Dutch, English, and Germans have in common, aside from the origins of their languages, is that they are acquisitive and have amassed extensive collections of cultural materials from their former colonies. So rich and varied are the cultures of the island of New Guinea that through the years they have fallen prey to collectors not only from the homelands of the colonizers but from a wide variety of other countries including Australia, Denmark, France, Hungary, Italy, Japan, New Zealand, Sweden, Switzerland, the United States, the Vatican, and Imperial Russia and its successor state the Soviet Union. Dramatic and awe-inspiring collections in international museums have had their origins in the villages of island New Guinea. Collections were acquired by all manner of explorers, missionaries, government officials, museum curators, adventurers, dealers, businessmen, and tourists. Their motives were various: to cleanse the villages of idols; demonstrate the kinds of things that the people in the colonies used in their everyday lives; as seizures of weapons of hostile peoples; as loot from conquest; by scholars seeking to illustrate artistic patterns; to situate groups on the evolutionary ladder, or to demonstrate specific kinds of technology such as maritime, pottery-making, and wood-carving skills. Reasons why we acquire exotic things are endless. Sadly, in only a few instances were the early collections of the nineteenth and twentieth centuries documented with notes, photographs, and details of provenance or use.

For the most part, the Europeans who sought to exploit New Guinea in one way or another from the 1870s onward seemed to have been poorly funded and sought to obtain cash by whatever means was at their disposal. And an easy way to remedy cash-flow problems was to obtain through theft, deceit, or purchase "native curios" that could be sold to collectors and museums.[1] Harvesting curios as a cash crop frequently brought about problems, particularly when artifacts were acquired by looting villages. When the next Europeans entered the locality they found the local population to be aggressively hostile. No doubt the predation by collectors was one of the reasons why the administration of Papua and then the Territory of New Guinea early in the twentieth century sought to regulate the trade in artifacts. Today there are approximately 215,000 objects from Papua New Guinea in fifty-three institutions in the United States, Canada, United Kingdom, Ireland, Australia, and New Zealand.[2] It is not known how many artifacts there are in Europe, but in just one museum in Basel, Switzerland, there are approximately 20,000 ethnographic specimens from New Guinea.

Barry Craig presents a fascinating account of the early collectors in New Guinea; the most notorious was Luigi Maria d'Albertis from the Kingdom of Savoy, now part of Italy.[3] He operated on the south coast of the island; some of his expeditions of discovery penetrated a considerable distance inland and, in the process, he amassed amazing quantities of natural history and ethnographic specimens. During his 1875 expedition, he traveled 160 miles (256 kilometers) up the Fly River, looting houses as he went. In one instance he located a longhouse and carried off as much as he could, leaving behind a few trade goods in exchange for various ornaments and human skulls overmodeled with clay features. In the following year, with the loan from the New South Wales government of the steamship *Neva*, Luigi again entered the Fly River and plundered empty houses. In one instance, he amassed so many weapons, clothing, ornaments, cooking utensils, smoking pipes, and human bones that they half-filled the *Neva*'s cabin. Luigi looted houses on multiple occasions and remarked that when returning to their villages he was surprised to be met by hostility. Men in eight canoes attacked his party when it returned after looting houses that they had missed when going up the river. By that time, he had purloined so many arrows from the villagers that even after he had retained the best, he was able to use the remainder as fuel for the ship's boilers and was rewarded with no less than two hours of steaming time! This is the man who was so patriotic that he wished to have New Guinea become a colony of his home country. Much the same kind of activity, that is, wholesale looting with poor if any documentation, was a feature of the early colonial days of both British Papua and German New Guinea.

Looted collections are not well documented; nor were the ethnographic artifacts that the administrator of Papua required his patrol officers as part of their official duties to forward to Port Moresby. Fortunately, the Victorian era was the age of gentlemen scholars and they tended to record at least some details of the artifacts that they obtained. Reverend George Brown, for example, in the course of his pastoral duties, acquired artifacts in southeastern Papua, in the Bismarck Archipelago, and German Samoa.[4] Although his collections were not well documented, Brown enhanced their value, through photographic documentation. The Australian Museum in Sydney purchased more than 600 photographic plates that he had made. Brown lived among the villagers of the Pacific, but the first anthropologist to do so is somebody that you cannot help but admire, and his legacy lives on with enduring ties between the scientific communities of Papua New Guinea and of Russia. Nikolai Nikolaevich Miklouho-Maclay, a Russian, spent fifteen months during 1871–1872 in a village on the northern coast of New Guinea observing daily life, collecting objects, and recording them. His diaries are truly fascinating, as they are an intimate portrayal of events when the members of two markedly different cultures meet for the first time. He approached villages on his own and he survived, at times just barely, being threatened with spearing, and ill from disease and poor nutrition. All told, he made three expeditions to New Guinea.[5]

The most notable for the English-speaking anthropological community is that of the Cambridge University Expedition of 1898 to the Torres Strait led by A. C. Haddon.[6] The reports document physical characteristics of the islanders and their arts, crafts, languages, magic, religion, and sociology.

During contemporary times, Michael Rockefeller is famous as a collector of artifacts for two reasons: that he came from one of the wealthiest and most avid collecting families in the world and that he disappeared during fieldwork, perhaps eaten by crocodiles or drowned and his body washed out to sea.[7] Twenty-three years of age, in 1961, Michael, as a photographer, had completed his work with the Harvard Peabody Museum Expedition to the highlands. He then commenced collecting ethnographic specimens on the southern coast of West Papua, the most visually impressive being the five-meter-high Asmat *bis* memorial poles. Michael disappeared when rafting across an inlet, and the search for him, or his remains, continued for a decade or more.

When undertaking an archaeological survey on the Trobriand Islands in 1967–1968, I unwittingly became a character in the novel *The Search for Michael Rockefeller* by Milt Machlin. The author has a depiction of a "young, totally bald archaeologist from Minnesota named Brian Egloff"—actually from Wisconsin, but near enough. At that time, my skills as a bartender were traded for lodging at the guesthouse operated by Tim Ward. I joined a bizarre crocodile-hunting expedition that involved a midnight boat trip to the reported lair of the predator that had recently attacked and killed a young village girl, and the dubious practice of wading ashore in the dead of night in search not of Rockefeller but of the crocodile. As an aside, it is worth quoting Machlin's impressions of the night in question:

> Moving with painful slowness, we got to within 12 feet. The croc's eyes looked to be more than a foot apart. I wondered how I would be able to move through the foot-gripping muck if he suddenly surged forward, but Tim had assured me that crocodiles seldom attacked under these circumstances.[8]

The crocodile got away, but I use this account to illustrate the kinds of places and people and happenings that punctuated fieldwork in the 1960s in coastal and island Papua. There are times when I wished that I had studied the colorful Westerners that I met hidden away on all but deserted bays and islands trying to "make a quid" out of rundown plantations, instead of recording the customs of villagers and searching for archaeological sites.

From my experience in the 1960s and 1970s, Australian, English, European, and American expatriate collectors operated in many different guises in Papua New Guinea. They were residents in the small towns and owned or managed trade stores and guesthouses, or if in the large district centers, the dealers operated mixed businesses trading in tourism and artifact sales and acting as hoteliers. Overseas dealers might meet up with resident collectors and exploit out-of-the-way places in search of the few remaining objects of high value. Dealers would then put together a shipment of artifacts and as soon as possible dispatch them out of the country by air cargo. Or they patrolled the coast in yachts, preying upon villagers and at times acquiring artifacts using coercive techniques with firearms blatantly in sight. No one was without guilt: from time to time academics tried to further their research by acquiring large collections that could be sold to defray fieldwork expenses, and some collections were acquired to meet with the requests of museums. As we will see later, these were not a just a few items here and there but could amount to a hundred carved wooden shields or large Hessian copra sacks filled with hundreds of pieces of traditional bone and shell jewelry or an aircraft-load of rare and highly valued wooden ancestral sculptures, drums, and masks.

ACADEMIC: "A LEARNED OR ERUDITE PERSON"

In 1965, the *Journal of Polynesian Studies* published a brief article based upon information supplied by the then owner of the Ambum Stone, Philip Goldman, accompanied by a high-quality photograph of the object by Werner Forman. The article has been variously attributed to three now deceased scholars: Mervyn Meggitt, Bruce Biggs (then the editor of the *Journal of Polynesian Society*), or Ralph Bulmer. Meggitt stated in correspondence to me that he was not the author of the article, and I think that it was most likely a collaborative effort by Ralph Bulmer and Bruce Biggs. Excerpts of the text are as follows:

> The figure was collected in 1962 from a cave in Yambu clan-territory in the Ambum (or Ambumu) Valley of the Western Highlands District of the Territory of New Guinea. The Ambum Valley is occupied by clans of the Mae Enga people . . . . The collector was a non-anthropologist who did not obtain any information from local people as to the stone's use or as to their beliefs concerning its origin.
>
> Prehistoric stone figures recovered from New Guinea include over twenty representations of birds and several anthropomorphic pieces, but only, so far as we know, one other which has been interpreted as a mammal. This is a figure from the Giriwo River headwaters, Eastern Papua, described

> by Etheridge (1908) and interpreted by him as a cuscus[9] or other marsupial. The Ambum stone is thus unique as a representation and is also clearly of quite remarkable aesthetic quality. However it does appear to share certain stylistic features (ridge-division running down the whole length of face; protuberant belly; representation of limbs and genitalia) with some other figures from the Highlands.
>
> Dr. M. J. Meggitt, in a forthcoming publication on Mae Enga religion, refers to the use of natural stones and prehistoric stone artefacts in fertility cults, which propitiate the ancestral dead.[10]

In the 1950s, Philip Goldman was a student at the University College, London (of Phyllis Kaberry, the authority on the life of the Abelam of the Sepik River), and he sought during the early years of his career as an art dealer to have the art of Papua New Guinea recognized as on a par with that of Africa and Oceania. The *Journal of Polynesian Studies* article raised the academic interest of the curator of the Museum of Primitive Art in New York, Douglas Newton, later to advise on acquisitions for the nascent Australian National Gallery. Newton pictured the Ambum Stone in "Pre-historic Stone Carvings and Their Relationship to the Ethnographical Art of New Guinea," a paper presented at the symposium, The Art of Oceania, held at McMaster University in 1974.[11] Thereafter, mention of the Ambum Stone was seldom made,[12] until in 1998 Wiessner and Tumu wrote *Historical Vines: Enga Networks of Exchange, Ritual, and Warfare in Papua New Guinea.*[13] This was the first meaningful attempt to place the category of cult object within a detailed social, historical, and ethnographic context. Increased interest in "tribal art" has resulted in the Metropolitan Museum of Art depicting four examples of carved stone artifacts from Papua New Guinea, including the Ambum Stone, as well as a pestle with a resemblance to the Ambum Stone.[14] The Jolika Collection in the de Young Museum, San Francisco, also features a carved stone similar to the Ambum Stone, but said to represent a female marsupial figure.[15]

POSTAGE STAMP: "A SMALL ADHESIVE LABEL"

The general public became aware of the Ambum Stone when it was pictured on a postage stamp issued in 1970 by the administration of Papua New Guinea; The Early History—New National Heritage Stamp Issue is comprised of five-cent, ten-cent, twenty-five-cent, and thirty-cent denominations.

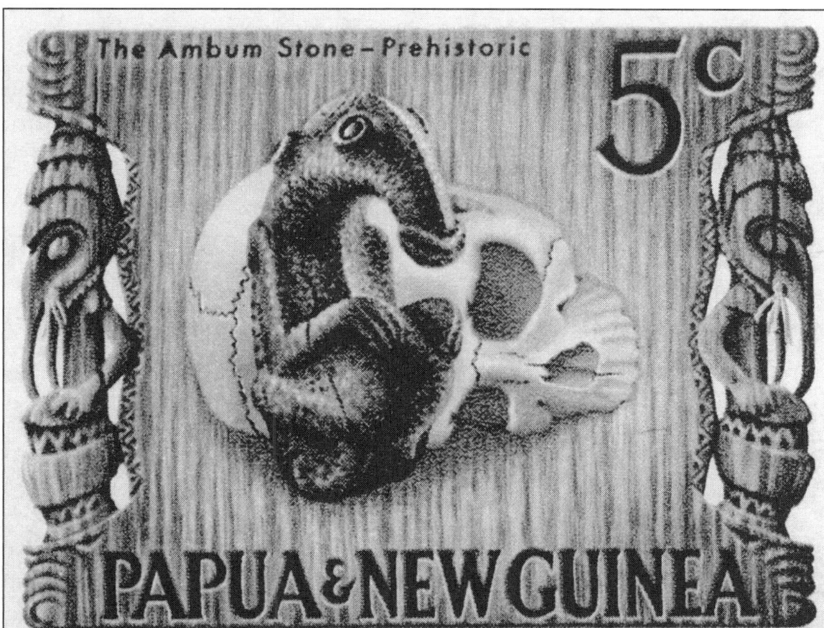

Figure 3.1. Ambum Stone postage stamp of the "Early History—New National Heritage Stamp Issue," released by the Department of Post and Telegraphs in 1970.

The five-cent stamp is described in the release brochure as follows:

> The Ambum stone is one of the finest carvings yet recovered from New Guinea. It was obtained in 1962 and is in the collection of Mr Philip Goldman of London. The figure is 20cm high and weighs 4 lbs 6 oz. It is one of five or six known pieces all from the Wabag subdistrict, which are believed to represent the Long-beaked Echidna or New Guinea Anteater (*Zaglossus*), a monotreme (egg-laying mammal) unique to New Guinea and now absent or very rare in most areas where there is any substantial human population.[16]

A picture of the Ambum Stone, and of a somewhat similar but considerably larger artifact from Paiela (Payala), was published in a booklet designed for secondary school students titled *Prehistory of Papua New Guinea.*[17] This photograph of the Ambum Stone was taken from a cast of the original artifact that had been supplied to the Papua New Guinea National Museum and Art Gallery by the owner, Philip Goldman. If I recall correctly, when Philip Goldman offered the Ambum Stone for sale to the Papua New Guinea Museum and Art Gallery, the question of the origin of the object and its transfer, purchase, and export was raised. In the 1970s, I was involved in the enforcement of the National Cultural Property (Preservation) Act 1965 but was unable to thoroughly investigate allegations that the Ambum Stone had been purchased and illegally exported without the required permit. Perhaps if I had, we would not be enmeshed in a tangled web that becomes more and more entrapping through time.

The gallery's offer to afford the museum first option on the purchase of the stone was rejected by the Trustees of the Papua New Guinea Museum and Art Gallery on the principal that they did not purchase artifacts for which there was no proof of legitimate export. Trustees of the museum were also concerned that the asking price seemed to be relatively high given a persistent rumor that the object had been purchased from a village elder for twenty shillings. Douglas Newton of the Museum of Primitive Art in New York, who was advising the Australian National Gallery on the purchase of artifacts, stated that the sale price was too high.[18] Philip Goldman to this day asserts that the object is truly unique and as such should have commanded a price similar to that of recently created modern art, with particular reference to *Blue Poles*. His viewpoint stresses the equation of the art of "primitive" cultures and Western societies.

YUPINI: "WICKER CULT FIGURE"

Detailed fieldwork by Wiessner and Tumu builds upon the research of Meggitt[19] and Gibbs[20] and confirms that carved stone objects are an integral part of the Enga ritual cycle along with the three-dimensional wicker figures known as *yupini*.[21] Carved-stone cult artifacts are found rather than made and are believed to be the "bones of the ancestors," as we have seen, something from the past or *time bilong tumbuna*. Gibbs describes the *kepele* ritual as directed at averting death and misfortune.[22] When the clan is subject to misfortune, such as deaths, landslides, when children die, and when the crops do not grow, the leaders will prepare for a *kepele* ceremony. Spirits are said to cause these misfortunes and the ghosts or spirit-beings must be put into a good mood. Six structures are built at the place where the ceremony is to be held. Each hut has a specific function that includes a place where the initiated men cook and eat the meat of possums, another where a pig is eaten, and in the large ceremonial house the *kepele* stone is kept in a leaf-lined hole in the ground during the ceremonies. A fence encloses the structures.

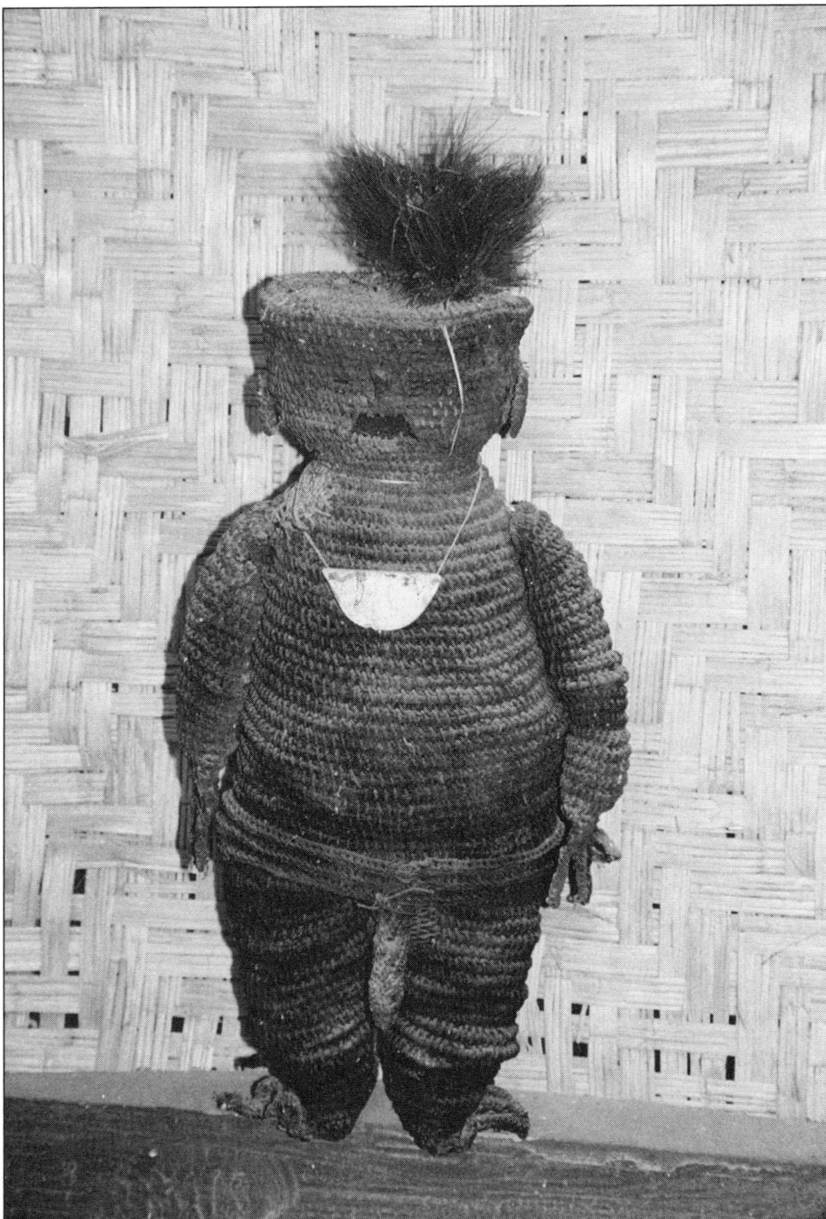

Figure 3.2. *Yupini* wicker cult figure, Enga Cultural Centre. Photograph by Polly Wiessner.

Cooking of pig meat, so that the smell of the roasting flesh can be eaten by the spirits, who then will be satisfied and stop causing trouble, is one of the key features of the *kepele*. The prelude to the ceremony is marked by two to three days of dancing where great care is given to the attire of the dancers. As the *kepele* progresses the *yupini* is taken from the men's ceremonial house, and a man carrying the wicker figure dances about displaying its male genitalia. It is then taken into one of the houses where it is fed pig fat and laid down next to the sacred stone, *kepele koulini*, with which it has sexual intercourse. Simulated intercourse between the *yupini* and the stone is orchestrated on four successive evenings, with one of the elders sleeping with the *yupini* to keep it company while the sacred stone is rubbed in fat and replaced in the leaf-lined hole. Gibbs recounts that:

> on the fifth day the *yupini* is returned to the men's house and the *kepele koulini* is buried. . . . This is the most elaborate burial ceremony because it is important that the *kepele koulini* should "sleep well." They say that if the stone is comfortable, then good times will come, but if the stone is not covered properly with fat, or if the fat is too old and dry, then good times will not eventuate. The test is whether things improve. If there is no change then the stone might have to be buried again properly.[23]

During the ceremony, spells are chanted urging the stone to stay hidden and be snug like a possum in its hole in a tree trunk. When feeding the *yupini* another spell is chanted:

> You are a good man *yupini*, Penis is erect,
> Teeth are on edge, make the teeth work.
> You are a good man *yupini*, Penis is erect, teeth are on edge,
> Penis is erect, make the teeth work, make the teeth work,
> The teeth work well.[24]

The stones are then buried in the ceremonial ground, or in the gardens, and are believed to enhance the fertility of the clan and to some extent foster positive intra- and extra-clan relations. The strength of the stones is expressed as:

The house stands,
green food is here.
I give, you give, all must give.
Greens, wild *korokas* and cordyline shrubs grow well
Everything grows well.
The *puli* tree grows well, come see it.
The *puli* tree is well, come and see.
I go to get good things, you follow.[25]

Cult objects are believed to wander, mate, and reproduce. For the villagers, perhaps this accounts for the absence of the Ambum Stone from its burial place in the clan ceremonial ground.

BONES OF THE ANCESTORS: "ENGA TERM FOR CLASS OF CULT OBJECTS"

Wiessner stresses that:

> the stones in the past were believed to be receptacles or abodes of the ancestors. They did not represent the ancestors. If a clan was driven off of its land, it was not concerned in taking the stones along—they found new ones in their new areas of residence. The stones were believed to have a life of their own, move around, mate and reproduce. These two somewhat contradictory concepts were not reconciled.
>
> In the case of theft, sale or destruction of the stones, punishment was believed to fall on the family of the thief, not

> the entire clan. The ancestors would find new residences. When the missions came, people welcomed the new religion and many do not seem to have been disturbed about giving up the stones together with fear of ghosts and ancestors. No doubt many people were quite happy not to have to kill precious pigs for that purpose! But older people still feel more secure if they know their ancestral stones are buried on clan land. Historical traditions give examples of stones being stolen or abandoned in the past. While the loss of traditional objects and subsequent compensation, reburial, etc. can be very important for indigenous groups in Australia and the United States as a part of a rallying point in a political struggle against the dominant group, this is not the case in Enga. The Enga are an extraordinarily powerful group in Papua New Guinea and have no lack of group identity!!! However, these objects are important to Enga history and should be preserved. I felt very distressed to hear that the Ambum stone had been broken.[26]

The Ambum Stone has been considered to represent many different kinds of things: a bird-like transformation;[27] a long-snouted echidna (*Zaglossus*);[28] a fetal extinct marsupial diprotodontid *Palorchestes*, particularly owing to the trunklike form of the nose;[29] fruit bat (*Cynopterus* sp);[30] an anthropomorphic form of the echidna; and a pig.[31] Rumors about stone carvings similar to the Ambum Stone would have one believe that there are many similar examples. However, less than a dozen reasonably intact examples are recorded, and one of these was destroyed in a fire. Gibbs states that most of those who practiced the *kepele* rituals now adhere to one of the Christian faiths and that the rituals have been abandoned, perhaps last practiced in the 1960s. Writing in the 1970s, he concludes that

> most of the *Yupini* figures are known to exist and many of the stones have been presented to missionaries as a sign of the people's desires to abandon traditional religious practices. *Yupini* figures have been exhibited in public . . . indicating that they have lost much of the sacredness which was attributed to them.[32]

First to reach the gaze of outsiders was the finely carved Ambum Stone that is the subject of this narrative. Then there is an intact stone with a find location believed to be Paiela (Payala), or perhaps Korombi, in Enga Province. It is roughly carved in a similar shape to the Ambum Stone but without the fine detail and is considerably larger in size.[33] The Papua New Guinea National Museum and Art Gallery has a cast of this artifact, and Paul Brennan states that the original was once in the Enga Cultural Centre.[34] Polly Wiessner has photographed artifacts in the center and agrees that the original artifact is not in the collection. James Specht of the Australian Museum states that it is not in their collection, as was once thought.

A similar specimen, auctioned by Sotheby's on 19 May 2000, is described as:

> a rare and important prehistoric New Guinea stone carving in the form of a highly abstract spiny anteater, rising from an ovoid torso, below relief carved arms meeting at the tapering loop head extending from defined rounded shoulders and joining the torso; encrusted and weathered patina.

The catalog entry lists its provenance as:

> collected by a patrol officer in the Tari Region, Southern Highlands, Papua New Guinea, 24 March, 1965. The collection note from the patrol officer reads "In relation to the

> unusual stone, I rescued this from being destroyed by a steel axe of a zealous native mission catechist intent on destroying it as evil . . . in an area known as Itapu which was approximately ten miles from Tari station.

The hammer price listed by Sotheby's is 27,200 USD.[35]

As the mid-1960s was a time when the Papua New Guinea Public Museum was actively adding to its ethnographic collections, all government officers had instructions to collect materials for the official collections (and not for themselves), it is highly unlikely that the Itapu specimen was either legally acquired or that the patrol officer received an export permit for it. Accounts of extensive collections by the Society of Divine Word and Lutheran missionaries have not been verified for the Ambum Valley. Missionaries in other parts of the highlands are known to have acquired carved stones and offer them for sale through Sotheby's in Sydney. It was widely known that some patrol officers and medical assistants were taking advantage of their official positions and authority to acquire artifacts under the guise of government actions. These same individuals would then offer the objects through sale by artifact dealers or they themselves would establish artifact-trading operations linked to tourism enterprises.

Mulangi, a broken (but all pieces present), deeply carved artifact similar to the Ambum Stone, was found by Paul Bokon of Sigiro Catholic Mission in the Ambum Valley and placed on loan with the Papua New Guinea National Museum and Art Gallery. Upon request it was returned to the owners via the local government administration. While in transit, it is alleged to have been destroyed in a fire that consumed the local police station. Radio New Zealand reports a lawsuit laid against the museum for the loss of the artifact:

> A Papua New Guinea tribe's 336-million US dollar court case against the national museum and art gallery for losing their cultural property, the Ambum Stone will be heard next month. The Post Courier paper reports, Michael Mangal on behalf of the Kunalini tribe of the Kompiam/Ambum district of Enga Province, filed the case in 2002 against the national museum.[36]

A carved stone, again like the Ambum Stone, found at Tukisenda, near Sirunki, Enga Province, is intact but heavily weathered on one side and is now in the collection of the Papua New Guinea National Museum and Art Gallery.[37] Another specimen is an exceptionally finely detailed artifact that has all the characteristics of being recently carved and does not feature the patina of age exhibited by the other specimens. It is listed in the holdings of the Masco Corporation collection and appears to be modeled after the Ambum Stone.[38] The Masco Corporation is a company founded by Detroit collector and art-gallery investor Richard Manoogian. Wayne Heathcoate, an artifact dealer, states that the carved stone was found during road construction in Enga Province and acquired by a missionary who then passed it on to him. The catalog indicates that Heathcoate is in possession of other similar pieces.[39] In April 2006 the Masco stone was advertised by Sotheby's for auction and then withdrawn.[40]

There are two objects like the Ambum Stone but with rounded pestle-shaped bases. One is in the collection of a missionary, J. Erkkila, who worked in the Tari area of the Southern Highlands in the 1950s. Sotheby's listed the article for sale by auction in 2000 with a price range of Australian $20,000–$30,000. It is thought that the carved stone was removed from sale following inquiries by the Papua New Guinea authorities.

A second Ambum-like Stone with a pestle base has exceptionally fine detail. From the Mendi region of the Southern

Highlands Province, it is pictured in the collection of the Metropolitan Museum of Art as an anonymous gift, 1984.[41]

The catalog of the Jolika Collection illustrates a "female marsupial figure, Enga Province, Central Highlands, Enga Area." Frank and Laura Martin found the stone during road works in the early 1960s and it remained in the possession of their daughter, Leslie Ann Martin.[42]

Kanopato Taneya, of the clan Lilyano from Pyakale, was photographed in 1969 or 1972, by John Womersley (former chief botanist) at Meriamanda near Wabag, holding a stone similar to the Ambum Stone. To the best of my knowledge this stone has not been reported as being held in any collection, nor has its photograph been previously published.

Chris Ballard, who completed his doctoral thesis on ritual and subsistence in the Southern Highlands, has photographed artifacts with the general conformity of the Ambum Stone in the Tari region of the Southern Highlands Province.[43] Two are similar to the Ambum Stone but are flattish and hooklike in shape, and neither has the detailed carving of the eyes, extremities, and nose that characterizes the Ambum Stone. Informants told Ballard that there are many artifacts of this kind in Southern Highlands Province.

The Ambum Stone is detailed in its carving and the only one of its kind to be independently dated; it has an authentic provenance and a trail of ownership that is all but complete. The research by Wiessner and Tumu shows that it is the only one known to have functioned as a cult object within contemporary Enga society.

PUGGLE: "MONOTREME YOUNG"

Let us think again about the image that the Ambum Stone conveys. It is fair to say that most of us have never seen either a young monotreme in the flesh or even a picture of a puggle. In Papua New Guinea and Australia, conjoined during the last glacial maxium, there are two kinds of monotremes (or mammals that lay eggs and have rudimentary milk glands): Continental Australia has the short-beaked echidna and the platypus, while the island of New Guinea has two kinds of echidnas, one with a long beak and one with a short beak, but not the platypus.[44] They are long-nosed, worm or ant eating, and have quills on their back and belong to the genus *Zaglossus* (Greek: meaning great tongue). *Nature Australia* published a short article, "The Trouble with Puggle," accompanied by a picture of a young short-beaked echidna.[45] As the Ambum Stone has been described as being similar to the fetal form of the long-beaked echidna, let us look more closely at the picture of the puggle. The infant echidna has more of a resemblance to a miniature beached elephant seal than it does to the Ambum Stone. Puggle has none of the distinctive features that mark the ancient carved stone—for example the long neck. Indeed, the infant echidna has no neck, as its body seems to merge imperceptibly with its head. Nor does it have a protruding snout; on the contrary, the puggle has a stumpy snout with sunken not protruding nostrils. As you would expect, given that the adult echidna is noted for disappearing vertically into the ground through its ability to burrow directly downward when threatened, the claws and stumpy limbs are the most prominent feature of the infant puggle. The Ambum Stone has long, thin appendages with no claws. It seems to me that it was most likely not patterned after a fetal echidna. But the Ambum Stone, whatever it is meant to represent appears to be in a contented, pregnant state with its arms resting comfortably on its large belly. So, it does signal fertility. But I have seen a fair few echidnas, and I have never seen one sitting on its haunches, like the Ambum Stone.

From the perspective of a natural scientist, Jim Menzies suggests that the Ambum Stone could be modeled after an extinct *Palorchestes*. This was a small cow-sized diprotodontoid herbivore whose remains have been found in prehistoric archaeological contexts in the highlands of New Guinea.[46] Menzies, an "old New Guinea hand," is well aware of the problems inherent in too-specific interpretation of artistic expression when searching the natural world for visual likeness for non-Western art. Tim Flannery, a zoologist, suggests that it "might be an anthropomorphized form of the echidna."[47] As we have seen throughout this story of the Ambum Stone, there is a grain of truth in even the wildest of expressions.

NOTES

1. Robert Welsch. 2000. "One Time, One Place, Three Collections: Colonial Processes and the Shaping of Some Museum Collections from German New Guinea." In Michael O'Hanlon and Robert L. Welsch (eds.), *Hunting the Gatherers: Ethnographic Collectors, Agents and Agency in Melanesia, 1870s–1930s*. Berghahn Books, New York and Oxford, 155–79.

2. Barry Craig. 1996. *Samting belong tumbuna: The Collection, Documentation and Preservation of the Material Cultural Heritage of Papua New Guinea*. Unpublished doctoral thesis, Flinders University of South Australia, 45.

3. Craig, *Samting belong tumbuna*, 75–76.

4. Helen Gardner. 2000. "Gathering for God: George Brown and the Christian Economy in the Collection of Artefacts." In Michael O'Hanlon and Robert L. Welsch (eds.), *Hunting the Gatherers: Ethnographic Collectors, Agents and Agency in Melanesia, 1870s–1930s*. Berghahn Books, New York and Oxford, 35–54.

5. Nikolai Nikolaevich Miklouho-Maclay. 1975. *New Guinea Diaries, 1871–1883*. Kristan Press, Madang, Papua New Guinea.

6. Alfred C. Haddon. 1901–1935. *Reports of the Cambridge Anthropological Expedition to Torres Straits*. The University Press, Cambridge.

7. Milt Machlin. 2000. *The Search for Michael Rockefeller*. Akadine Press, Pleasantville, New York.

8. Machlin, *The Search for Michael Rockefeller,* 76.

9. *Kuskus* is the Melanesian pidgin word for the tree-kangaroo, or in keeping with its wide-eyed appearance of looking through spectacles also refers to a clerk in an office.

10. Anon. 1965. "A Remarkable Stone Figure from the New Guinea Highlands." *Journal of the Polynesian Society* 74:76–77; photographs by Werner Forman are available on www.werner-forman-archive.com/Oceania.htm (accessed on 30 January 2007).

11. The published version is "Prehistoric and Recent Art Styles in Papua New Guinea." In S. M. Mead (ed.), *Exploring the Visual Art of Oceania*. University of Hawaii Press, Honolulu, 32–57. Also refer to Newton. 1974. "Pre-historic Stone Carvings and Their Relationship to the Ethnographical Art of New Guinea." Paper presented at a symposium, The Art of Oceania, McMaster University, 22 August 1974.

12. T. Jentsch and R. Doetsch. 1986. *Keman, Eine Siedlung im Hochland von Papua-Neuguinea: Bestandsaufnahme und Untersuchung des kulturellen Wandels*. Dietrich Reimer Verlag, Berlin.

13. Polly Wiessner and Akii Tumu. 1998. *Historical Vines: Enga Networks of Exchange, Ritual, and Warfare in Papua New Guinea*. Smithsonian Institution Press, Washington, DC, and London.

14. From www.metmuseum.org/toah/hd/ngss/hd_ngss.htm (accessed on 30 January 2007).

15. John Friede et al. 2005. *New Guinea Art Masterpieces from the Jolika Collection of Marcia and John Friede* (2 vols.). Fine Arts Museums of San Francisco in Association with 5 Continents Editions, Milan, Italy, 2:84.

16. Department of Posts and Telegraphs, Territory of Papua New Guinea, Government Printer, G.P.-10533.

17. B. Egloff and J. Egloff. 1978. *The Prehistory of Papua New Guinea*. Trustees, National Museum and Art Gallery, Boroko.

18. Douglas Newton to Brian Egloff. Correspondence of 29 September 2000 and 6 April 2001.

19. Mervyn Meggitt. 1956. "The Valleys of the Upper Wage and Lai Rivers, Western Highlands, New Guinea." *Oceania* 27: 90–135.

20. Philip Gibbs. 1978. "The *Kepele* Ritual of the Western Highlands of Papua New Guinea." *Anthropos* 73: 434–48.

21. Two *yupini* figures are pictured in the Jolika Collection at the de Young Museum in San Francisco. See Friede et al. *New Guinea Art Masterpieces from the Jolika Collection of Marcia and John Friede,* 190–91.

22. Gibbs, "The *Kepele* Ritual of the Western Highlands of Papua New Guinea," 435.

23. Gibbs, "The *Kepele* Ritual of the Western Highlands of Papua New Guinea," 439–40.

24. Gibbs, "The *Kepele* Ritual of the Western Highlands of Papua New Guinea," 445.

25. Wiessner and Tumu, *Historical Vines*, 179, quoted from Gibbs, "The *Kepele* Ritual of the Western Highlands of Papua New Guinea," 447.

26. Polly Wiessner to Brian Egloff. E-mail of 1 August 2002.

27. Douglas Newton (author given as "D.N."). 1978. (No title). In *Genesis of a Gallery, Part 2: A Touring Exhibition from the Collection of the Australian National Gallery*. Australian National Gallery, Canberra, 26–27.

28. Anon. 1965. "A Remarkable Stone Figure from the New Guinea Highlands"; Goldman to Egloff. Correspondence of 3 October 2000.

29. J. I. Menzies. 1987. "Reflections on the Ambun [*sic*] Stone." *Science in New Guinea* 13(2): 170–73.

30. Dr. R. M. Husson, Curator of Mammals, Rijksmuseum van Natuurlijke Historie, supported by L. D. Brongersma of the same institution (Brongersma to Goldman. Correspondence of 3 June 1965).

31. Opinion of Chris Ballard mentioned in Newton, correspondence of 29 September 2000.

32. Gibbs, "The *Kepele* Ritual of the Western Highlands of Papua New Guinea," 447.

33. This artifact is illustrated in Newton, "Pre-historic Stone Carvings and Their Relationship to the Ethnographical Art of New Guinea"; and Egloff and Egloff, *The Prehistory of Papua New Guinea*.

34. Wiessner and Tumu, *Historical Vines*, 47; Paul Brennen, Polly Wiessner, and James Specht. Personal communications.

35. From www.sothbys.com, African and Oceanic Art (NY7474) New York, Lot 144, sold for $27,200.

36. *Post-Courier*. 10 May 2002. In Radio New Zealand 26 April 2006. From www.rnzi.com/pages/news.php?op=read&id= 23676 (accessed on 12 February 2007).

37. Artifact recorded and photographed in 2000 by Glenn Summerhayes, The Australian National University.

38. From www.maineantiquedigest.com/articles/soth0398.htm (accessed on 30 January 2007).

39. Allen Wardell. 1994. *Island Ancestors: Oceanic Art from the Masco Collection*. University of Washington Press in Association with the Detroit Institute of Arts, Seattle and Detroit.

40. Sotheby's sale no 8190, 4/26/2006. Lot 24; and Rex Dalton. Personal communication.

41. From www.metmuseum.org/toah/hd_ngss.htm (accessed on 30 January 2007).

42. Friede, *New Guinea Art Masterpieces from the Jolika Collection of Marcia and John Friede*, (vol) 2: 84.

43. Chris Ballard. *Death of a Great Land: Ritual, History and Subsistence Revolution in the Southern Highlands of Papua New Guinea*, Appendix C7, A Survey of Archaeology in the Tari Region. Unpublished doctoral thesis. The Australian National University.

44. John Long, Michael Archer, Timothy Flannery, and Suzanne Hand. 2002. *Prehistoric Mammals of Australia and New Guinea: One Hundred Million Years of Evolution*. The Johns Hopkins University Press, Baltimore and London, 44–47.

45. G. H. 2003–2004. "The Trouble with Puggle." *Nature Australia* Summer: 82–83.

46. J. I. Menzies.1987. "Reflections on the Ambun [*sic*] Stone."

47. Tim Flannery. Personal communication of 8 March 2007.

FOUR

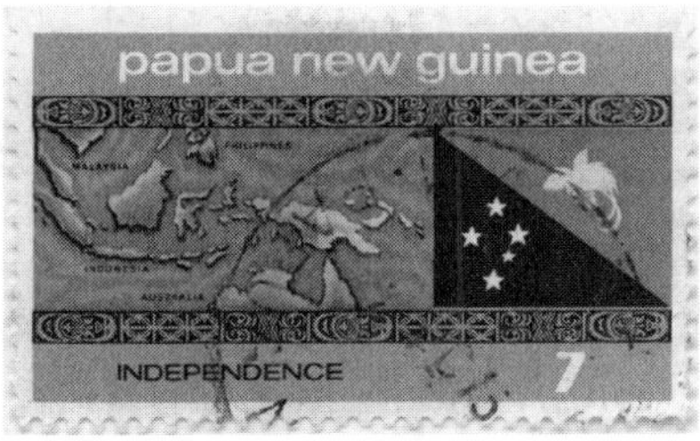

Laws, Museums, and Galleries

Papua New Guinea has an astounding repertoire of distinctive cultural materials that function both as utilitarian objects and as highly significant ritual objects. It is predictable that, given the extraordinary richness and variety of cultural material found in many of the Pacific and African territories of the British Empire, the colonizers would seek to control the artifact trade. Such efforts are longstanding in the Antipodes, for as early as 1824, Governor Lachlan Macquarie of New South Wales had taken steps to curtail the trade in tattooed Maori heads (the islands of New Zealand were then part of the Australian colony).[1]

ANTIQUITY: "THE QUALITY OF BEING ANCIENT"

In 1913 J. H. P. Murray, being aware of the Maori Antiquities Act of 1908, drafted the Papuan Antiquities Ordinance.[2] The definition of antiquities was broad and was followed in 1918 with regulations that included a Schedule for an Application for Permit to Export Papuan Antiquities. It was further defined and expanded in 1939 and again in 1940. The New Guinea Antiquities Ordinance 1922, for the Trust Territory mandated by the League of Nations, followed the Maori-Papuan model; it was illegal to export a wide range of material from the Territory without first offering it for sale to the administrator.

From its inception the legislation was taken seriously and enforced by the administration of the Territory. The *Sydney Sun* on 9 February 1923 reports an altercation between Judge Murray, the administrator of the Territory, and Captain Frank Hurley, the renowned photographer (he had accompanied the Mawson expedition to Antarctica and photographed action on the Western Front and in the Middle East with the Australian Imperial Force during the First World War).[3] The *Sun* expressed the issue succinctly as "the main contention, being the confiscation of Hurley's ethnological collection by the Acting Papuan Administration." A photograph under the heading "Official Piracy" accompanies the article; its caption reads:

> Convicts removing Captain Hurley's purchase (a long canoe) for the Australian Museum, by order of the Acting Administrator of Papua. The canoe was bought from the chief of Totani, Arama. It is the finest . . . of carved native workmanship seen during the expedition and is 40 feet in length.

On Tuesday 13 February the *Sun*, supporting Hurley's case, quotes him:

> As for calling myself an explorer—well, if the press and public wish to honour me by that calling it is no fault of mine, but I would point out to my critics that my honorable reputation has been won on sterner fields, to which Papua is a mere playground.

What a sly dig at Murray, Hurley implying that Papua is a "playground" compared to the Western Front and Antarctica! Hurley alleged that the Papuan administration had not correctly mapped the area, had no idea at all about the local language, and had collected artifacts without properly compensating the villagers:

> As for the Administration securing curios which we could not buy at any price, it appears that they are simply confiscated, and whatever the official thinks they are worth is left in their stead. . . . I can enumerate many articles that have been secured in this way, and which are at present in the official Papuan collection at the Australian Museum.

The discussion in the press is manifestly one-sided, that of Captain Hurley, with the collection being restored to Hurley perhaps through the pressure of the press. Or maybe by Murray wishing to maintain a reasonable relationship with the Australian Museum (which was holding for safekeeping a substantial part of the official Papuan collection until such time as a museum could be constructed in Port Moresby).[4] Unfortunately, construction was indefinitely delayed, as in Papua, like in Australia, development ground to a halt during the First World War and, as recovery was slow, many projects were put on hold, only to be further curtailed by the depression and then by the Second World War.

Antiquities legislation for the League of Nations–mandated Territory of New Guinea written in the 1920s was comprehensive and detailed, specifically considering "carvings, paintings or other representation on rocks or caves of living beings or inanimate objects." Upon discovery, immediate disclosure to the nearest district officer was a requirement of the ordinance.[5] The Territory of Papua New Guinea Antiquities Ordinance (No. 53 of 1953) brought together the Papuan statutes with those of New

Guinea into a single instrument, in turn replaced by the National Cultural Property (Preservation) Ordinance of 1965. The legislation continues today as Chapter No. 156 in the laws of the Independent State of Papua New Guinea.[6]

There is confusion in the literature as to when legislation was enacted to protect National Cultural Property. For instance, Robert Welsch states "Around the time of Papua New Guinea independence in 1975, the national parliament established National Cultural Property (NCP) legislation aimed at preventing old and important cultural artifacts, carvings, and art objects from leaving the country."[7] The general requirements of the ordinance did not change greatly through the various iterations of the legislation with respect to the discovery and transfer of categories of antiquities. In 1965 the definition of antiquity was narrowed to exclude from control modern artifacts made for the tourist trade.

ENFORCE: "TO COMPEL OBSERVANCE"

During the 1970s, the national museum of Papua New Guinea was given carriage of the National Cultural Property (Preservation) Ordinance of 1965, and actively policed the legislation. The seizure by Customs and Dirk Smidt, director of the museum, on 10 June 1972, of a large quantity of cultural property in seventeen cases of "consigned air cargo" at Madang airport, included a carved wooden mask, *Gweim*, from the village of the chief minister, Michael Somare. *Gweim* was so highly valued in the Sepik community that only initiated men were allowed to see it. The offending dealers in Papua New Guinea and abroad were not compensated for their loss.[8] Artifacts from that one police operation provided sufficient major pieces to constitute an exhibition at the Papua New Guinea National Museum and Art

Gallery, entitled the "Seized Collection."[9] This in turn raised the government's awareness of the illegal export of cultural property, gaining the support of customs, police, the courts, and political leaders. Happening so close to home, so to speak, it may well have spurred on the prime minister to undergo initiation and to give his unqualified support to policing the legislation.[10] At the first Oceanic Art Symposium at McMaster University in Hamilton, Ontario on 28 August 1974, Somare spoke in these terms:

> We are people. We do not like the way in which we have been regarded as passive objects of research and study by experts. We view our masks and our art as living spirits with fixed abodes . . .
>
> I would ask you to co-operate with us in returning our ancestral spirits and souls to their homes in Papua New Guinea. It is not right that they be stored in New York, Paris, Bonn or elsewhere. You can't make a fish live on land. It does not belong there.[11]

The establishment of a museum in Papua enjoyed the support of the highest authorities from the time of the inception of British and Australian colonization, through self-government in the 1960s and 1970s and until well after independence in 1975.

MUSEUM: "SEAT OF THE MUSES"

Although the various administrators had acquired extensive collections for the country, and there were plans dating to the 1920s for the construction of a museum building in Port Moresby, it was not until the enactment of the Public Museums and Art Galleries Ordinance of 1954 that a national institution was officially established. In 1965 the trustees of the Papua and New Guinea

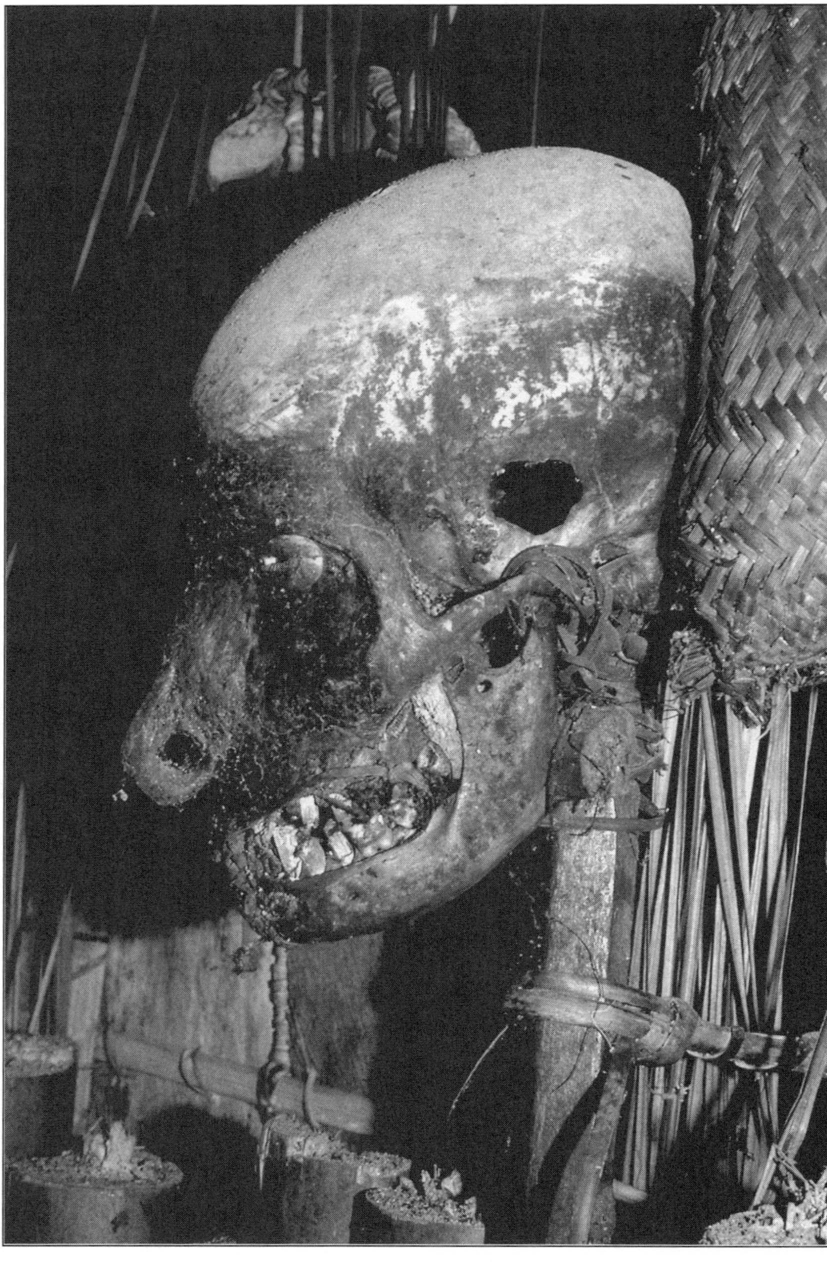

Figure 4.1. Human skull over-modeled with clay and an example of artifacts sought by collectors from the Gulf of Papua. Photograph by the author.

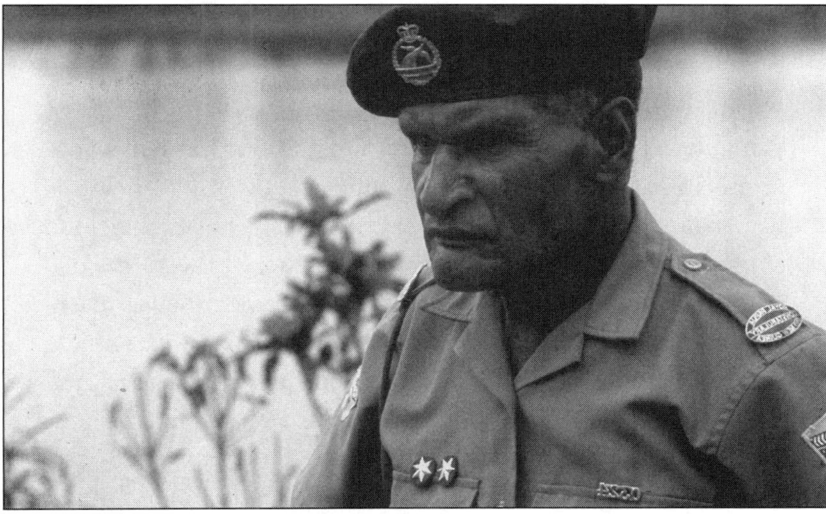

Figure 4.2. Corporal with twenty years service, Royal Papua New Guinea Constabulary on patrol with the author in the Gulf District.

Museum and Art Gallery published their first annual report for the years 1963–1964 (prior to this just a few typewritten pages had been submitted to the administrator). Thereafter reports were illustrated with photographs of key acquisitions of both cultural and natural history specimens. A catalog of artifacts detailing the collection as of October 1965[12] and a preliminary catalogue of archaeological monuments as of February 1966[13] were published. Reading the reports of the Trustees for the 1960s is fascinating, as they sought to cope with the conflicting interests of stimulating the economic activities of villagers to produce artifacts for the art market while restricting the export of cultural property. Trustees were also concerned that while the Department of Native Affairs Circular Instructions of 1962 (as prepared by Charles Julius, government anthropologist, and first issued in 1953), had once brought into the museum well-documented specimens, the level of recording of essential information had diminished through the years.

The Annual Report of 1963–1964 provides an account of the early years of the museum:

> With the resumption of civil administration, the collection of specimens was resumed as an official activity. In 1953, the Department of Native Affairs organised this collecting on a continuous and systematic basis by its field officers during their routine duties. One year later, official approval was given to the establishment of a museum for the Territory, which was confirmed by the adoption of the *Public Museums and Art Galleries Ordinance 1954*. By courtesy of His Honour the Administrator, two buildings in the Government House grounds were made available as temporary Museum buildings and since then, the official collections have been retained in this Museum or in Canberra. The cataloguing and supervision of the Museum was assigned to a Native Clerk, under the supervision of the Government Anthropologist. In 1959, space was assigned for the Museum in the basement of the old European Hospital building and, after extensive renovations, the present establishment was opened on 15th October, 1960.[14]

With opening hours from 2 p.m. to 7 p.m. each day, the museum was overseen and reviewed by the Trustees, who consisted of no less than Sir Alan Harbury Mann, chief justice of the Territory; Miss Ruth Carter, principal librarian of the Public Library; J. K. McCarthy, director of District Administration; Charles Julius, government anthropologist; Dr. Dorothy Shaw, principal plant pathologist; and Dr. J. J. H. Szent-Ivany, the senior entomologist. One cannot help but get the impression that the museum received genuine support from the highest levels of the territory administration and that if you wished to succeed in your government position it would be wise to contribute both artifacts and time to the museum. But as we have seen earlier, all too often government officers choose to profit from their position by illegally acquiring artifacts, and a few went so far as to establish artifact businesses. In 1965, the J. K. McCarthy Museum opened in the highlands at Goroka and housed the extensive collection of J. K. McCarthy, director of District Administration and trustee of the Papua and New Guinea Museum and Art Gallery.

Professionalism of the museum was enhanced with the appointment of Roy D. Mackay (previously of the Australian Museum in Sydney) as the preparator in charge, the employment of the able Christina Wright as administrative officer, followed by Dirk Smidt (now of the Rijksmuseum voor Volkenkunde, Leiden) and myself as curators in 1971 and 1972. The museum then took on its "modern" organizational shape as the anthropology, archaeology, and natural history collecting institution that it was to retain until the new museum facility was opened and substantial pieces of modern art were added to the collection. In 1974 a guide to the collections was published that documents the displays in what had been the old European hospital building and had become the House of Assembly.[15]

The era of make-do museology drew to a close in 1973 when Australia provided an independence gift of $5 million (Australian) for cultural development that was matched by $3 million from the Papua New Guinea government.[16] Funds were allocated to establish the National Cultural Council, National Arts School, Institute of Papua New Guinea Studies and the National Museum and Art Gallery.

Approximately $2.25 million was allocated for the construction of a museum facility. This was completed in 27 June 1977, two years after it was started. By then the collections had grown from 5,000 items in the 1960s to 20,000. The new museum had a 150-seat theatre, education and library facilities, sophisticated lighting and air-conditioning, extensive exhibition and storage space, and a courtyard with a dozen or so pairs of brightly colored parrots, donated by their owners when they "went finish" to Australia. Storerooms were earth-integrated to enhance thermal stability, while the exhibition area featured a ceiling with a curved shape reminiscent of traditional spirit houses of the Sepik River district. The plan, by Martin Fowler, was a masterpiece in functionality and security, designed to the UNESCO specifications for museums in developing countries. Staff, like the new building, took on a national characteristic with Joseph Mokuma from Bougainville as an education officer; curators Resonga Kaiku, from the inland of the Huon Peninsula on the northern coast of New Guinea, and Soroi Eoe, from coastal southern Papua; Geoffrey Mosuwadoga, as director, from the Trobriand Islands; Simon Poraituk curator of the natural history collections; and Francis Bafmatuk as a conservator.

Meanwhile the collections, based upon artifacts acquired by government officers in the 1960s, were growing every day through donations, repatriations from overseas museums,[17] seizure of illegal exports[18] as well as through expeditions planned and executed by the museum curators.[19] There were massive collections in Australia that belonged to Papua New Guinea, but until the new building was constructed there had been no place to house them. Under the direction of Sir William MacGregor, administrator and then lieutenant governor from 1888 to 1889 of British New Guinea, some 8,000 artifacts were acquired as the basis of the official Papua collection. The collection was sent to the Queensland Museum for curation, where it remained for eighty years. Once the museum was established in Port Moresby, the trustees sought return of the collection, only to be thwarted in their efforts until selections were made by both museums. Between 1979 and 1992, 3,297 items were returned to Papua

New Guinea and 2,675 were retained in Queensland, with 2,217 awaiting selection.[20]

A second official government collection had been acquired by Sir Hubert Murray, chief justice and lieutenant governor of Papua, from 1904 to 1939. That collection also had been transferred to Australia for safekeeping. Initially the collection was stored at the Australian Museum in Sydney, and then all but 400 artifacts were shifted to the Institute of Anatomy in Canberra. A third collection, earlier thought to have been lost in the Second World War, surfaced in Australia; this had been a collection maintained by the government administrators in Rabaul. Following the First World War, Rabaul on the island of New Britain served as the administrative center for the Mandated Territory of New Guinea. The Rabul collection was also on deposit at the Institute of Anatomy. Both the Murray and the Rabaul collections were assumed to be part of the Australian national collections. Barry Craig documents that:

> extensive correspondence in 1969 and 1970 between authorities in PNG and Australia indicates that the former, by advice from K. A. Green (Chief Archivist in PNG), believed that the MacGregor and Murray collections were sent to Australia for safekeeping for a future museum in the Territories, whereas the Commonwealth's Attorney General came to the conclusion that the collections were the property of the Queensland government and Institute of Anatomy respectively.[21]

Pressure was exerted by the Papua New Guinea National Museum and Art Gallery and eventually the major parts of each collection were repatriated (but not without considerable effort on the part of the museum). By the mid-1970s the museum had established itself internationally through its scientific research and by maintaining a publication series that highlighted its research activities.[22] Astoundingly, more than 11,000 copies of *Papua New Guinea's Prehistory* were circulated, for the most part within the country.[23]

GALLERY: "BUILDING DEVOTED TO THE EXHIBITION OF WORKS OF ART"

Until federation in 1901, the operation of museums and galleries was the function of the various colonies that came to comprise the states of Australia. On 18 September 1912, following the decision to locate the national capital at Canberra, the federal government's Commonwealth Art Advisory Board (CAAB) was founded. The board pressed for the construction of a national gallery in Canberra[24] and acquired works by both international and national artists. It did not restrict acquisitions to the Western art world. In the 1970s, it dispatched collecting expeditions to the islands of Melanesia and to the Territory of Papua New Guinea in particular:

> In the light of the fact that PNG was hurtling towards independence, the policy was to obtain great collections from that region before it was too late—Australia was already well endowed with Melanesian collections held by other public institutions. This policy may have reflected a belief that the last great "primitive art" (a term which still had some currency, though debatable) was to be found in the archipelago to the north of Australia, and not within the confines of its own shores.[25]

James Mollison was appointed in 1971 as acting director of the Australian National Gallery and shortly thereafter the plans for the gallery were given a boost when the newly elected prime minister, Gough Whitlam, as minister for the arts, threw his formidable physical and intellectual presence behind the effort to establish the gallery:

> Into the 1970s the National Gallery's Acquisitions Committee (which superseded the CAAB) and later the Interim Council, developed more sharply focused acquisition policies and were provided with the wherewithal to execute them, and a number of exceptional works entered the collection.
>
> Among these are the so-called *Ambum stone* from the western highlands of Papua New Guinea, dated to about 1508–1438 BCE.[26]

Wally Caruana, curator at the National Gallery of Australia, discusses the distribution of two major collections when he writes:

> After Papua New Guinea gained its independence in 1975 the National Gallery and the Commonwealth government talked of the repatriation of the relevant collections. Indeed a number of works collected in Port Moresby and intended for Canberra are now permanently housed at the PNG National Museum.[27]

His first sentence refers either to the official Papuan collection that was assembled by Sir Hubert Murray, or perhaps to the earlier MacGregor collection.[28] In the second sentence, he probably is referring to the controversy that developed in the early 1970s when the trustees of the Papua New Guinea Public Museum refused to provide export permits for artifacts collected by agents of the Commonwealth Art Advisory Board. This blocking action might have been precipitated by alleged budgetary imbalances that provided more funds to the Commonwealth

Art Advisory Board for collecting in Papua New Guinea than were available to the trustees for the operation of the Papua New Guinea Public Museum.[29]

ORDEAN AL SOL: "PERU'S HIGHEST AWARD"

In 2003, Colin Renfrew (Lord Renfrew of Kaimsthorn), former Disney Professor of Archaeology at the University of Cambridge, accused museums and private collectors of indirectly funding the looting of archaeological sites.[30] "The loss to our knowledge and the damage is appalling," as antiquities are ripped from their original context and surreptitiously entered onto the world art market. Not only are artifacts looted from archaeological sites sold to galleries, but so are antiquities stolen from national museums. In 1973, three unique woven textiles were stolen from the Museo Nacional de Anthropología y Arqueología, in Lima, Peru. One of those textiles was acquired by the Australian National Gallery in 1975. By 1976 the government of Peru knew that the textile was in Australia and raised this matter with the gallery, seeking return of the mantle. It took a decade of effort by the government of Peru supported by Australian archaeologists before the textile was correctly identified.

During prehistoric times, approximately 2,000 years ago, peoples of the Paracas civilization of the southern coastal reaches of Peru wrapped their dead in exceptionally fine woven textiles and interred them in communal tombs. Elaborate, highly ritualized burial practices continued into historic times and were described by the Spanish invaders. Burial shrouds, or mantles, have survived due to the cool and dry coastal desert conditions. Their large size, often in excess of 2.5 by 1.25 meters, varied natural colors, and highly complex embroidered decorative motifs mark each textile as unique. Ancient textiles are highly sought after and command exorbitant prices on the international art market. Tombs are regularly subject to looting and those items not considered of commercial value are smashed and left behind by the looters. Prehistoric fabrics are also the focus of studies by archaeologists. Each textile is hand-woven with intricate and individualized motifs that to a curator's trained eye are readily recognizable.

In 1973, the Dumbarton Oaks conference "Death and the Afterlife in Pre-Columbian Peru" presented a paper by Jane Powell Dwyer and Edward B. Dwyer entitled "The Paracas Cemeteries: Mortuary Patterns in a Peruvian South Coastal Tradition." Drawing upon earlier published works by Julio Tello of 1928 and 1959 as well as other specialists describing Peruvian burial textiles, the Dwyers illustrated the mantles that were stolen at a later date from the Museo Nacional de Anthropologia y Arqueología. At the time that the particular Paracas mantle was acquired by the Australian National Gallery in the 1970s, there was archaeological information suggesting that it once was in the national collection of the government of Peru.

The campaign by the Peruvian government for the return of the mantle was aided by the advocacy of Jane Dwyer of Brown University:

> In 1982 the Government of Peru requested the return of the textile from the Australian National Gallery and produced a negative print of a part only of a textile for purposes of comparison. Unfortunately, the photograph produced was clearly of a similar textile, No. 219-8 which was still in the National Museum in Lima.
>
> As a result, the Australian National Gallery replied on 15 July that while there were similarities, the two textiles were distinctly different. This assessment is correct as the photograph was clearly of textile No. 319-8.[31]

Correct as the gallery was in its focused assessment, the archaeologists perceived that it was not being proactive in resolving this matter, nor did it willingly help the archaeologists who did their best to put together a case for the restitution of the burial mantle. Then in 1987, the National Gallery of Australia was approached by Ian Farrington and Helen Parrott from The Australian National University with a detailed report and irrefutable evidence that the gallery had in its collection one of the woven textiles that had been stolen from the Museo Nacional de Anthropologia y Arqueología in Lima, Peru. The report points out that Peru's antiquity legislation dated to 13 June 1929 and prohibited the export of artifacts such as burial mantles. Their detailed report, "The Paracas Textile Held by the Australian National Gallery, Canberra, Australia—an Examination of the Case for Its Restitution to the Government of Peru," included previously published articles and illustrations of the stolen textiles.

Events in the past are often recalled by the participants in diametrically opposed ways. The Honorable Gough Whitlam, once prime minister of Australia and minister for the arts, recalls the return of the burial shroud as one where "the ANG has acted in accordance with its spirit" (referring to the 1970 UNESCO convention), "by returning the illicitly acquired Paracas mantle to Peru and is most scrupulous to check the provenance of its proposed acquisitions."[32] Farrington and Parrott worked diligently on behalf of the Peruvian government to interpret the archaeological reports and to fully document the identity of the textile. Matters obscuring the documentation were an incorrectly identified photograph that was submitted to the gallery followed by a reversed image of the Paracas textile. As of 2005 the textile is in the collection of the Museo de la Nacion in Lima, where it is the centerpiece of the new museum's displays. The government of Peru was so pleased with the action of the archaeologists that they received the Ordean al Sol, Peru's highest award.

Today, as seemingly always, the crux of the problem is that the looting of archaeological sites and the theft of materials from museums is rampant. Yes, it has happened again. "At dawn of Friday, October 15, 2004 there was an organized heist of three textiles, the most impressive fabrics on exhibit in the Regional Museum of Inca, Peru."[33] The task faced by archaeologists and the governments of "donor" nations is overwhelming.[34] Unless proactive support is forthcoming from recipient galleries and museums, a substantial amount of time and energy is sidetracked into dealing with what one would think are relatively well-documented and straightforward efforts toward restitution of stolen antiquities; there is little time left for the more difficult cases let alone original research and documentation of collections.

LOOT: "ILLICIT GAINS"

Colin Renfrew, one of the United Kingdom's foremost public archaeologists and a vocal critic of the trade in looted antiqui-

Box 4.1

THE RED LIST (LISTE ROUGE) AND INTERPOL

An initiative by ICOM (International Committee for Museums) that is supported by the U.S. Department of State, the Red List has proven to be a useful tool in combating the trade in illicit artifacts. It "describes the general types of artifacts most favored by the illegal antiquities market, so that they may be identified and detained whenever they surface." In 2007 the types of objects most likely to have been stolen and illegally exported from Iraq are listed on the ICOM museum website. Interpol provides stolen art information on CD-ROM.

ties, with his archaeological colleagues, has undertaken studies, and published widely, on the destructive impact of illicit trade on archaeological knowledge. Renfrew's forceful argument is summarized as an "ethical crisis in archaeology":

> Crisis is not too strong of a word to use when we speak of the predicament which today faces the historic heritage in nearly every country on earth. The world's archaeological resource, which through the practice of archaeology is our principal source of knowledge about the early human past, is being destroyed at a formidable and increasing rate. It is destroyed by looters in order to serve the lucrative market in illicit artifacts through which private collectors and, alas, some of the major museums of the world, fulfill their desire to accumulate antiquities.[35]

Dramatically, Renfrew illustrates his point by a review of the case of the Salisbury Hoard, which commenced with the sale to the British Museum of a previously unrecorded series of twenty-two bronze miniature shields from the British Iron Age. The price paid was £55,000. Fortunately—but not as common as we would hope—in 1988 the shields were brought to the attention of a curator who sought the truth of their origin. Ian Stead, the British Museum's Iron Age specialist, pursued this case with an interest reinforced by his view that the items were unique.[36] After considerable detective work, it emerged that the pieces were part of a larger hoard that had been looted by "nighthawks" employing metal detectors. The culprits then sold the loot to less-reputable dealers, who then sold the tainted goods on to reputable dealers until the antiquities acquired a thin veneer of respectability. As so much of the antiquities trade by dealers is conducted in secret, as indeed is the purchase of objects by collecting institutions, with false trails being laid, the contents of the hoard and the extent of its distribution to dealers, museums, and collectors was not immediately apparent. But indeed, Stead did follow many leads, looking for the truth about the "ownership" and the prehistoric context of the hoard.

If the Salisbury Hoard was a single find, then it was unique because it comprised many types of artifacts, which typically dated to about 2,000 years older than the miniature shields—known to derive from 200 BCE. If it had been disinterred from a single cache, then it must have been buried during the pre-Roman British Iron Age, and must have contained items collected together over an extended period.[37] His inquiries were directed at determining just what constituted the hoard and whether it had indeed come from one find spot. If all of the known finds came from one place, then the hoard was not some quickly hidden set of family valuables, but spoke of an Iron Age collection of remarkable diversity: perhaps even a votive offering with religious connotations, maybe even belonging to a sanctuary. So unique was this hoard that Stead had to prove the single-find-spot proposition beyond any doubt. But could the single-find-spot theory be demonstrated given that by 1988 there was every indication that items from the hoard had been widely dispersed by various dealers? Some pieces had crossed the Atlantic to the United States.

Stead met with shady dealers in shadowy places and gradually pieced much of the story together. The looters were tried and convicted. But only one of the dealers was convicted. Distribution routes are illustrated by Stead so that the agents, or prime movers, of the antiquities and recipient collecting institutions are identified. The chart lists dozens of individuals, well-known dealers, auction houses, and institutions that were connected with receiving parts of the Salisbury Hoard.[38]

As every attempt had been made to disguise the location, it was no easy task locating the original find spot. First accounts stated that the farmer who owned the property did not wish to be identified; it then unfolded that the owner knew nothing of the clandestine activities of the looters and had a legitimate title to the goods that were stolen from his property. The British Museum returned the goods to the owner, but when it requested a refund, the museum did not receive a reply. Earlier, when the British Museum had received the grant from the National Memorial Heritage fund to purchase the twenty-two miniature shields, the director of the fund expressed concerns with the lack of provenance for them. Had the British Museum heeded the director's concerns, it would have saved the English taxpayers £55,000 pounds, as that is the sum that the estate of the owner sought and received in tax relief. The British Museum issued the following statement:

> The British Museum deplores the deliberate removal of ancient artifacts from British soil other than by properly directed archaeological excavation, especially when the context of those artifacts is thereby left unrecorded and severely damaged. However, although the unauthorized excavation of such material from a scheduled monument is illegal and can never be condoned, much of what is discovered elsewhere is brought to light lawfully; persons in possession of it often have a legal title to dispose of it as they think fit. In these circumstances, the Museum has an overriding duty to try to acquire such finds as it considers to be appropriate to the national collection. To refuse to follow this course would entail a serious loss to our heritage, since we would then lose the chance to see and record a great many objects. The Museum understands, and shares, the concern of the archaeological world, but since there is a ready-market both here and abroad, the

> situation will not be remedied by a museum embargo. Selective acquisition remains, in our view, not only the practical, but also the proper course.[39]

In 1994, Stead undertook controlled excavations at the 23 February 1985 find spot, eight miles southeast of Stonehenge. His first task was to locate precisely the hoard pit and demonstrate that all of the artifacts had come from that place. A broken piece that matched one of the unique objects ascribed to the hoard was recovered, offering convincing evidence that this was the place where the many different kinds of artifacts in the hoard had been buried. Piecing together all of the various kinds of information that had come to light, Stead determined that the Salisbury Hoard indeed was a massive find of close to 500 objects. What every archaeologist (or "nighthawk") dreams of finding, just once in a lifetime!

Now, what about the law? Persons who take things are regarded as thieves and are prosecuted accordingly. Legitimate finds must be reported to the property owner and to the local coroner who may seek advice from the British Museum. If the antiquity is acquired by the Crown, the person who found it, or on whose land it was found, receives a bounty. But just how does the Treasure Act of 1996—formerly "Treasure Trove" regulations—apply to the Salisbury Hoard?

The Treasure Act did not apply to the Salisbury Hoard as finds have to be made of silver or gold, not bronze, to be covered by the Treasure Act; a very big loophole indeed! Stead advocates that the Treasure Act be extended to cover all antiquities and that all finds be reported to a museum, not the coroner, where the antiquities would be identified by archaeologists and those worthy of entering public collections would be set aside, the owners given fair compensation, and following documenting the remainder would be returned to the owners.

Three or more salient points, already discussed with respect to highly valued objects, are reinforced by the complexities of the Salisbury Hoard case. First, why are not more established galleries and museums undertaking detailed investigations when possibly they have suspicions that tainted material is brought before them? Second, the number of supposedly reputable individuals involved in a less than transparent way with this case is astonishing; it gives no credence to the notion that the traffic in illicit artifacts is being controlled or lessened. Third, the case demonstrates that it is only through immediate and determined investigations that the truth, or at least part of it, will become known.

Antiquities of silver or gold are regulated by the United Kingdom statute, but those made of other materials are not. One of the most widely recognized of British archaeological treasures is the Lewis chess pieces made of the ivory of sea mammals. Sometime before 1831 a hoard of elaborately worked chess pieces was found in the vicinity of Uig on the Isle of Lewis in the Outer Hebrides of Scotland. Consisting of four incomplete sets, the pieces were probably made between AD 1100 and 1200 in Norway.[40] Protecting only gold and silver antiquities contrasts sharply with the laws in countries where all antiquities are protected. Legitimization of the wholesale use of metal detectors to recover archaeological materials is contrary to regulations in other countries where antiquities are protected from unauthorized excavators.

Stead's investigation of the Salisbury treasure emphasizes the loss of information resulting from clandestine looting and breaking up of coherent and complex archaeological information to facilitate the sale of individual finds as commodities. This case questions the notion that an increase in supply of antiquities through legitimate trade, perhaps including duplicate artifacts released from museums and sold on the open market, would lessen the predation on archaeological sites and that the trade in tainted antiquities would diminish.[41] Yes, museums have many artifacts that perhaps they wish that they did not have to curate. But few of those would be of collectable quality and dealers know that unique, more intact and rare pieces bring the greatest profits.[42]

Only the primary dealer in the Salisbury Hoard case was prosecuted. Probably the others were not dealt with because of the difficulty in demonstrating beyond a reasonable doubt that secondary dealers knew that the antiquities were stolen property. Consider the defense often claimed by dealers, curators, and gallery directors that they did not know that the goods were stolen loot. In the Salisbury Hoard instance it probably was too difficult for the authorities to deal with. Investigators must have wondered how any reasonably knowledgeable person, one who regularly deals in antiquities, could believe that the Bronze and Iron Age antiquities were chance finds or stumbled across in "my Aunt's attic." Until recently, courts were not prosecuting unscrupulous dealers if they claimed to be witless and hapless victims. But that is no longer the case if the defendant by virtue of their work is expected to be knowledgeable; as dealers, curators, and directors are paid to be. Courts are beginning to take seriously the obligations of dealers in antiquities. Courts in the United States are prosecuting individuals charged with importing stolen goods or with incidences of incorrect customs declarations. The landmark case is that of Frederick H. Schultz Jr., who in 2002 was charged with conspiracy and receiving and dealing in stolen goods from Egypt. Members of the jury received careful instructions from the judge:

> A defendant may not purposely remain ignorant of either the facts or the law in order to escape the consequences of the law.[43]

Schultz, president of the National Association of Dealers in Ancient, Oriental, and Primitive Art, was found guilty and served his sentence, being released in 2005.

Stead's archaeology of the Salisbury Hoard demonstrates just how much there is to learn about prehistoric Iron Age settlements from a reasonable understanding of the context of the find. Despite his limited excavations at the find spot, he was able to show that the small pit that had held the hoard had been dug into a much larger Iron Age grain storage pit. To explain the presence in the hoard of 2,000-year-old Bronze Age artifacts, Stead speculated that the farmers had found them in the course of tilling their land and had purposefully incorporated them into what might have been a community collection with sacred connotations.

All told, the story of the Salisbury Hoard lasted some thirteen years from the date that the looting commenced in 1985 to the close of the investigations. Not that the case ever really will be closed, as sadly, at least 188 pieces of the Salisbury Hoard are in private hands.[44]

NOTES

1. Ngahuia Te Awekotuku. 2002. "More Than Skin Deep: *Ta Moko* Today." In Elazar Barkan and Ronald Bush (eds.), *Claiming the Stones, Naming the Bones*. The Getty Research Institute, Los Angeles, 243–54.

2. Barry Craig. 1996. *Samting belong tumbuna: The Collection, Documentation and Preservation of the Material Cultural Heritage of Papua New Guinea*. Unpublished doctoral thesis, Flinders University of South Australia, 111.

3. James Specht, former Curator of Anthropology at the Australian Museum, now an associate, kindly provided the newspaper clippings upon which this discussion is based.

4. *Papuan Annual Reports* for the years 1922–1923, 1923–1924 and 1924–1925 do not mention the confiscation of the Hurley ethnographic collection; also Michael Quinnell. 2000. "Before It Has Become To Late." In Michael O'Hanlon and Robert L. Welsch (eds.), *Hunting the Gatherers: Ethnographic Collectors, Agents and Agency in Melanesia, 1870s–1930s*. Berghahn Books, New York and Oxford, 81–102.

5. Craig, *Samting belong tumbuna*, 115.

6. Craig, *Samting belong tumbuna*, 117–18.

7. Robert Welsch. 2005. "One Symphony from Many Voices: Collectors, Collecting Activities, and the Culture of Collecting since 1870." In John Friede et al. *New Guinea Art Masterpieces from the Jolika Collection of Marcia and John Friede* (2 vols.). Fine Arts Museums of San Francisco in Association with 5 Continents Editions, Milan, Italy, 2:23.

8. Craig, *Samting belong tumbuna*, 163–64.

9. Dirk Smidt. 1975. *The Seized Collections of the Papua New Guinea Museum*. Creative Arts Centre and Papua New Guinea Museum, Port Moresby.

10. Michael Thomas Somare. 1975. *Sana: An Autobiography of Michael Somare*. Niugini Press, Port Moresby.

11. Resonga Kaiku. 1980. "Restoration of National Cultural Property: The Case of Papua New Guinea." *Preserving Indigenous Cultures: A New Role for Museums*, UNESCO Regional Seminar, 10–15 September 1978, Adelaide, Australia, 175.

12. Papua New Guinea Museum. 1965. *Catalogue of Artefacts in the Papua New Guinea Museum* (with details of data required for specimens in the future). Acting Government Printer, Port Moresby.

13. Papua New Guinea Museum. 1966. *Preliminary Catalogue Archaeological Monuments in the Territory of Papua New Guinea*. Government Printer, Port Moresby.

14. W. F. Ellis. 1965. "Comments on The Papua New Guinea Public Museum and Art Gallery with Proposal for Future Development." In *Annual Report of the Trustees of the Papua New Guinea Museum and Art Gallery, 1963–1964*, Port Moresby, 19–32.

15. The Trustees. 1974. *Guide to the Collections*. Papua New Guinea Public Museum and Art Gallery, Port Moresby.

16. A. L. Crawford. 1977. *The National Cultural Council, Its Aims and Functions: With Guidelines for Establishing and Operating Cultural Centres within Papua New Guinea*. National Cultural Council, Port Moresby.

17. Craig, *Samting belong tumbuna*.

18. Smidt, *The Seized Collections of the Papua New Guinea Museum*.

19. Brian Egloff and Gava Aura (eds.). 1977. *Pottery of Papua New Guinea: The National Collection*. Papua New Guinea National Museum and Art Gallery, Port Moresby.

20. Quinnell, "Before It Has Become To Late," 97.

21. Barry Craig. 1990. "The Return of Ethnographic Material to Papua New Guinea." *Bulletin of the Conference of Museum Anthropologists '89* 23: 84.

22. Dirk Smidt. 1977. "The National Museum and Art Gallery of Papua New Guinea, Port Moresby." *Museum* 29(4): 226–39.

23. Pamela Swadling et al. 1981/1986. "Papua New Guinea's Prehistory." Papua New Guinea National Museum and Art Gallery in association with Gordon and Gotch, Boroko, Papua New Guinea; and correspondence of Pamela Swadling to Brian Egloff, 7 February 1989.

24. Ann Gray. 2003. "Truly National." In Pauline Green (ed.), *Building the Collections*. National Gallery of Australia, Canberra, 73–115.

25. Wally Caruana. 2003. "The Collection of Indigenous Australian Art: Beginnings and Some Highlights." In Pauline Green (ed.), *Building the Collections*, National Gallery of Australia, Canberra, 193.

26. Caruana, "The Collection of Indigenous Australian Art," 194.

27. Caruana, "The Collection of Indigenous Australian Art," 194.

28. Craig, *Samting belong tumbuna*.

29. "Acquisition of PNG Artefacts—Relations between CAAB (Commonwealth Art Advisory Board) & PNG Authorities," file A3757 (A3753/13) 1972/1700, National Archives of Australia.

30. Jeremiah Crim. 2003. "Scholar Accuses Museums of Looting." *The Daily Pennsylvanian*, 22 October. www.dailypennsylvanian.com (accessed on 27 October 2003). Refer also to Colin Renfrew. 2000. *Loot, Legitimacy and Ownership: The Ethical Crisis in Archaeology*. Duckworth, London; and Renfrew. 2001. Forward. In Neil Brodie, Jennifer Doyle, and Colin Renfrew (eds.), *Trade in Illicit Antiquities: The Destruction of the World's Archaeological Heritage*. McDonald Institute Monographs, Cambridge.

31. I. Farrington, and H. C. Parrott. 1989. "The Paracas Textile Held by the Australian National Gallery, Canberra, Australia—An Examination of the Case for Its Restitution to the Government of Peru." Unpublished manuscript, 6–7; and Helen Parrott. 1990. "The Restitution of a Paracas Textile to Peru—the Australian International View." *Bulletin of the Conference of Museum Anthropologists '89* 23: 88–96.

32. Hon. E. G. Whitlam. 1990. "National Collecting Institutions" (First Keith Myer Lecture, 5 April 1990). Whitlam Institute, The University of Western Sydney.

33. Ann H. Peters. 2004. "Textile Theft in Inca, Peru: A Threat to Heritage and Its Conservation," www.elcomercioperu.com.pe/EdicionImpresa/Html/2004-10-15/impNacional0206946.html (accessed on 12 December 2006).

34. Christopher Chippendale and David W. J. Gill. 2000. "Material Consequences of Contemporary Classical Collecting." *American Journal of Archaeology* 104: 463–511.

35. Renfrew, *Loot, Legitimacy and Ownership*, 9.

36. I. M. Stead. 1998/2000. *The Salisbury Hoard*. Stroud, Tempus.

37. Stead, *The Salisbury Hoard*, 9.

38. Stead, *The Salisbury Hoard*, Figure 6.

39. David Wilson. 1989. *The British Museum: Purpose and Politics*, 33–34, cited by Stead, *The Salisbury Hoard*, 16.

40. Neil Stratford. 1997. *The Lewis Chessmen and the Enigma of the Hoard*. The British Museum Press, London, 4–11.

41. Patrick O'Keefe. 1977. *Trade in Antiquities: Reducing Destruction and Theft.* Unesco Publishing, Paris and Archetype Publications, London, 103.

42. Kathryn Walker Tubb and Neil Brodie. 2001. "From Museum to Mantelpiece: The Antiquities Trade in the United Kingdom." In Robert Layton, Peter G. Stone, and Julian Thomas (eds.), *Destruction and Conservation of Cultural Property*. Routledge, London and New York, 106–7. Also refer to Tubb (ed.). 1995. *Antiques Trade or Betrayed: Legal, Ethical and Conservation Issues*. Archetype Publications, London.

43. Peter Watson and Cecilia Todeschini. 2006. *The Medici Conspiracy: The Illicit Journey of Looted Antiquities from Italy's Tomb Raiders to the World's Greatest Museums*. Public Affairs, New York, 238–40.

44. Stead, *The Salisbury Hoard*, 106.

FIVE

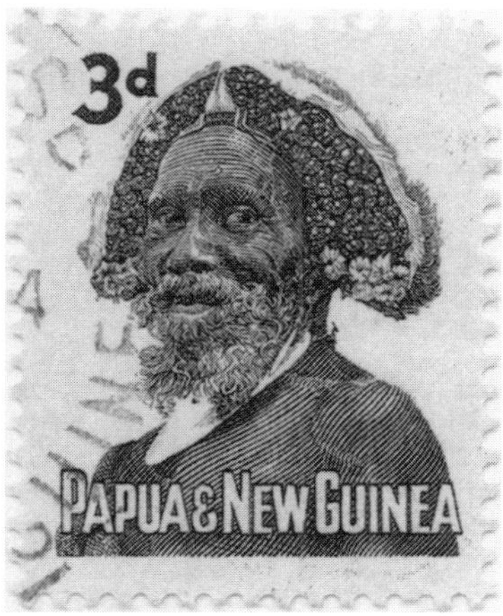

Romancing the Stone

From ancient times to the present, the Ambum Stone has given power to whoever has possessed it. It is the reaction of each individual that has come into contact with the stone, either through possessing it, or wishing that they had it, or in seeking to know more about it, that enlivens the story of the Ambum Stone. The romancing of the stone no doubt started in distant prehistoric times in the remote highlands of New Guinea, and continues to this day with its exhibition at the National Gallery of Australia. Where and when to commence this story is not an easy choice to make. I have decided to restart the story with the art dealer who first brought the Ambum Stone to the attention of the scientific world, then to let the narrative unfold from London to Australia to the highlands of New Guinea and back to Australia. Of utmost importance to the story is the interplay between the Papua New Guinea National Museum and the Australian National Gallery as well as the information that was provided to the gallery by its advisors. The advice was provided over a number of years and took on an added urgency when funds to purchase the Ambum Stone became available. Here I rely upon the detailed accounts contained in documents acquired under the Freedom of Information Act. Let us start in London with the art dealer who was the first Westerner to fully appreciate the aesthetic and cultural value of the Ambum Stone.

ROMANCE: "TO EXAGGERATE OR INVENT"

Philip Goldman provides the following account of the Ambum Stone through telephone conversations and e-mail correspondence with me throughout 2000 and 2001. He stressed that, as these events took place some twenty-five to forty years ago, he might not correctly recall details. Goldman's narrative begins with an account of a collecting trip to Papua New Guinea in the early 1960s, when he was shown, or later sent, a picture of the Ambum Stone by a person whose name he could not at that time recall. At that time it was not for sale. He was then offered the object in 1962 or 1963 after, in his words, "it had been exported." With the purchase of the artifact, he received a map with place names indicating the "cave" where the object was said to have been found. He supplied information to the *Journal of the Polynesian Society* along with a three-quarter front photographic image taken by Werner Forman.[1] Some time later he offered the object to the British Museum and states that Bryan A. Cranstone, assistant curator of anthropology, was unwilling to purchase the stone, being concerned that it was of prehistoric nature and had not been excavated by archaeologists and as such had no established provenance.[2] Barry Craig dedicated *Children of Afek: Tradition and Change among the Mountain-Ok of Central New Guinea* to the memory of Bryan Cranstone, adding:

> Part of the collection he made was allocated to the (then) Papua New Guinea Public Museum and Art Gallery, perhaps the earliest comprehensive collection of the material culture of a particular group of people [referring to the Tifalmin] given to that museum and one that set the standard for many ethnographers who have worked in Papua New Guinea since then.[3]

The stone was offered to and purchased by the Australian National Gallery.[4] At about the same time, 1975–1977, according to Goldman, a museum in Basel became interested in the Ambum Stone.

In November 1978, when I had only recently left the Papua New Guinea National Museum and Art Gallery, Professor Ralph Bulmer of the Department of Anthropology, University of Auckland, sent to me in Australia a copy of correspondence with Paul Brennan, a linguist and founder of the Enga Cultural Centre collection. Apparently Brennan had written to Bulmer to determine what he knew about the Ambum Stone. Bulmer wrote:

> My suspicion was that it was the Danish journalist Jens Bjerre . . . who seems to have been collecting out from Laiagam in about 1962, accompanying Denys Faithful the kiap (ADC?) there. However Meggitt pointed out that there was a Catholic Mission and leprosarium in Yambu territory that he understood the S.V.D. priests to have acquired an extensive collection of stone objects.
>
> Latter correspondence (in August 1968) with Sir Alan Mann, then Chief Justice of the Territory and Chairman of Trustees for the Museum, indicates that he had seen a similar but not identical anteater figure in possession of Denys Faithful. Clearly Mr Faithful is one person who might be able to

shed further light on the matter, as he was Bjerre's guide and had also himself seen these kinds of stones.[5]

The Annual Report of the Trustees of Public Museum and Art Gallery of Papua New Guinea for the year 1967 records "a beautiful black stone from the Laiagam area in Western Highlands, lent by Mr. D. Faithful" as entering the collections. It is likely that the object referred to by Sir Alan Mann was this stone pestle with a carved bird at its head and not an echidna-shaped artifact. I confirmed this information by telephoning Denys Faithful in 2001. Faithful asserts that he only lent the pestle to the museum. The entry in the museum catalog reads "stone bird pestle, E2082OAH.01, from Nere people in West Laigap, between Strickland and Pogera, Enga Province, height 21.5cm, collected by Dennis Faithful, 1963."[6] Along with other stone artifacts, the pestle was stolen from the museum in 19 May 2003.

Why was a linguist who had worked with the Lutheran missionaries in Enga corresponding about the whereabouts of the Ambum Stone? Paul had been the initial force in acquiring the collections that were later to comprise the Enga Cultural Centre, but why in 1978 was he interested in the Ambum Stone? The answer may lie in the correspondence of Anthony Forge, professor of anthropology at The Australian National University, when two years later he wrote to Brennan, then a member of the Information Review Committee in Port Moresby, stating that "The stone certainly is in the possession of the National Gallery of Australia." This would appear to indicate that, as late as 1980, there was some doubt in the minds of officials in Papua New Guinea as to the whereabouts of the Ambum Stone.[7] How could this be so if the stone was on exhibit at the Australian National Gallery? Or, had there been an inadvertent breakdown in communications?

MAP: "REPRESENTATION OF EARTH'S SURFACE OR PART THEREOF"

Arriving in a thick brown-board envelope, postmarked 9 February 2000, as "printed matter" addressed by Philip Goldman to my University of Canberra office, the map is no simple hurried sketch of an artifact find spot, but it is detailed and complete with symbols designating "roads," "rivers," "villages," "govt. stations," "airstrip," "mountains," and "tracks." At the top in a wide marker pen are written the words "MAP. P Goldman 1962" and added in an aged and less than firm hand, the same that addressed the envelope, "Sorry A Poor Reproduction 1962 pg."

On the find-spot map, Wabag is more or less central, with its airstrip a short distance to the northwest. Also indicated is the village of Sari on the road running northwest to Laiagam. The Ambum and the Lai rivers are shown, as is the track to Monogam and the road to Tsikiru. To the northwest is a distant cluster of mountains. But who drafted the map? It is apparent, that the map was drawn by an individual with a degree of experience with cartography and a broad knowledge of the local terrain. Perhaps, it might have been drawn for another purpose: After all why indicate a far distant place like Monogam when the find spot of the Ambum Stone, as marked on the map was less than a mile from Wabag. Yes, a short distance north of the Lai River, "KENEIDEN PIO" is written in uppercase with a cross marking the find spot a short distance further north on the track to Tsikiru, and a bold arrow overmarking a lighter arrow with the words "STONE FOUND HERE." At the time that the map was drafted, presumably the early 1960s, Wabag was the government administration center with satellite missionary settlements a short distance away.

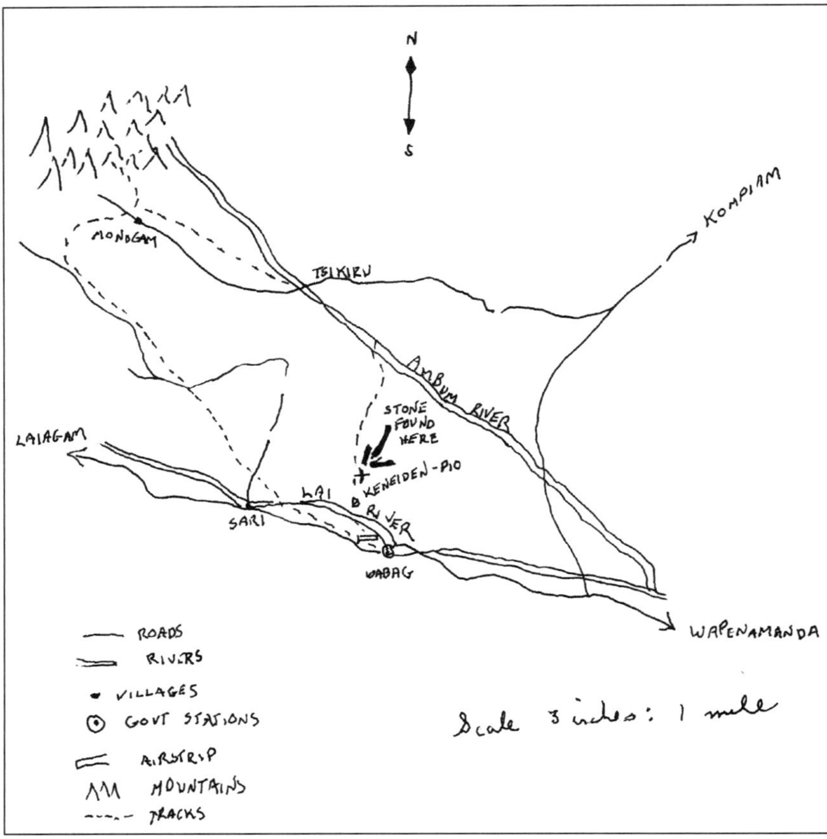

Figure 5.1. Hand-drawn map of the find spot of the Ambum Stone, probably based on a Papua New Guinea patrol report map.

Keith Buxton arrived in Papua New Guinea in 1956 as a medical assistant with the Public Health Department, then worked as a Hospital Administrator. In *Papua New Guinea, the Golden Years* he briefly touches upon his time in the highlands, stating that "Wabag presented the most opportunities to carry out extensive patrols." He illustrates his book with a picture of the Wabag airstrip in 1963. That was the year that President Kennedy was assassinated, and presumably one year after the map of the find spot of the Ambum Stone was annotated. Buxton left the government service to enter the travel industry, with a sideline as an artifact dealer.[8]

Beverly Lawrence, whose husband operated the village trade store, well remembers her years at Wabag. During the mid-1960s their business was the only commercial operation in the town, selling trade goods, petrol and acting as the manifest agents for the airlines and as the post office. She and her husband worked out of their home. It was of modern construction, meaning not made of bush materials, with the business below on the ground floor along with a lockup that had been built by the previous operator, Ron Ingles, to store artifacts that he had acquired through trade with the local highlanders. The dusty airstrip was immediately across from the house. Their home and the houses of the two administrative officers and the government teacher along with their families were the only other constructions of modern materials in the town. The Australian National University had a house constructed of bush materials for their researchers, then occupied by an English couple. The roads were atrocious; they led westerly to the Catholic mission at Sari and southeasterly to Wapenamunda. None of these places had any Western-style buildings.

BROTHER: "MALE BEING RELATED TO AN OTHER"

A photocopy of the map of the supposed find spot of the Ambum Stone was sent to Polly Wiessner who was on her way to do field work with the Enga. She was familiar with the clan territory marked on the map and was able with the help of Akii Tumu to go directly to the location indicated on the map. However, this was not a cave as Wiessner had expected given the information provided to Goldman and reiterated by the Australian National

Gallery. It was a clan ceremonial ground! Quite a difference; one that we will discuss later. When she and Tumu questioned the villagers in 2001, two individuals stepped forward and stated that as boys they were encouraged by the teachings of missionaries to take the stone from where their father had buried it in the clan ceremonial ground and sell it to the owner of the trade store in Wabag, whom they identified as Ron Ingles. They were paid 20 shillings for the Ambum Stone, the older brother received 12 and the younger 8 shillings.

Although the name and location of the ceremonial ground is known, as is the name of the father of the brothers and their names, as is the name of the store owner and the sum of the transaction, it was not known until this narrative was all but complete who exported the Ambum Stone or who sold it to Philip Goldman. Goldman was keeping faith with his supplier and, in spite of many hours of discussion with me, he would not reveal the individual's identity. But there could have been no more than half a dozen persons who were in Wabag during the early 1960s who would have had the inclination to acquire the Ambum Stone. Virtually all that was known specifically about the Ambum Stone had been based upon the information that Philip Goldman supplied to the editor of the *Journal of the Polynesian Society*. Presumably he obtained the map and the information that the stone had been found in a cave from the same individual that sold him the stone. Goldman states that he cannot recall the name of the vendor or details of the sale, such as price and shipping arrangements. Published ethnographic studies of Mervyn Meggitt provide a description of the Enga in the 1960s, but with the focus of his research on warfare he did not directly address the role and significance of sacred cult objects. Philip Goldman corresponded with Mervyn Meggitt and was frustrated that no one was interested in pursuing further investigations into the nature of these stones. Unfortunately *Historical Vines: Enga Networks of Exchange, Ritual, and Warfare in Papua New Guinea* was not as widely read as it should have been following publication in 1998.[9]

Apparently Ralph Bulmer, when professor of anthropology at the University of Papua New Guinea became interested in the Ambum Stone, he corresponded with Paul Brennan, a linguist who was working on the establishment of an Enga cultural center. It was in this correspondence of 1978 that Bulmer stated that inquiries should start with the Danish adventure author Jens Bjerre[10] and the guide that Bjerre in *Savage New Guinea* mentions as Patrol Officer Denys Faithful.

By the late 1990s, our ethnographic understanding of the role of these carved stone objects in Enga society had been greatly expanded by the field research undertaken by Polly Wiessner in concert with Akii Tumu, the curator of the Enga Cultural Center.

Just how ancient are the carved stones of the highlands? Jack Golson during his excavations of the agricultural drainage systems at the Kuk Site, a few miles from Mt. Hagen, recovered a collection of stones "conservatively dated to around 7000–7500 BP." It included:

> the rim of a stone bowl, which thus becomes one of the few examples of the well-known but poorly understood New Guinea mortar and pestle complex to be dated, and certainly the oldest, to be found in archaeological context.[11]

REVEAL: "TO DISCLOSE OR MAKE KNOWN BY DISCOURSE OR COMMUNICATION"

In my Freedom of Information request to the National Gallery of Australia,[12] I sought access to documents relating to the Ambum Stone, specifically those:

- Pertaining to the provenance of the Ambum Stone
- Pertaining to the acquisition and transfer of the Ambum Stone
- Relating to the legal status and ownerships of the Ambum Stone
- Documents relating to the loan of the Ambum Stone to other institutions

On 10 April 2002, a list of 122 documents was supplied by the National Gallery of Australia[13] along with copies of the majority of those documents or parts thereof.[14] Documentation commences in 1974 with a letter from B. E. W. Kelson, secretary of the Commonwealth Art Advisory Board, to Philip Goldman of Gallery 43 in London. This correspondence initiated the process that led four years later to the acquisition by the Australian National Gallery of the Ambum Stone:

> As you know, the Commonwealth Art Advisory Board is interested in acquiring important works of ethnic art for the Australian National Collection. Our attention has been drawn to an article in the *Journal of the Polynesian Society* for 1965 describing a sculptured stone figure from the Ambum Valley in the New Guinea Western Highlands which at that time was in your possession. The Board would be grateful to know if you still have this piece and, if so, whether you would consider offering it to us.[15]

Philip Goldman responded that "offers will be considered in excess of £50,000."[16] On 12 November 1974, James Mollison[17] then director of the Australian National Gallery, wrote to Goldman to determine if the piece was available and at the same time to Douglas Newton, director of the Museum of Primitive Art, to ask his advice on the "offer in excess of £50,000." The letter must have crossed paths with that from Goldman dated 18 November to Kelson asking if the board was still interested.[18] Correspondence from Goldman to Mollison dated 21 November states that "I have been in touch with the owners of the Ambum stone who inform us that at present it is still available."[19] Goldman had been asked by the gallery if the Ambum Stone was available and replied with a sale price at what he believed from his extensive knowledge of the European art market to be reasonable. Newton took exception and mistakenly referred to the price as "terms."

The letter of 19 November 1974 from Douglas Newton to Mollison raises interesting points and although lengthy is worth quoting:

> Your two letters, 11 and 12 November—Goldman is getting ambitious. The first price I heard on that figure was 20,000 pounds, the latest US$100,000. Intrinsically it is the finest New Guinea stone sculpture yet found and it is a superb work in its own right. I have had it in my hand twice, and have been able to take a very good look at it; it holds up magnificently. I think it is a masterpiece in anybody's terms.
>
> There are a few points to be considered. It is not strictly speaking unique; there are to my knowledge about five other similar pieces, or fragments, and I am told there are more. Two (see enclosed) have just been sold for $20,000 each. Therefore one never knows whether a better one might not turn up; but if it did, I doubt if it could be exported from PNG legally. Another thing that worries me about Goldman's price, apart from its dimensions, is that it would be bound to become public, and this would undoubtedly stimulate the search for more such things, consequently wrecking of potential sites, smuggling, and all the other bad things.
>
> As you can see, my feeling is that the object is intensely desirable, but that the price is indecent, and I am very apprehensive about the consequences of buying it on Goldman's terms.[20]

These recommendations by Newton were considered, and negotiations continued. Further correspondence between Goldman and the gallery followed,[21] then a telegram dated 5 February 1975 from Mollison to Goldman stating that "no action on Ambum stone was possible before July 75."[22] Goldman responded in June when no further words had arrived from Mollison, reminding him of his "cable of February 75." Mollison concluded in correspondence to Goldman with "the price is high and I am apprehensive about the consequences of recommending its purchase."[23] Goldman responded to Mollison's concern[24] with a pointed comment referring to the substantial price paid by the Australian National Gallery for Jackson Pollock's *Blue Poles*: "If the available funds are better spent on recently dead Modern artists, then perhaps you have a point."[25]

Mollison then wrote to Michael Somare, Chairman of the Trustees of the Papua New Guinea Public Museum and Art Gallery writing, "I did not feel that I was able to proceed at all with the consideration of the Stone without first consulting your institution." And that we would "naturally stand down if your Museum is interested in its acquisition." [26]

On 22 September the director, Geoffrey Mosuwadoga, responded[27] with "unfortunately in the light of our present financial situation, the expressed £50,000 is well beyond our budgetary capacity." Mosuwadoga adds in closing "We appreciate your thought to advise us before your consideration of the Stone and suggest if the Australian National Gallery is interested they proceed."

Alan R. Dodge, as Senior Research Officer at the Australian National Gallery, then prepared a "Curator's report on works of art offered for acquisition" dated 23 October 1975, quoting the 22 September letter from Mosuwadoga and suggesting that the director offer "$70,000 Aust" for the Ambum Stone.[28] On 26 November there was a second letter from the Australian National

Gallery to the museum asking if the Papua New Guinea Public Museum and Art Gallery would be interested if the price were "£25,000–£30,000."[29] Mosuwadoga, perhaps now more fully aware of the situation, or perhaps better advised, wrote on 18 December:

> I refer to your letter of 26 November, 1975 concerning the Ambin [*sic*] Stone offered to the Australian National Gallery Interim Council for £50,000. While I was in Canberra on the 5 December, I discussed this matter with Mr. Dean. I told him that if you could forward to us a photograph of this piece, I could then present it to the Trustees for further discussion.
>
> I also mentioned that it would be preferable that we have the address of the dealer to enable us to negotiate with him directly. You may be able to act on our behalf after this if we haven't received satisfactory results.
>
> I am concerned that, even though I believe that the object has been publicized a great deal, it lacks information; for example, the exact location it comes from, its uses etc. Artistically, the piece is beautiful, but without any documentation there would not be justification in paying this large amount of money. It may be hard to convince the Trustees as to its importance from a cultural view with no information.
>
> However, I would like to try to negotiate with the dealer if possible and would appreciate if you could forward me his address.[30]

No answer to this letter is present in the FOI documents. It is not impossible that Mosuwadoga was fishing for information that would allow him to fully document the Papua New Guinea museum's priority for acquisition.

From this time onward there appears to be no further correspondence between the Australian National Gallery and the

Papua New Guinea National Museum and Art Gallery with respect to the acquisition of the Ambum Stone. As mentioned earlier with respect to the correspondence from Professor Anthony Forge of The Australian National University and Paul Brennan, it appears that, as late as 1980, it was not widely known that the Ambum Stone was in the collection of the Australian National Gallery. The comments in the letter written by Mosuwadoga are very much a warning to the Australian National Gallery that they are preceding with the purchase of an artifact at an exceptionally high price without independently investigating the provenance of the object. The question of who originally owned the object and whether or not it was legally exported from Papua New Guinea apparently was not easily clarified at the time as the events had happened a decade earlier. Correspondence at this time from Newton steadfastly stands by his earlier advice; do not buy at this price.[31]

Although the Australian National Gallery apparently did not respond to the correspondence from Mosuwadoga, Mollison did transmit his concerns with the contents in correspondence with Newton of 15 January 1976 stating:

> Mr Mosuwadoga is pressing to negotiate with Goldman directly. What are your thoughts on all of this? What should we do now?[32]

There appears to be no response from Newton as Mollison writes and raises the same matters on 25 March:

> The position of the Ambum stone is as follows: Although we asked you to begin serious negotiations for this piece, we felt that it was proper, out of its importance to Papua New Guinea Art Gallery, and considering Geoffrey Mosuwadoga's remarks about the work, that it be offered to that nation in the first in-

> stance. Geoffrey Mosuwadoga has said he would like this piece for the Papua New Guinea Gallery and would like to buy it. Whatever [photocopy is indistinct] are entirely up to him, if the Papua New Guinea Art Gallery is unable to finalize this purchase, our attitude is that we should certainly buy the piece.[33]

Apparently without further correspondence with the Papua New Guinea Public Museum and Art Gallery, V. Leehy, secretary of the Australian National Gallery Interim Council, writes to Newton requesting a report and advising:

> It appears that the Papua New Guinea people are not in a position to buy it and Goldman is now pressing for a decision.[34]

Leehy, in subsequent correspondence, informs Newton that the government has given the gallery $3.5 million for acquisitions and associated costs.[35] With this allocation of funds in hand, the gallery moves to clear the £50,000 purchase price. In telegraph cables between Goldman and the Australian National Gallery, Goldman states that due to the devaluation of the English pound, the original price is no longer acceptable, and that the value was set two years ago at US$115,000 and that is what the owners expect to receive for it today.[36]

Advice from Newton over two years[37] claimed that Goldman's price was too high. Seeking a more supportive "expert," the gallery sought an evaluation of the Ambum Stone from Michel Strauss, of London, who responded:

> However, due to the rarity of such pieces, any price is very speculative and I believe that if it is so important and rare, it could very well be worthwhile paying over the odds for it, such as $50,000 or $60,000.[38]

Presumably this price was in United States dollars. Strauss's advice is much the same as that provided by Newton and perhaps not what the Australian National Gallery wanted to hear, as they considered the information that the artifact was worth only half of what the gallery was in the process of paying. The context of this advice from Newton has been omitted in the FOI document. However, the part provided restates Newton's longstanding position:

> In the circumstances I think an offer of half Goldman's asking price would be fair. What do you think?[39]

There then follows a flurry of cables and letters between Mollison and Philip Goldman discussing when the sale would take place and the method of payment. A submission was redrafted and submitted requesting permission to purchase at the current higher price, which was more in Australian dollars than the original asking price. Included in that submission was a "curator's report on work of art offered for acquisition" dated 23 October 1975. Apparently that report may not have been updated with respect to the correspondence from Mosuwadoga that expressed the interest of the Papua New Guinea National Museum and Art Gallery in the Ambum Stone.

But all was not going smoothly, for records of the Australian National Gallery Council meeting in Canberra on 31 May–1 June 1977[40] state: "Council was aware of Mr. Newton's expressed concern at the price of the Ambum stone received over a number of years" and "agreed to obtain a written report from Mr. Newton confirming his verbal advice that the Ambum Stone is worth $US115,000."[41]

Mollison then dispatched a cable to Newton:

> Council anxious to acquire Ambum stone and submissions to Minister must have report from you in writing the $US115,000 is in fact reasonable price having in mind quality and uniqueness of object. Minister concerned that in 1972 you recommended that stone was overpriced at $50,000.[42]

Yet another cable when the earlier one was unanswered, then another on 19 July,[43] before the Australian National Gallery received the awaited response:

> Strongly recommend purchase of Ambum stone figure at price stated if no negotiation possible stop object unique and first class quality.[44]

Reading between the lines, it is possible that Douglas Newton was being careful not to say that the Ambum Stone was worth the asking price.

The gallery then submitted a proposal to the minister requesting that the Ambum Stone be acquired for $US115,000, as the vendor was not prepared to reduce the price. For some unstated reason, the following portion of the minutes is censored. In closing, there is mention of the attachment of Newton's cable.[45] It appears that also attached to this submission is "Extract from Submission of 20 March 1977" stating:

> Before proceeding with the negotiations we approached Mr Michael Somare stating that we would stand aside if New Guinea wished to acquire it. Subsequently we were advised that if the Australian National Gallery were interested in the piece it should proceed.[46]

The prime minister then approved the purchase in accordance with the submission of 10 August 1977.[47]

At this stage in the proceedings, August 1977, Philip was overseas recovering from a near-fatal accident and was not able to directly supervise the sale that had shifted from London to Switzerland. Payment by blank check was agreed upon as were arrangements for shipping the object from Geneva, Switzerland, be put into effect.[48] What follows is somewhat confused—like when there was an attempt to pick up the artifact from Goldman's business, Gallery 43 in London. A dozen or more cables crossed half the globe clarifying the handover of the stone and the payment by check. Eventually the check was tendered in payment, with the object being dispatched by Henri Harsch via Hong Kong from Geneva on 22 September 1977 to the Australian National Gallery. Harsch was instructed to clear the shipment through customs. Odd, but there is no record on file of it being cleared through customs, though the shipper was asked by the Gallery to do so.

Meanwhile, the Papua New Guinea Museum and Art Gallery was undertaking its own investigations while awaiting a reply from Mollison to Mosuwadoga's letter of 18 December 1975. Having had no response, the museum could have surmised that the gallery was considering its intentions to purchase the stone and was unaware that the Australian National Gallery was negotiating to purchase the object. However, at some time in the process the museum in Port Moresby received from Philip Goldman a superb cast of the Ambum Stone, made by the British Museum.

There is no more relevant correspondence on the gallery file until 1994, when Goldman wrote to the "Department of Tribal Art" asking if it was interested in purchasing further objects.[49] It appears, although I cannot be certain, that at that time Goldman included the copies of correspondence that he had had in the 1960s seeking further information on carved stone artifacts from the highlands as well as possibly including the map of the find spot of the Ambum Stone.

NOTES

1. From www.werner-forman-archive.com/Oceania.htm (accessed on 29 January 2007).

2. Philip Goldman. Personal communication.

3. Barry Craig and David Hyndman (eds.). 1990. *Children of Afek: Tradition and Change among the Mountain-Ok of Central New Guinea*. Oceania Monograph 40.

4. For description of the Ambum Stone refer to Douglas Newton (author given as "D.N."). 1978. (No title). In *Genesis of a Gallery, Part 2—A Touring Exhibition from the Collection of the Australian National Gallery*. Australian National Gallery, Canberra, 27.

5. Ralph Bulmer to Paul Brennan (copy to Brian Egloff). Correspondence of 10 November 1978.

6. Douglas Newton. 1979. "Prehistoric and Recent Art Styles in Papua New Guinea." In S. M. Mead (ed.), *Exploring the Visual Art of Oceania*. University of Hawaii Press, Honolulu, image 3Ibs; and color photograph published in Pamela Swadling et al. 1981/1986. *Papua New Guinea's Prehistory*. Papua New Guinea National Museum and Art Gallery in association with Gordon and Gotch, Boroko, Papua New Guinea, 55.

7. Anthony Forge to Paul Brennan. Correspondence of 13 August 1980.

8. Keith Buxton. 2002. *Papua New Guinea, the Golden Years*. Keith Buxton, Maryborough, Queensland, 51–53 and 167.

9. Polly Wiessner and Akii Tumu. 1998. *Historical Vines: Enga Networks of Exchange, Ritual, and Warfare in Papua New Guinea*. Smithsonian Institution Press, Washington and London.

10. Jens Bjerre. 1964. *Savage New Guinea*. M. Joseph, London.

11. Jack Golson. 2000. "A Stone Bowl Fragment from the Early Middle Holocene of the Upper Wahgi Valley, Western Highlands

Province, Papua New Guinea." *Australian Archaeologist: Collected Papers in Honour of Jim Allen*. Coombs Academic Publishing, The Australian National University, 231

12. Brian Egloff to Brian Kennedy. Correspondence of 3 December 2001.

13. The Australian National Gallery Act was passed in 1976; the name was changed in 1982 to the National Gallery of Australia.

14. John Santolin, FOI coordinator, was responsible for responding to the request. The extensive collection of documents no doubt reflects a diligent and complete search of the Gallery files.

15. B. E. W. Kelson to Philip Goldman. Undated. FOI document 3.

16. Philip Goldman to B. E. W. Kelson. 10 September 1974. FOI document 4.

17. James Mollison to Philip Goldman. 12 November 1974, FOI document 5; James Mollison to Douglas Newton. 12 November 1974. FOI document 5.

18. Goldman to Kelson. 18 November 1974. FOI document 7.

19. Philip Goldman to James Mollison. 21 November 1974. FOI document 9.

20. Douglas to James. 19 November 1974. FOI document 12.

21. FOI documents 14, 16, and 17.

22. Mollison to Philip Goldman. 5 February 1975. FOI document 18.

23. James Mollison to Philip Goldman. 9 July 1975. FOI document 20.

24. Philip Goldman to James Mollison. 16 July 1975. FOI document 22.

25. Philip Goldman is referring here to the purchase of the Jackson Pollock painting *Blue Poles: Number 11* for a sum in excess of Australian $1 million. In 2000, he made this same point in a telephone conversation with me.

26. James Mollision to Michael Somare. 4 September 1975. FOI document 23.

27. Geoffrey Mosuwadoga to James Mollison. 22 September. 1975. FOI document 24.

28. FOI document 26.

29. V. Leehy to G. Mosuwadoga. 26 November 1975. FOI document 29 (file reference 75/768).

30. G. Mosuwadoga to V. Leehy. 18 December 1975. FOI documents 33.

31. The Museum of Primitive Art to James Mollison. 10 November 1975. FOI document 30.

32. James Mollison to Douglas Newton. 15 January 1976. FOI document 34.

33. James Mollison to Douglas Newton. 25 March 1976. FOI document 35 (reference 959169, 73/4838).

34. V. Leehy to Douglas Newton. 9 April 1976. FOI document 37 (reference 75/768).

35. V. Leehy to Douglas Newton. 24 June 1976. FOI document 38 (reference 75/768).

36. FOI documents 40–45, in particular: Philip Goldman to James Mollison. 17 November 1976. FOI document 46 (reference 18 Aus/AMB).

37. Documents apparently relating to this process were excluded from the material received under FOI.

38. Michel Strauss to V. Leehy. 24 September 1976. FOI document 47 (reference 15/768).

39. The Museum of Primitive Art to James Mollison. 11 August 1976. FOI document 48, provided in part (reference 72/997).

40. Provided in part under FOI.

41. Australian National Gallery. 31 May–1 June 1977. Extract from Agenda, FOI document 60, censored in part.

42. FOI document 62.

43. Mollison to Newton. Undated. FOI document 62. Also 11 July 1977. FOI document 65. Also 19 July. FOI document 66.

44. Newton to Mollison. 5 August 1977. FOI document 67.

45. James Mollison to the Minister. 10 August 1977. FOI document 69 (reference 75/768).

46. Extract from submission of 20 March 1977, FOI document 68.

47. B. E. W. Kelson to the Director. Undated. FOI document 73.

48. Rosalind Goldman to Mollison. Cable received 26 August 1977. FOI document 80.

49. Philip Goldman to Wally Caruana. 22 July 1994. File number 83/998, FOI documents 116, 117, 118, 119, and 120.

SIX

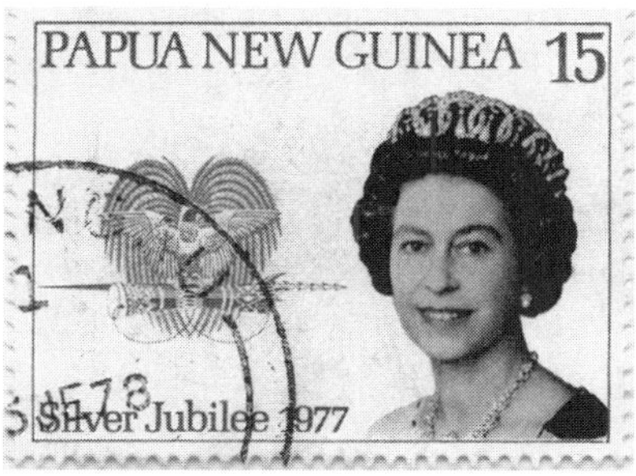

Fitting the Pieces Together

Of particular concern to me was the response by the National Gallery of Australia to my efforts to reach a better understanding of the provenance of the Ambum Stone. On 10 March 2001, I sent a letter to Brian Kennedy, director, National Gallery of Australia:

> This correspondence is a request to access the records of the NGA pertaining to the cultural associations, and the acquisition and transfer of the Ambum Stone. This relatively unique artefact was acquired by the NGA in the mid 1970s. At approximately the same time, I received correspondence from Professor Ralph Bulmer, one of the pioneering anthropological researchers in the western highlands of Papua New Guinea that provided me with valuable clues pertaining to the initial acquisition of the artefact by Europeans. Shortly after receiving the correspondence, I left the National Museum and Art Gallery of Papua New Guinea and was unable to follow-up the leads that he provided. I am now in a posi-

tion to do so and need to have at hand all relevant information in order to facilitate further field research with the Mae Enga.

It is intended that this research will take place in July. As the key informants are aged, this could be the last opportunity to bring together and verify oral testimony from a variety of sources. It is my understanding that there is little information at hand pertaining to the cultural associations of the artefact, its acquisition by Europeans and its transfer out of Papua New Guinea. What little information has been made public definitely needs to be verified by field research.

Any information found in the course of the field research will be made available to the NGA. Thank you for your kind attention and co-operation.

That letter elicited the following response:

It has been brought to my attention that you are currently undertaking independent research into the history of prehistoric stone sculptures from Papua New Guinea, focussing especially on the National Gallery of Australia's Ambum stone. Confidential information about the purchase of NGA acquisitions, including the Ambum Stone, cannot be made readily available to members of the public on request.

While we wish you well on any project on PNG cultural artefacts which you may wish to pursue, I must inform you officially that you should not state or imply in any way that your research is supported or sanctioned by the National Gallery of Australia, or suggest to them that you are carrying out your research in the NGA's interests or with the NGA's encouragement.

As you are aware, the Ambum Stone was damaged while on loan to a French public museum last year. The results of conservation tests carried out on the object during the process

> of restoration will soon be published and I am sure you will find them very interesting. You should feel free to contact NGA curators Wally Caruana or Robyn Maxwell if you have questions about this letter.

For security reasons, galleries and dealers may choose to protect their sources from theft or harassment while museums may welcome researchers. I then addressed correspondence to the curators specified in the director's letter and received no response. At the same time as my request was referred on, in keeping with the current information policy, the gallery released to the press details of the recent acquisition of *After Cezanne*, a painting by Lucien Freud, including the original asking price, the acquisition price, and the name of the dealer. By an odd quirk of fate, in the same issue of *artonview* that details the conservation of the Ambum Stone, there is an article entitled "In Search of Lucien Freud."[1]

BROKEN: "SEPARATED FORCIBLY INTO PIECES"

When valuable art objects are lent by one gallery to another, the usual practice is for them to be accompanied by a courier, generally speaking, either a curator or assistant curator from the lending institution, whose task it is to ensure that the loans are correctly and safely installed. An article entitled "Precious Artefact Broken by French Was Already a Bust" offers an account based on preliminary staff advice:

> A precious artefact from the National Gallery of Australia had been broken before it was dropped at a French museum while on loan last month. The NGA's director Dr. Brian Kennedy, said two of last month's three breaks on the Ambum stone,

> a prehistoric sculpture from the western highlands of Papua New Guinea, occurred where previous mending had been done. It had been broken before the gallery acquired it in 1977, he said. The Musée D'Arts Africains, Océaniens, Amerindiens [*sic*], in Marseilles, was running behind schedule in setting up an exhibition when the sculpture was knocked off of its stand on April 13, the morning of the exhibitions opening. The accident happened after the Australian courier left the stone on a cushion on the museum floor, at the request of the exhibition organisers, because more work needed to be done on its glass display case. The Ambum stone is one of the most prized pieces in the NGA's Melanesian collection.[2]

The matter reached the attention of the Senate Estimates Committee, the body that overseess expenditure by government agencies; and questions were placed on notice to be answered by the National Gallery of Australia. Answers on notice to parliament and recorded in Hansard offer this account in reply to the question raised by Senator Schacht:

> The work was safely installed in a display case. . . . It was subsequently damaged when a museum employee accidentally knocked it when attending another object in the case.[3]

As the exhibition must go on, so to speak, the Musée repaired the breaks and in due course informed the National Gallery of Australia of the accident. What is interesting in the account is the initial advice of the staff of the National Gallery of Australia that the Ambum Stone "had been broken before it was dropped at the French Museum while on loan last month." Douglas Newton specifically mentions in correspondence that he had handled the object when it was on loan to the Museum of Primitive Art, yet makes no comment during the dozen or more communications with the Australian National Gallery that the object had been broken or repaired. Nor is any breakage recorded in curator's report prepared on 27 October 1975 by Alan Dodge.

During 2001 and 2002, while I was searching for clues that would provide a trail of information on the transfer of the stone from the Ambum Valley to Canberra, conservation of the broken object was underway.

CONSERVATION: "PRESERVATION FROM DESTRUCTIVE INFLUENCE"

Damage had been done. In France, the Ambum Stone, now in three pieces, was repaired to some extent, returned to Canberra and then submitted to further conservation treatment. This appears to be the first time in more than twenty-five years that the gallery sought a better understanding of the Ambum Stone. Museum and gallery curators seek to understand the collections, and conservators keep them intact, with both specialists being responsible for their safekeeping. Conservators have expertise in materials and museum environments, while curators are intellectually involved in historical and social processes that add to the understanding of the context and the particular circumstances of an artifact. Conservators need to have at their disposal a considerable amount of information before they can proceed with the conservation treatment. Aside from having to have a thorough understanding of the materials that comprise the object, conservators need to be informed of any previous treatments as well as the environmental context of the object when it was being used. At the time that the conservation treatment was being undertaken, 2000 and 2001, there had been no further investigation of the original provenance information beyond that which was provided by Goldman and published in the *Journal of Polynesian Studies* in 1965. As such, the conservators thought that the object had been "collected in 1962 from a cave in Yambu clan-territory."

Conservators undertake incredibly detailed work, maintain records of the condition of objects before they go out on loan and then assess the objects when they return. Although the Musée had adhered the pieces together, serious bruises were apparent. The gallery conservator reports that

> the stability of the adhered joins was unclear. It was therefore decided to take the broken sections apart and readhere them under a careful controlled environment.
>
> The restoration was taken apart by placing the object in a saturated atmosphere of acetone vapours to minimise the risk of solvent staining of the surface. After 92 hours the adhesive softened and the broken sections were separated.
>
> After de-assembly, it became apparent that the sculpture had not been broken before, as was previously assumed.[4]

Taking the opportunity provided by the fresh surfaces provided by the breaks, the stone was analyzed and micro-organic material that had found its way into one of the fracture lines provided organic material for dating:

> Analysis identified the rock from which the Ambum stone was carved as a volcanic sandstone or crystal tuff. Its mineralogical composition is consistent with the geology of the area of the find. The break occurred largely along a natural line of weakness, which had been penetrated by water and plant activity during the period of burial before the Ambum Stone's discovery.
>
> The small amount of plant material found in the crack of the sculpture provided an opportunity for radiocarbon

dating. The results of the analysis indicate the plant material to be approximately 3,500 years old.[5]

The date of 3,500 years ago, given that it was derived from a small amount of material found in a crack in the artifact following various chemical conservation treatments, is reasonable from what we know about highlands prehistory. When considering the reliability of this date, it is necessary to be mindful that the stone had undergone previous treatments, in particular the process of making copies at the British Museum and then the repair by the Musée, and who knows what substances had been used to clean it or were applied to it during its use as a cult object in the highlands. Being in a saturated vapor of acetone for ninety-two hours could influence the radiocarbon age estimate. Interferences with the natural qualities of the stone and the plant material residues could have introduced ancient hydrocarbon contaminants that would have had the effect of producing an older age result. The date is acceptable but is approximately 3,500 years younger than that obtained for a fragment of a stone bowl, or mortar, excavated by Jack Golson at a prehistoric site near Mt. Hagen (dated to 7,000 to 7,500 years ago).[6] Swadling and Hide point out that ancient carved-stone artifacts are more broadly distributed than are figures carved like the Ambum Stone that are confined to the Western and Southern Highlands of Papua New Guinea.

LEGALITY: "THE QUALITY OF BEING LEGAL"

No evidence has come to light that the Ambum Stone was acquired or transferred within, or exported from, the Territory of Papua New Guinea with the required permission or export permit. The lack of such documents could be a factor of the 1960s export date but more likely is due to the object being surreptitiously or unwittingly exported. Nor are there any documents in the Freedom of Information material alerting the customs service of a highly valued object even though the Australian National Gallery had requested that the shipping agent clear the shipment through customs. Staff of the National Gallery of Australia are quoted as "Mr Caruana and curator of Asian Art, Dr Robyn Maxwell, disputed yesterday Dr Egloff's charges, saying that he had got the sequence of events wrong. It is reported that Dr Maxwell said that Australian legislation for cultural heritage agreements post-dated the gallery's acquisition of the stone."[7] The article is referring to the 1970 UNESCO Convention on the Means of Prohibiting the Illicit Import, Export and Transfer of Ownership of Cultural Property, that Australia came to ratify sixteen years later when the government of Australia enacted the Protection of Movable Cultural Property Heritage Act of 1986. This is not the relevant instrument to refer to, as an international treaty regulating the transfer of cultural property had little bearing on an incident that took place in the 1960s and 1970s when Papua and New Guinea was a territory of Australia or as a newly independent nation that maintained a special customs relationship with Australia. The press article implies that in 1977, when the Ambum Stone was imported into Australia, the UNESCO convention (had it been ratified by Australia) was the only regulation that would have pertained to the import of artifacts from Papua New Guinea. But this emphatically was not the case!

Australia had and continues to have a customs regulation specifically designed to deal with artifacts illegally exported from Papua New Guinea and imported into Australia. The *Annual Report to the Trustees from the Director of the Papua New Guinea National Museum and Art Gallery* for the period 1 July 1974 to 30 June 1975 states that the Museum's efforts to effect a change of the *Australian Customs Act 1901–1974* have been successful. Under new regulations, National Cultural Property exported from Papua New Guinea as a prohibited export automatically becomes a prohibited import into Australia. If the Australian Customs Authority seizes this material it will be sent back to Papua New Guinea.

Prott and O'Keefe refer to the regulation:

> Australia, an important geographical transit State for material from Papua New Guinea, has imposed import controls on cultural materials from that country since 1975.[8]

And, elsewhere, they remark that

> sometimes co-operation between institutions occurs not merely on occasions . . . but on a long-term basis. Thus the Australian Museum in Sydney has particularly good relations with the National Museum of Papua New Guinea in Port Moresby. It has been prepared to return to some Pacific countries material, which had been quite properly acquired . . . is vigilant not to acquire, authenticate or value objects, which have been illicitly exported . . . and will assist the Australian Customs Service in identifying material from Papua New Guinea subject to the prohibition of the *Australian Customs (Prohibited Imports), Regulations.*[9]

Information received from the Australian Customs Department:

> On 22 April 1975, at the request of the Chief Minister of Papua New Guinea, Item 9A of Schedule 3 of the customs (Prohibited Imports) Regulations 1956 was enacted to pro-

> tect articles of PNG cultural property. The control gives the Australian Customs Service the authority to intercept, seize and return items of national cultural significance if requested by the PNG authorities.
>
> Prior to the introduction of these border controls, Customs had no authority to detain or seize PNG heritage goods. Item 9A cannot be applied retrospectively to goods imported before the Gazettal of this control in 1975.[10]

The Ambum Stone was imported into Australia two years after the regulation was in place and, if the government of Papua New Guinea had been aware of the transfer of an item of national cultural property to Australia, Prime Minister Somare would have carefully considered requesting its return.

Arrangements with Australian customs authorities had been realized as early as 7 June 1974, when a shipment of fourteen crates of artifacts aboard the Australian naval barge HMAS *Wewak* was unloaded and subsequently impounded in Townsville.[11] Australian customs was concerned, as in February a similar shipment of fifteen crates had been dispatched from Daru to Cairns as personal affects. Of particular interest were fifteen items including *kundu* drums and elaborately carved ceremonial *gopi* boards. Investigations concluded that the shipment of objects had originated at the Hotel Daru and were consigned to officers of the naval vessel for transportation to Australia. It was suggested that the vessel's mess received cases of grog and a hi-fi set in return. Needless to say, Australian naval authorities were reluctant to discuss this case because HMAS *Wewak* apparently was not scheduled to discharge cargo at Townsville. Follow-up discussions led me to believe that the officers of the vessel had been transferred to the United Kingdom, perhaps to place them at a distance from any judicial inquiries. I then sought a search warrant and with police in attendance seized further items that were in the hotel and prepared for shipment. The matter was resolved in the Daru court with the successful prosecution of the hotel manager under the National Cultural Property (Preservation) Ordinance.

The Townsville-Daru seizures did not reach the same degree of national prominence as did a case where it was alleged that artifact collectors had threatened villagers with guns and forcefully acquired national cultural property. The three unidentified offenders sailed off in their vessel. The Deputy District Commissioner of the Gulf District prepared a detailed and lengthy report of the incident. A year or so later, believing, correctly, that the statue of limitations had expired on the violation of the National Cultural Property (Preservation) Act, the offenders returned to Port Moresby, presumably on another collecting expedition. The detailed report by the deputy district commissioner enabled the customs authorities to seize the vessel and arrest the three individuals, not under the National Cultural Property (Preservation) Act, as the statue of limitations had indeed expired, but charges were laid against the suspects for conspiracy against the Crown. They forfeited their passports, were released on bail, and promptly fled the country. This embarrassed the government of New Caledonia, where the culprits were resident, to such an extent that all artifacts in possession of the suspects were seized and transported to Port Moresby aboard a French naval vessel where they were added to the national collections.

BLUE POLES: "A PAINTING BY A RECENTLY DEAD MODERN ARTIST"

Not all investigations led to positive outcomes, although many did in one way or another. Relating tangentially to the Ambum Stone were two incidents, one in 1971 and the second in 1972, involving the illicit removal of carved wooden figures and masks from the small island of Tabar, lying to the east of New Ireland.[12] Documents testify that as early as 1971, under the auspices of Roy Mackay, preparatory in charge, the museum was taking every step possible to enforce internationally the cultural property export controls, as well as vigorously pursuing objects that had been illegally exported and identified as being in the hands of galleries or collectors:

> In May 1971, an exhibition of eight carved wooden heads and masks from Tabar (New Ireland District) was held at the Galerie Jacques Kerchache in Paris. The Director of the International Council of Museums drew the attention of the Australian delegate to UNESCO to this exhibition and said, "that he was anxious to make some enquiries concerning the acquisition of these artifacts, since the Director of the Galerie Jacques Kerchache had gained, particularly in Africa, a reputation for unscrupulousness in this regard."[13]

The response from New Ireland District headquarters at Kavieng to inquiries made by Mackay indicates that "M. Jacques Kerchache and another (Frenchman) in collaboration with Mr. B. Birve (Tabar resident) purchased artifacts on Tabar approx. July/August 1970" and "the artefacts are alleged to be a quantity of 'grave sculptures' of some significance."

As permits had not been issued for the transfer, acquisition, or export of these objects, it was obvious that the National Cultural Property (Preservation) Act had been violated. However, no action took place until March 1974 when the objects were thought to have been seized by United States customs but were in fact in the hands of a new owner.

Interpol had been requested to assist and had traced one of the masks to America. As events unfolded, it became apparent that United States customs could not intercede on behalf of Papua New Guinea as the object had been legally imported into their country. Although a signatory to the UNESCO convention, the United States had not enacted legislation that would allow it to put into effect the provisions of the convention.[14] In other words, it could not seize the objects. Advice from the Crown Solicitors office in Port Moresby was that it would require lengthy and expensive court proceedings in the United States to have any chance at all of recovering the carved mask. Indeed it was most unlikely that such action would meet with success.

Investigations indicated that Ben Heller Inc. of New York had purchased the mask from Galerie Jacques Kerchache in Paris on 16 October 1973. This is the same Ben Heller who gained fame in Australia for buying in 1957 the Jackson Pollock painting *Blue Poles* for reportedly slightly more than $200,000 and reselling it in 1973 for more $1.34 million dollars to the Australian National Gallery. "How *Blue Poles* Polarised Australia" reports that at that time the highest price paid for a Picasso was $500,000.[15] The article mentions the speculation, since disproved, "that Pollock and his friend Tony Smith painted *Blue Poles* in a drunken frenzy." After the sale, Heller is reported to have said that it was like losing one of the family. It is this sale that Philip Goldman refers to as that of a "recently dead Modern artist," in his correspondence to the gallery, as one of the reasons that justifies his asking price for the Ambum Stone or perhaps it was the perfectly reasonable perception, at that time, that the Australian National Gallery was a ready customer for quality art!

Increasingly throughout the 1970s, the Papua New Guinea Museum perfected its systems of export controls and was able to garner major pieces and in fact entire galleries of masterpieces for its collections. In 1972, two collectors not associated with

Kerchache acquired artifacts on Tabar and the neighboring islands. Mackay traveled to Rabaul and inspected the artifacts. He reserved for the museum collections valuable pieces, including two exceptionally rare wooden carvings "which were part of the forked branches acting as gateways into the stone walls of the men's sacred enclosures." These carvings have been on display in the masterpieces collection of the museum and were illustrated in the 1969–1972 *Annual Report of the Trustees*. The report documents the actions by the museum to enforce the cultural property legislation that received the wholehearted support of the government of Papua New Guinea.[16] Collectors then began to shift their collecting expeditions to other countries, such as Indonesia, where there were abundant fine textiles and carvings to be collected and the chances of having one's goods confiscated were minimal.

CONFUSION: "TO MIX-UP IN THE MIND"

The Jolika collection has been discussed by various individuals. There seems to be some confusion as to how much of the collection could be regarded as the national cultural property of Papua New Guinea. Perhaps the most exhaustive consideration is a communication from Evan J. Paki (Papua New Guinea ambassador to the United States) to John E. Buchannan, Jr. (director of the de Young Museum). In his letter, Paki states that:

> Even if those few pieces in the Jolika Collection are ultimately proven to have been NCP objects, the question that may be asked is what to do with those few works of art. It is quite possible that the NCP objects, if any, in the entire Friede collection may previously have been the subject of unauthorized

exporting by certain art dealers or collectors and then sold to others outside of the country, who in turn may have sold them to others, including Mr. Friede. Unbeknownst to him Mr Friede may well have innocently acquired those few NCP objects.

Paki continues:

> It is thus irresponsible and perhaps defamatory, in our view, to point to a few pieces in the Jolika Collection and imply that a man who is not only of extreme repute in the art community but a philanthropist may have been involved in illegal exports of NCP objects or may have knowingly acquired them from others who may have illegally exported cultural artifacts from PNG.[17]

Paki indicates that the majority of the artifacts in the Jolika collection has been acquired by Friede after they had been exported. The collection is breathtaking and the exhibit at the de Young is of international standard. It is understood that the de Young Museum is making arrangements such that there will be a lasting and mutually beneficial relationship with the Papua New Guinea museum. The question of national cultural property is clouded by the fact that there are two kinds of national cultural property in Papua New Guinea. Paki is discussing the kind of national cultural property that is individually listed as exceptional objects. The other kind of national cultural property covers virtually all objects that were made and used for traditional purposes.

The correspondence stresses that:

> The overriding interest is—and should still be—the preservation, protection and promotion of PNG's unique art and art history as a crucial component of our cultural heritage.

Repatriation enters the consideration in the following statement:

> It appears that the appropriate circumstances do not presently exist there for the few NCP artifacts, if any, in the Jolika Collection to be repatriated to PNG at this stage. . . . The National Museum is in a rebuilding and expansion mood, and is trying to secure additional space for its various collections.

Papua New Guinea has a large and fully modern museum facility with extensive earth-integrated and thermally controlled storage rooms. But in common with all museums, it is short of storage space in part due to the monumental size of many of the traditional works in the collection: canoes, large spirit-house painted gables and carved house posts as well as hundreds of masks, carved wooden bowls, and ceramic pots. Nevertheless, I would have thought the primary consideration would be an enforcement of the laws of the land buttressed by a timely, comprehensive, and detailed investigation of the allegations. Where has the notion of truth, so stressed by Coggins, gone?[18] It needs to be stressed that there is no simple answer to the matters raised in the press. Certainly I do not wish to diminish the philanthropic efforts of John Friede, but in keeping with the notion that we should search for the truth, further inquiries would seem to be appropriate.

Robert Welsch writes that:

> Another factor is also relevant to an understanding of the importance of the Jolika Collection. Around the time of Papua New Guinea independence in 1975, the national parliament established National Cultural Property (NCP) legislation aimed at preventing old and important cultural artifacts, carvings, and other art objects from leaving the country. When the

> Friedes starting collecting New Guinea art, not only had the best old pieces already been bought out from the villages but the national laws would have made their export illegal if they had been there. Again, then, field collecting as presently governed would have made it impossible to assemble the Jolika Collection today through that means alone.[19]

It is not apparent why the earlier antiquities legislation was not mentioned. Welsch coedited a publication entitled *Hunting the Gatherers: Ethnographic Collectors, Agents and Agency in Melanesia, 1870s–1930s* containing an article in which Michael Quinnell discusses the early efforts by the administrator of Papua to acquire a collection of artifacts for the government museum and to enforce the antiquities legislation.[20]

Remember that antiquities legislation in Papua dates to 1913 and to the Mandated Territory of New Guinea to 1922, and covers not only antiquities, but all objects made by natives for traditional purposes. In other words, the purchase and export of all artifacts was controlled. In the 1960s, the antiquities legislation was redrafted and the ethnographic, geological, and archaeological objects more correctly described as national cultural property.

The Papua New Guinea National Cultural Property (Preservation) Act of 1965 appears to be in conformity with the UNESCO convention of 1970. However Papua New Guinea has not acceded to the convention. Writing in 1989, Prott and O'Keefe explain that

> in the case of many smaller or poorer States this may well be because the lack of resources does not make it easy to participate very actively in Unesco's work, but the view has also been expressed by some that there is no point in accession to the Convention when most of the important cultural material has

> long since been taken. Some States are far more concerned with the "realities" issue, and less with the non-retrospective scheme of the 1970 Convention, which they see as bringing them, at this stage, very little advantage. The reason may also be a certain disenchantment with the final text of the Convention: one commentator from Italy, which is party to the Convention, has suggested that, even if all States scrupulously carried out the obligations under Articles 5 to 8, the larger part of the illicit trade would continue.[21]

Instead of a blanket proscription on the purchase and export of all artifacts, the Papua New Guinea legislation enumerates various categories. Artifacts made for traditional purposes were controlled, and modern artifacts made for the tourist market were excluded; as such, the essential elements of cultural property controls remained unchanged from earlier instruments that made no provision for exclusion of modern artifacts. Ceremonial masks, carved stone objects, decorated parts of men's houses, large ceremonial slit drums, human remains; all the "treasures" sought after by dealers where substantial profits were to be made were controlled. But the export of these artifacts was strictly controlled. If national cultural property was found in a shipment, the objects were seized without compensation being paid to the errant dealers.

Now that we have a bit better understanding of the early antiquities ordinances of Papua and New Guinea followed by the transformation of those instruments into the National Cultural Property (Preservation) Ordinance of 1965, it is worth applying our newly acquired skills to an analysis of the controversial Jolika collection. With a detailed, well-illustrated, and comprehensive catalog, the Jolika collection by John Friede at the de Young Museum in San Francisco is ideal for analysis, as there is a picture of each item and provenance information where available, details about the collector, date of collection, collections that the artifact has belonged to, as well as venues where it has been exhibited. John Friede is to be commended for making such an effort to describe in detail the collection.

The Friede bequest to the de Young Museum has raised questions over artifacts illustrated in the catalog that are reported as being of such importance that at least two were individually listed in the government gazette as the national cultural property of Papua New Guinea and a total of nine are considered to be national cultural property.[22] Acting on comments by Barry Craig of the South Australian Museum, the media published statements that nine artifacts in the collection were national cultural property of Papua New Guinea. Craig collected in New Guinea for the Commonwealth Art Advisory Board in the 1970s, the predecessor of the National Gallery of Australia, and in the 1980s served as a curator for the Papua New Guinea National Museum and Art Gallery. In the 1970s, an effort was made to catalog significant pieces that remained in the villages. Photographs were taken of the objects and details of cultural affiliation and ownership were recorded. If the allegations are correct, then the artifacts were illegally acquired, transferred, and exported, most likely within the past two or three decades. Being individually listed provides the highest level of protection that can be afforded under the National Cultural Property (Preservation) Act. Listing in the government gazette sends a clear and unambiguous signal that the object must remain in its context and it cannot be acquired without permission of the trustees of the national museum. Craig knows what he is talking about. Appendix 2.3 of his thesis lists all of the artifacts entered in the government gazette as national cultural property. The list commences in 1967 with petroglyphs, grave-markers and megalithic structures being entered, and ends in 1982: a total of ninety-seven objects in all. On the downside, and this is a real problem, publication of national cultural property in the government gazette provides unscrupulous dealers with a shopping list of the most valuable items of cultural heritage remaining in the villages.

The reported national cultural property in the Jolika collection comprises slightly more than 2 percent of the listed objects. The allegations are a bit vague, so let us look more closely at the collection, as there appears to be considerable confusion as to just what is national cultural property. The Papua New Guinea ambassador has stressed that only a few objects were possibly national cultural property.

The Jolika catalog lists 598 pieces, with material ascribed to New Guinea, Papua, West Papua (Indonesia), and the Torres Strait (Australia). All pieces are pictured and described, but the information on the provenance and collector is adequate for only a minority of pieces. For instance, only about 6 percent of the objects have a collector listed. But as Friede has brought this collection together relatively recently, during his adult lifetime, many of the pieces have been exhibited in museums or are listed as once having been in another collection or are described as having been exhibited in a commercial gallery. This kind of a pedigree has been provided for 37 percent of the objects.

New Guinea is listed as the source for the majority of the material: approximately 517 items. Thirty-seven objects are likely to have been collected before the enactment of the antiquities legislation in 1922. About 51 pieces were collected from 1922 to 1960 and would have been subject to the antiquities legislation, and 90 were collected after 1960 and would have been categorized as national cultural property; about 227 have no dates but for the most part are presumed to be national cultural property. We have to be careful, because an object made for sale to tourists that has never functioned in a traditional setting is exempt from the provisions of the National Cultural Property (Preservation) Act. Without a close scrutiny of the objects it is difficult to know if there are any modern artifacts in the collection.

One of the more common practices of artifact dealers in Papua New Guinea was to employ traditional carvers from villages that produced notable art and have them carve old-style works. Some pieces would be left as new and sold to tourists, while the better pieces might be artificially aged by allowing downspouts from the dealer's house to direct water over them, burying in organic rich mud and rubbing with various self-made ageing compounds to obtain an aged look and a patina of authenticity. As such, if there were "fakes" in the collection or pieces made to look like traditional objects, they would not be categorized national cultural property. The year 1960 is used as a time marker because that is the start of the decade when the Papua New Guinea Museum was being formalized by the administration of the territory and policing of the act was more stringent than previously.

For Papua, twenty-five pieces are likely to have been collected prior to 1913 and the enactment of the antiquities legislation; eight in the period from 1913 to 1960; and thirty-nine after 1960, with the majority of the last category comprising acquisitions from the Gulf of Papua that are of such high quality that it would have been difficult to acquire export permits for them. At times, the Papua New Guinea National Museum and Art Gallery did allow exceptionally high-quality objects to leave the country if prior permission was obtained from the trustees to acquire a collection—for a public institution—and if major pieces from the collection were donated to the museum.

In summary, approximately one-tenth of the Jolika collection would not have had their purchase and export controlled, as they were acquired prior to the enactment of the antiquities legislation. However, the remaining would have been controlled as either antiquities or national cultural property. A buyer or dealer would have been required to have permission to purchase the objects and would have been required to have export permits because although not listed in the government gazette, the artifacts are clearly produced for traditional purposes.

Many of the artifacts have gone through the hands of more than one owner and a few excellent artifacts are listed as deaccessioned museum pieces—in at least one instance from a collection of a missionary association. It is well known that some museums are so cash-strapped that duplicates in their collections—and some of these are exceptionally fine artifacts with established pedigrees—have been sold to raise funds.

NATIONAL IDENTITY: "A ONENESS"

Papua New Guinea is divided both by natural features and colonial processes that continue to plague this relatively new nation. It is separated into two halves by a mountain range that is rugged beyond belief, dissected by major waterways and deep gorges, and distanced by straits and seas from its constituents on the Admiralty Islands, New Britain, New Ireland, and Bougainville. With its numerical weakness, 3 million versus 180 million Indonesians, and its relatively undeveloped economy compared with Australia's, it is a given that the country will have difficulty feeling complete and equal to its neighbors. The uncomfortable border issues, the extraordinarily rich cultural diversity, and an unheard-of multiplicity of languages make it appear that the inhabitants of Papua New Guinea have little in common with each other except a shared colonial past and the turbulent birthing pains of nationhood. More recently, efforts toward national unity have been frustrated by the decade-long secessionist struggle of copper-rich Bougainville. With no common religion, ethnicity, or language, or indeed a universal sharing of cultural attributes, Papua New Guinea does not have the obvious prerequisites for a united nation-state.

Creation and maintenance of a shared vision of nationhood has been a task of the government since well before independence in 1975. Michael Somare, chief minister during the days of self-government that preceded independence and then the first prime minister, stated that:

> Strong steps have been taken to help preserve and develop our culture and thereby our national identity. The national museum is building up a growing collection of art works from Papua New Guinea, and we have started to negotiate with Australia and other countries for the return of some of our art that was carried away during colonial times.[23]

Somare considered that the creation of a constitution that suited the village-orientated peoples of Papua New Guinea was an all-important initial step in nation building. The opening words of the constitution are:

> We, the people of Papua New Guinea—united in one nation, pay homage to the memory of the ancestors—the source of our strength and origin of our combined heritage; acknowledge the worthy customs and traditional wisdoms of our people—which have come down to us from generation to generation; pledge ourselves to guard and pass on to those who come after us our noble traditions and Christian principles that are ours now.[24]

Attributes considered to contribute to a shared identity are: a respect of the ancestors; a reciprocal sharing of wealth, community values and self-reliance, authority vested in the elders, strength of kinship ties, expansive trade systems that connect the country like a spider's web,[25] tolerance of religious diversity, the "Melanesian way" of consensus during conflict mediation, and a richness of oral and visual art and dance traditions.[26] Considerable importance is given to the continuation of the artistic past into the present, with Papua New Guinea playing a major role in the Pacific Island arts festivals. Lindstrom in "Pasin Tumbuna: Culture and Nationalism in Papua New Guinea" writes:

> In Papua New Guinea, the exercise of nationalist imagination has in large part fixed upon culture. In this, national identity is located within cultural traditions (or *ol Pasil bilong ol tumbuna*—"the ways of the ancestors").[27]

But Lindstrom notes that:

> discourse that devalues tradition is a popularized version of the 19th-century social evolutionism that portrays Papua New Guinea as the land of the primitive: "the Stone Age in the Space Age." This perspective tends to depict Melanesian cultures in terms of what they lack: no law, no government, no economy, morals, sense of time, individuality, and so forth. National culture is haunted by specters of primitiveness, sorcery, cannibalism, and savage feuding. These images have been fed by a century of social theory that seized upon PNG as the epitome of The Primitive.[28]

It is easy to understand why for Papua New Guineans, objects like the Ambum Stone have all of the attributes that constitute what they as a nation value in a shared past. And that pieces from their ancestral past are so highly valued and take pride-of-place in the National Gallery of Australia must considerably heighten their pride. Nations may on the one hand be arbitrary constructs, but on the other hand the "reason nations matter is that they matter to *people*."[29] But there certainly is a downside. Papua New Guineans cannot be anything but chagrined that one of the few similar pieces of intact quality was destroyed during a conflict that resulted in the police station where it was in safe-keeping being burned down. If the past and its material representations are so valued by the nation, then why has the national museum—a show piece located adjacent to the national parliament in Port Moresby—been allowed to drift into such a parlous state that it cannot prevent the theft of exhibits and equipment, nor ensure the safety of its staff and visitors?

Exhibitions such as the Jolika at the de Young Museum will fuel mixed emotions in Papua New Guineans. On the one hand there is pride in the artistic and symbolic achievements of their ancestors, on the other hand there are concerns with the depiction of the art as "primitive"—is the term "tribal" likely to be less offensive? Display of trophy human skulls is no doubt less than welcomed, given that indigenous peoples around the world have been making concerted efforts to have ancestral remains returned or at the very least removed from display. And, there is the added discomfort of knowing that their own national museum has operational challenges and that a considerable quantity of their national cultural property lies outside of the country.

The National Cultural Property (Preservation) Act of 1965 and its predecessors (dating back to 1913) were exemplary in their simplicity, adaptability, and ease of enforcement. Aside from the problems that have emerged by the listing of valuable pieces remaining in the villages, the act can be administered with surprisingly few resources assuming that the customs and police departments have the capacity to extend full cooperation to the national museum. It is difficult to believe that there could be any misunderstanding about the nature of the instruments that have regulated the trade in Papua New Guinea cultural materials for almost a century. The legislation has been widely discussed in national as well as international publications and the monumental compendium by Prott and O'Keefe.[30] Less than twenty pages in length, including the regulations and subsidiary legislation, the act is surprisingly economical and easy to grasp. It is much the same as its predecessors with respect to the definition of national cultural property, earlier referred to as "antiquities":

> "National cultural property" means any property, movable or immovable, of particular importance to the heritage of the country, and in particular (but without limiting the generality of the foregoing) includes
> (a) any object, natural or artificial, used for, or adapted for use for, any purpose connected with the traditional cultural life of any of the peoples of this country, past or present; and
> (b) any mineral specimen or fossil or mammal remains of scientific or historic interest to the country; and
> (c) any other collection, object or thing, or any collection, object or thing of a class, declared to be national cultural property.[31]

Every traditional object in Papua New Guinea is national cultural property unless it has been exempted by the head of state upon the advice of the trustees and by notice in the *National Gazette*. What could be more explicit!

Where the national cultural property legislation poses an ethical concern is with its restrictions on the activities of nationals—as Mark Busse points out,

> the importance of restricting acquisition, ownership and movement of certain objects and categories of objects thought to be important to a wider segment of people than those individuals or groups who owned or controlled them.[32]

Blanket control of individual property rights is something that might be acceptable to the colonial administration but it does pose problems within a free and newly independent nation-state. Also, Westerners that dealt in illicit cultural property were prosecuted and had their goods seized, but what about the nationals that sold the goods, assuming that they were not stolen, in the first place? They were never prosecuted, unlike Italians that are prosecuted under their laws for selling prohibited artifacts to foreigners. So there is an uncomfortable double standard here that perhaps could be excused in the past through the villagers not being aware of the legislation. But does that excuse hold true today?

For perhaps the last twenty years, the cultural property legislation of Papua New Guinea has not been consistently enforced due to the national museum's lack of capacity to do so. But it is surprising how few resources are required to police the legislation internally. From personal experience, I would estimate that application of the act requires no more resources than those so readily allocated to a single member of parliament. The courts in Papua New Guinea are sympathetic to national interests and perhaps lean toward the prosecution of Westerners that have infringed the laws of their country. To prosecute cases internationally in foreign courts and recover national cultural property that has been spirited abroad is another matter. It can be an endless saga with high costs for possibly little return.

GOVERNANCE: "METHOD OF MANAGEMENT"

To ensure that suspect material does not enter museum collections, effective management frameworks are most important. Management knowledge and skill is necessary to deal with the complexities of trade in national cultural property and the instruments that guide and legislate best practice. Standards of good governance assert that two principles are fundamental: the need for adequate disclosure and the need for appropriate checks and balances in the governance structure.[33] If you pause to think about those two requirements, you will note that the adherence to these two principles is not particularly noticeable in the operations of many collecting institutions. There seems to be a notion that commercial confidentiality is required even though in most instances public or institutional funds are being expended, or taxation relief is being given, and the taxpayer one way or the other is footing the bill. Our cases of tainted material entering collections would have had different outcomes if there had been adequate public disclosure, and a culture of adherence to the spirit of legal instruments and professional guidelines.

There is a strong congruence between what is sought in corporate and international governance and what archaeologists in particular and museum authorities in general seek in the administration of collecting institutions. Governance literature stresses that the major change over the past decade (referring to the 1990s) is through the voluntary acceptance of codes of conduct. In the international world of financial governance there is a real carrot:

> The World Bank promoted the development of good governance in general and good corporate governance in particular as part of the recommendations for the transformation of economic systems in developing countries, particularly in the 1990s.[34]

That kind of incentive, a flow of funds, is not present in the world of collecting institutions. Few governments or institutions that fund museums and galleries seem to be particularly worried if tainted material enters their collections unless they have had a particularly gruesome, prolonged, and expensive experience dealing with the aftermath of an inappropriate acquisiton. An open adherence to such codes may signal the quality of an operation.[35]

It is interesting to consider what has been the impact of highly publicized financial scandals. There have been scandals comparable to that of Enron, in collecting institutions. *The Medici Conspiracy*, for example, has touched various large museums and galleries. Have these scandals contributed to the adoption by organizations of codes of good governance, and adherence to the spirit of international instruments such as the 1970 UNESCO convention and UNIDROIT?

Cuervo-Cazurra and Aguilera observe that there is difficulty changing legal systems that are embedded within the tradition of a country. This may be one of the reasons why international agreements cannot be as specific as we might wish and that they appear to have no teeth, that they clash with state legal systems.[36] For instance, countries with strong centralized governments may find it easier to enter into international agreements that have forceful compliance terms, but nation-states that cannot mandate certain kinds of conditions to their provinces may find it more difficult to comply with such international agreements. Codes are more easily transferable between countries with similar legislative systems and institutions, such as those countries once part of the British Empire that maintain common law as a basis of their legal systems. Codes are necessary when the legal systems of countries cannot cope with irregularities that are extraterritorial and when nation-states are not willing to accede to international agreements such as UNIDROIT.

Why from a corporate governance perspective are there instances when legislation and codes are not being followed, especially when there are efficiencies to be gained by not spending

Box 6.1

UNIDROIT

The loophole in international law that allows title to stolen or looted goods if acquired in good faith in a country such as Switzerland has been recognized for many years. UNIDROIT's Convention on International Return of Stolen or Illegally Exported Cultural Objects of 1995 represents at the international level a concerted action to remedy the problems caused when nation-states have conflicting interpretations of property and ownership. Its primary purpose through the "harmonizing" and coordinating law between states is to facilitate the restitution of stolen cultural objects and the return of cultural objects that have been removed contrary to laws regulating the export of cultural goods. The convention allows states that are parties, or their citizens, to request the return of goods that under the terms of the convention have been illegally exported or stolen. Although sixty-one nations have acceded to the UNIDROIT statute, not all member states are parties to the 1995 convention. Notable exceptions are the United Kingdom and the United States, while Spain, France, Netherlands, and Italy, as well as nations that suffer from the illicit trade such as Guatemala, Nigeria, Peru, and El Salvador, are parties to the convention.[1]

1 Refer to UNIDROIT. 1995. Article 1, on www.unidroit.org; and Tubb and Brodie (eds.). *Illicit Antiquities: The Theft of Culture and the Extinction of Archaeology*. Routledge, New York.

time in defending an institution against litigation? I suggest that this may be due to an institutional culture that stresses acquisition over other values. It is not unusual for a museum or gallery to seek to balance its collections after the initial period of exuberant acquisitions is over.

"Leadership Run Amok: The Destructive Potential of Overachievers" is a fascinating evaluation of how employees goaded on by the rewards of the management system can do incredible damage to an organization's finances and good name.[37] How can one recognize these individuals?

> Overachievers tend to command and coerce, rather than coach and collaborate, thus stifling subordinates. They take frequent shortcuts and forget to communicate crucial information, and they may be oblivious to the concerns of others.[38]

There is a recognized downside of achievement as outlined by McClealland, the late Harvard psychologist. They are:

> the tendencies to cheat and cut corners and to leave people out of the loop. Some high achievers are so fixated on finding a shortcut to the goal . . . that they may not be too particular about the means they use to reach it.[39]

Overachievement is on the rise in the corporate world according to Spreier, Fontaine, and Malloy. If overachievement is one of the key factors in the acquisition of tainted materials, through a reward feedback process between the individual and institutional culture, then we can expect an increase in the rules being stretched to accommodate individual values and perhaps a greater sophistication being employed in covering one's tracks.

NOTES

1. Brian Kennedy. 2001. "In Search of Lucian Freud." *artonview* 26: 28–31.

2. Kelly Burke and Peter Gotting. 2000. "Precious Artefact Broken by French Was Already a Bust." *Sydney Morning Herald*, 11 May, 3.

3. Commonwealth of Australia, Senate Legislative Committee 2000–2001 Environment, Communication, Information Technology and the Arts, Answer to Questions on Notice, Supplementary Budget Estimates, Thursday, 30 November 2000, ECITA 296-3001, Hansard, 30/11/00, question 128, page no. 212.

4. "Ambum Stone" National Gallery of Australia http://nga.gov.au/ConservationArt/ambum.htm (accessed on 12 February 2007).

5. Beate Tworek-Matuszkiewicz. 2001. "The Ambum Stone." *artonview* 26: 58–59.

6. P. Swadling and R. Hide. 2005. "Changing Landscape and Social Interaction: Looking at Agricultural History from a Sepik-Ramu Perspective." In Andrew Pawley, Robert Attenborough, Jack Golson, and Robin Hide (eds.), *Papuan Pasts Cultural, Linguistic and Biological Diversity of Papuan-Speaking Peoples*. Pacific Linguistics, Canberra, 289–327. Also refer to Pamela Swadling, Polly Wiessner, and Akii Tumu. n.d. "Prehistoric Stone Artefacts from Enga and the Implications of Links between the Highlands, Lowlands and Islands for Early Agriculture in Papua New Guinea." Unpublished manuscript.

7. Helen Musa. 2000. "Foetal 'Echidna' Repairs Complete." *Canberra Times*, 21 September, 3; and Musa. 2001. "PNG Artefact Found to Be 3500y Old." *Canberra Times*, 1 May, 3.

8. Lindel V. Prott and P. J. O'Keefe. 1989. *Law and the Cultural Heritage*. Volume 3, *Movement*. Professional Books Limited, Oxford, 567.

9. Prott and O'Keefe, *Law and the Cultural Heritage*, 3:664–65.

10. Information received from the Australian Customs Department, dated 13 October 2003.

11. Information is from reports to the trustees of the Museum: "Report on Inspection of Artefact Shipment, Townsville, 3–5 July 1974, Brian J. Egloff" and "Report on the Inspection of the Hotel Daru, Western District, 17–19 July 1974 (including the application for a search warrant), Brian Egloff."

12. Activities of Roy Mackay toward the enforcement of the National Cultural Property (Preservation) Ordinance of 1965 are reported at length in Barry Craig. 1996. *Samting belong tumbuna: The collection, Documentation and Preservation of the Material Cultural Heritage of Papua New Guinea*. Unpublished doctoral thesis, Flinders University of South Australia.

13. Australian Embassy, Paris: Memo No.708, File No: 223/3/63—copy not dated but certainly between early June and early July 1971.

14. Craig, *Samting belong tumbuna*, 174.

15. Amanda Dunn. 2001. "How *Blue Poles* Polarised Australia." *The Age*, 25 January, Green Guide, 14.

16. *Papua New Guinea Annual Reports of the Trustees of the Papua New Guinea Public Museum and Art Gallery to the High Commissioner of Papua New Guinea from the President of the Board of Trustees 1969 to 1972.*

17. Evan J. Paki to John E. Buchannan, Jr. Correspondence of 21 April 2006.

18. Clemency Chase Coggins. 1995. "A Licit International Trade in Ancient Art: Let There Be Light. *International Journal of Cultural Property* 1(4): 61–79.

19. Robert Welsch. 2005. "One Symphony from Many Voices: Collectors, Collecting Activities, and the Culture of Collecting since 1870." In John Friede et al. *New Guinea Art Masterpieces from the Jolika Collection of Marcia and John Friede* (2 vols.). Fine Arts Museums of San Francisco in Association with 5 Continents Editions, Milan, Italy, 2:22.

20. Michael Quinnell. 2000. "Before It Has Become To Late." In Michael O'Hanlon and Robert L. Welsch (eds.), *Hunting the Gatherers: Ethnographic Collectors, Agents and Agency in Melanesia, 1870s–1930s*. Berghahn Books, New York & Oxford, 81–102.

21. Prott and O'Keefe, *Law and the Cultural Heritage*, 3:784.

22. Margaret Mackenzie. 2007. "Jolika Collection of New Guinea Art, de Young Museum, San Francisco, California, Opened October 2005." Book and Media Reviews. *The Contemporary Pacific* 19(1): 345–35; and Rex Dalton. 2006. "Guinea Experts Cry Foul on Tribal Exhibits." *Nature* 440(6 April): 722–23.

23. Michael Thomas Somare. 1975. *Sana: An Autobiography of Michael Somare*. Niugini Press, Port Moresby, 135.

24. Lamont Lindstrom. 1998. "Pasin Tumbuna: Culture and Nationalism in Papua New Guinea." In Virginia R. Domínguez and

David Y. H. Wu (eds.), *From Beijing to Port Moresby: The Politics of National Identity in Cultural Policies*. Gordon and Breach, Amsterdam, 151.

25. Wari Iamo and Jacob Simet. 1998. "Cultural Diversity and Identity in Papua New Guinea: A Second Look." In Virginia R. Domínguez and David Y. H. Wu (eds.), *From Beijing to Port Moresby: The Politics of National Identity in Cultural Policies*. Gordon and Breach, Amsterdam, 195.

26. Iamo and Simet, "Cultural Diversity and Identity in Papua New Guinea"; and Lindstrom, "Pasin Tumbuna."

27. Lindstrom, "Pasin Tumbuna," 143.

28. Lindstrom, "Pasin Tumbuna," 159.

29. Kwame Anthony Appiah. 1997. "Cosmopolitan Patriots." *Critical Inquiry* 23(3): 624.

30. Refer to Susan Bulmer. 1969. "New Guinea's Laws Concerning National Cultural Property." *Man in New Guinea* 1(3): 2–4; Papua New Guinea Museum. 1974. *Guide to the Preservation of National Cultural Property in Papua New Guinea and Guide to the Collecting of Artefacts for the Papua New Guinea Museum* (leaflet). Papua New Guinea Museum, Port Moresby; Resonga Kaiku. 1980. "Restoration of National Cultural Property: The Case of Papua New Guinea." In Robert Edwards and Jenny Stewart (eds.), *Preserving Indigenous Cultures: A New Role for Museums*. Australian Government Publishing Service, Canberra, 175–83; and Mark Busse. 2000. "The National Cultural Property (Preservation) Act." In Kathy Wimp and Mark Busse (eds.), *Protection of Intellectual, Biological and Cultural Property in Papua New Guinea*. Pacific Area Press, The Australian National University and Conservation Melanesia, Inc., Port Moresby, 81–95.

31. Independent State of Papua New Guinea, Chapter No. 156. National Cultural Property (Preservation) Act, 5.

32. Busse, "The National Cultural Property (Preservation) Act," 83.

33. Refer to Alvaro Cuervo-Cazurra and Ruth Aguilera. 2003. "The Worldwide Diffusion of Codes of Good Governance." In Anna

Grandori (ed.), *Corporate Governance and Firm Organization: Microfoundations and Structural Forms*. Oxford University Press, Oxford, 318–48, quoting A. Cadbury. 2000. "The Corporate Governance Agenda." *Corporate Governance* 8: 9.

34. Cuervo-Cazurra and Aguilera, "The Diffusion of Codes of Governance," 323.

35. Cuervo-Cazurra and Aguilera, "The Diffusion of Codes of Governance," 321.

36. Cuervo-Cazurra and Aguilera, "The Diffusion of Codes of Governance," 320.

37. Scott W. Spreier, Mary H. Fontaine, and Ruth L. Malloy. 2006. "Leadership Run Amok: The Destructive Potential of Overachievers." *Harvard Business Review* June: 72–82.

38. Spreier, Fontaine, and Malloy, "Leadership Run Amok," 72.

39. Quoted without reference in Spreier, Fontaine, and Malloy, "Leadership Run Amok," 76.

SEVEN

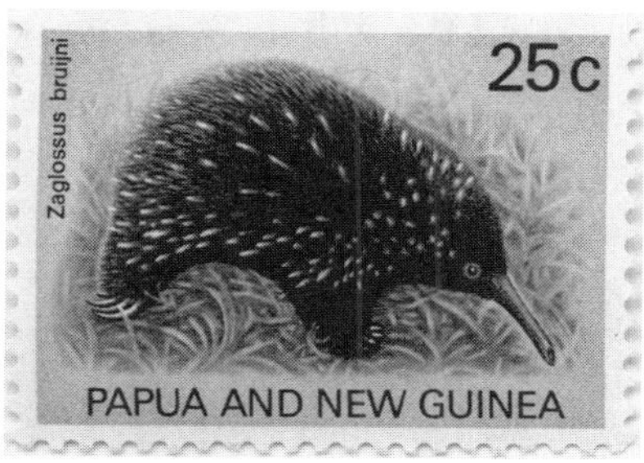

Had Enough Romance?

The description of the Ambum Stone being found in a cave was accepted by Goldman and by the Australian National Gallery. It became the provenance given in catalogs, press releases, and journal articles for four decades. When acquiring the stone Goldman had openly advertised it, sought advice from colleagues and the wider Oceanic art world. No further information came forward. But on the other hand, it is convenient to find something in a cave, because it implies that it has no owners: the Indiana Jones romance of the find was thus initiated. Odd, as we will see later in the Epilogue to this story, the Ambum Stone was not the only stone artifact to be acquired in the 1960s and ascribed to a "cave"—"Enga"—"Wabag."[1] When staking such a large sum of money on the purchase of an artifact, the most thorough verification is required. But, and this is the rub, the Australian National Gallery had no staff devoted to Oceanic art and it had to rely upon outside expertise that, although acceptable in the first instance, may not have been briefed to conduct detailed and ongoing investigations into the provenance. Collecting institutions in general should build up fields of strength and only in exceptional circumstances move outside of their range of expertise. There is no information in the FOI documents that the gallery was aware of the customs regulation that would call for the confiscation and return of the object to Papua New Guinea. But why is there no record of a response to Mosuwadoga's request of 18 December 1975 for information?

HOLE: "CAVITY IN SOLID BODY"

The 2001 conservation report on the damage repaired by a conservator repeats the misinformation that the stone "was discovered in 1962 in a cave."[2] Was there any grain of truth in the assertion that the Ambum Stone was found in a cave? Polly Wiessner was informed by the villagers that there were no caves near to the place where the Ambum Stone was said to have been found. Now imagine this scenario: two young brothers influenced by the local missionary surreptitiously dig up the stone, most likely in daylight as any activity of that kind at night would have been fraught with danger from malevolent spirits even with the Christian gods on your side. The boys then take the stone to the local trade store and ask for money in exchange for the artifact. The merchant is no fool. He probably realizes that the object is worth far more if it has a find spot, so he asks the boys in Tok Pisin, "*Yu kisim dis pela tumbuna long we*"—"You find this ancient thing where?" They reply, "*Mi kisim long hul bilong graun*"—"We took it from a hole in the ground (cave)."

The owner of the trade store then asks the boys further questions, enough to ascertain the location. Someone then placed this information on the map dated 1962 that came into the

BOX 7.1

TOK PISIN

Neo-Melanesian (New Guinea Pidgin) or *Tok Pisin* has its roots in the Pacific Islands and Queensland, where it proved to be an effective mechanism for communication between peoples from various Melanesian Islands and entrepreneurs who exploited the natives as a source of cheap labor. *Tok Pisin* incorporates words and expressions from Melanesian, German, English, Malay, and other European and island languages. It was used as the second language of administration in German New Guinea until the First World War. Following the war it rapidly spread through the Mandated Territory of New Guinea and into the coastal and island reaches of the Territory of Papua.

possession of Goldman, who then sent a copy to the Australian National Gallery. Goldman also gave a copy of the map to me and I sent a copy to Wiessner. I leave it for the reader to decide if the boys told the trade store owner that they took the Ambum Stone from the clan ground or if they said that they found it in a cave or if the trade store owner romanced the location. Or, could it simply be a case of *hul bilong graun* referring to the hole the boys dug to obtain the stone or the villagers dug to house the cult object; it is unlikely that the trade store owner simply misunderstood the boys and genuinely thought that the boys' "*hul bilong graun*" referred to a cave.

Steinbauer, in his Neo-Melanesian Dictionary defines *hul* as "hole, pit, cave, grave." But there should have been a difference in expression since the boys dug the hole. There is another puzzling side to the transaction, in that the boys were paid twenty shillings for the stone. It was my experience that trade store operators in the late 1960s, and I assume by extension in the early 1960s, seldom paid for services or goods in cash but invariably in tobacco, cloth, axes, bush knives, or similar goods. However, I am assured that cash payments were made in the 1960s and perhaps the boys did not want trade goods. Sudden riches in the form of trade goods would have been a declaration of the brothers' transgression of the sacred values of their community, while currency could have been hidden from other members of the community.

ETHICS: "SCIENCE OF HUMAN DUTY"

In many situations the law is considered to be an inappropriate means to right the wrongs of the past in distant places. Nevertheless, in some cases there is a feeling that an injustice has been done and that the wrongs of the past should be compensated for. Codes of practice for ethical conduct have been drafted over the past thirty or more years, particularly following identification of the many holocaust art works that have found their way into the holdings of public institutions. Norman Palmer, discussing holocaust art thefts and the holding of objects by museums, stated that collecting institutions must display transparency with an acceptance of responsibility, accept a formal recognition of morality, as well as take seriously attempts to correct errors or lack of provenance with respect to objects.[3] Palmer emphasized the "Tort of conversion"; this means that, if the trail of legal ownership is broken, purchase of an item in good faith requires the buyer to be certain that the ownership transfer process has been correct. If the first transaction is tainted, the line of title is invalid; this is referred to as a "title flaw." He continued: should individuals or institutions wish to profit from circumstances of hardship or misunderstanding, such as buying a piece from an incompetent person (including minors), or from individuals who sell while under duress, that these cases are considered as being different from normal financial transactions involving goods, and their ownership of the object may be legally challenged.

The Code of Professional Ethics of 1986 states that "Due Diligence" is the fundamental requirement, that every endeavor must be made to establish the facts of a case before deciding a course of action, particularly in identifying the source and history of an item offered for acquisition or use before accepting it.[4] "Cultural Heritage" is described as any concept or thing, natural or artificial, that is considered to have aesthetic, historical, scientific, or spiritual significance. The section dealing with acquisitions is particularly apposite:

> A museum should not acquire any object or specimen by purchase, gift, loan, bequest, or exchange unless the governing body and responsible officer are satisfied that a valid title to it can be obtained. Every effort must be made to ensure that it has not been illegally acquired in, or exported from, its country of origin or any intermediate country in which it may have been owned legally (including the museum's own country).
>
> A professional conflict can exist when an acquisition, highly desired by a museum, lacks provenance. However, the ability to establish legal title to the item must be an overriding factor when considering acquisition.[5]

Brodie, Doole, and Watson in 2000 sketch the background to "the end of the age of piracy," a term coined by Thomas Hoving, director of the Metropolitan Museum of Modern Art, in *Stealing History: The Illicit Trade in Cultural Material.* The authors point out that, in the early 1960s museum curators and archaeologists were particularly frustrated as they tried to make sense of objects pouring into museums. These treasures all too often raised more questions than they answered:

> There was a growing realisation that unprovenanced museum acquisitions provided fertile ground for unverifiable and thus sterile speculation, but were of little use for productive research.[6]

Researchers were particularly concerned that museums were supporting, and in many way encouraging, the trade in illicit artifacts that was contributing to the ongoing destruction of historic places and monuments, something that continues into this millennium. Brodie, Doole, and Watson recommend that the government of the United Kingdom consider whether tax benefits should accrue to individuals in respect of unprovenanced material donated to public institutions, and whether it is appropriate for the "Indemnity Scheme" to continue to cover loans of unprovenanced material.[7] At the same time, there was a developing awareness by donor countries that their heritage was being systematically plundered. The authors argue that attitudes toward the acquisition of tainted artifacts changed in the 1970s as ICOM issued "an influential statement on the ethics of museum acquisitions." Many institutions incorporated the spirit of the UNESCO convention into their ethical codes even though their nation-states were not yet signatories to the convention.

Brodie and his coauthors refer to the UNESCO Convention as "changing forever the ethical landscape of the museum world." Apparently, this is the convention that is referred to in the *Canberra Times* article of 21 September 2000 as not being relevant to the 1976 purchase of the Ambum Stone, as Australia did not become a signatory until after the Ambum Stone had been acquired by the Australian National Gallery. The impact of the convention was being seen in Papua New Guinea in the 1970s, as collecting institutions were adopting formal procedures to ensure that objects were acquired and exported legally.

In the mid-1970s, Douglas Newton of the Museum of Primitive Art regularly requested from the National Museum verification of the status of artifacts, sending a photograph with a description of the artifact. Similarly, the gallery contacted the museum with respect to their pending purchase of the Ambum Stone.

The "universal heritage" of mankind is a difficult concept to deal with as it is employed by Western institutions in defense of their acquisition of the cultural property of other peoples or nations. The argument raised against the repatriation of objects or skeletal materials is couched in terms of the universal value of the objects outweighing the needs of particular peoples or interest groups. How can the Greeks claim that the Parthenon sculptures (Elgin Marbles) belong to them alone when sculptures from the Parthenon epitomize the values that underpin all Western civilization?[8] An interesting argument to keep in mind, but does it have any force? Museum directors would seem to think so!

DILEMMA: "A SITUATION REQUIRING A CHOICE"

All highly prized objects have multiple values and more often than not those values are in conflict with one another. Claire L. Lyons of the Getty Research Institute, in *Claiming the Stones, Naming the Bones*, explores a case that reached the United States Supreme Court (*United States v. An Antique Platter of Gold*).[9] A shallow bowl dated to the third century BCE had passed through the hands of various dealers and eventually sold for $1.2 million. While at the conservation facility of the Metropolitan Museum of Art in New York, the bowl became the defendant in a forfeiture case following a request for restitution by the Republic of Italy. Of particular interest is the decision by the American Association of Museums and other professional museum associations to enter the case in support of the dealer and in opposition to the return of the object to Italy. This action, according to Lyons, spurred the Archaeological Institute of America to support the Italian claim for restitution.

Lyons succinctly characterizes four of the many kinds of stakeholders: dealers, museum curators, gallery collectors, and academic scientists, each having a distinct and at times opposing set of values. Roughly speaking, the dealer operates in a commercial capacity, the curator seeks to understand, the collector wishes to obtain the object and display it, while the scientist is driven to understand its physical properties. All love and cherish the piece and might view their role as central and their values as preeminent. But with respect to the Ambum Stone, as an item of "living heritage," there is a fifth group of stakeholders: the members of the community that once owned and valued the object for its spiritual significance. Following from the well-publicized attempts to have holocaust art works returned to their original owners,[10] there have been increasing demands that objects acquired under duress or tainted circumstances in colonial countries should also have their ownership renegotiated. Foremost among apposite cases are those of the Benin bronzes of Nigeria, and the Elgin Marbles of Greece. "Museums Face New Clamor to Return Plunder" is a headline that no doubt raised concerns among museums.[11] In 2002, the Museums Association, a professional organization based in England, published a set of guidelines stipulating that curators should "recognize the interests of people who made, used, owned, collected or gave items in the collections."[12]

The National Gallery of Australia has assured the press that "no concern has been raised on the ownership" of works of art on a risk list of plundered Nazi art. Apparently, eighty-six "works have gaps in the history of their ownership between 1933 and

1945," and an article entitled "Gallery Brushes Off 'Nazi Plunder' Threat," indicates that the gallery is actively working with the International Art Loss Register in New York in an open and transparent fashion to determine if these art works are tainted.[13] Investigations by the National Gallery of Australia are in keeping with current protocols. Comments in *Building the Collections*, twenty-first anniversary publication of the gallery reinforce the position that the Ambum Stone continues to be regarded as a masterpiece. Sasha Grishin, an academic, writes:

> The Gallery's advisor on Primitive Art, Douglas Newton . . . [wrote] of the Ambum stone . . . : "Intrinsically it is the finest New Guinea stone sculpture yet found, and it is superb work in its own right . . . it holds up magnificently, I think it is a masterpiece in anybody's terms."[14]

The second paragraph of that letter by Douglas Newton reads:

> There are a few points to be considered. It is not strictly speaking unique; there are to my knowledge about five other similar pieces, or fragments, and I am told there are more. Two (see enclosed) have just been sold for $20,000 each. Therefore one never knows whether a better one might not turn up; but if it did, I doubt if it could be exported from PNG legally. Another thing that worries me about Goldman's price, apart from its dimensions, "is" that it would be bound to become public, and this would undoubtedly stimulate the search for more such things, consequently wrecking of potential sites, smuggling, and all the other bad things.
>
> As you can see, my feeling is that the object is intensely desirable, but that the price is indecent, and I am very apprehensive about the consequences of buying it on Goldman's terms.

This is another instance of the complexities of the international art market. Also, Douglas Newton is deceased and as such he is not be able to respond to any comments that might arise.

In that same article Grishin mentions *Bird in Space, 1931–1936*, by Constantin Brancusi as a notable acquisition in 1973.[15] Forgotten in the mists of time is the controversy over the export of the artwork from India. *Art Newspaper* subheadlines an article on the Brancusi birds as follows:

> In 1973 the Tate wanted to buy Brancusi's black marble "Bird in Space" through the dealer Richard Feigen. The sale fell through because the trustees believed the work had been "smuggled" out of India.[16]

How interesting is the world of art when the full story is told about the history and acquisition of masterpieces, as most have twisted tales to tell. Alan Dodge is open and frank about the purchase of the most notable of the gallery's acquisitions, *Blue Poles*. He provides us with an interesting and somewhat humorous perspective, one that is not widely known. In 1972, Alan had acquired what he termed a dream job, and commenced work at the National Gallery of Art in Washington, D.C. The following year, in 1973, it was understood that *Blue Poles* would be donated to the National Gallery of Art, and the gallery was hosting American Art at Mid Century:

> A special wall had been erected to display the star of the exhibition, a painting by Jackson Pollock *Blue Poles* 1952. The presentation was to impress Ben Heller, the owner of the painting. It was believed at the time that Carter Brown was angling to have Heller present the painting to the National Gallery as a gift for the new wing. But is seems that Heller had

other ideas and a month before opening, as the exhibition was being installed, news broke around the world that James Mollison, the Director of something called the Australian National Gallery, had purchased *Blue Poles* for what was then a huge record price for a work of modern American art—US$2 million (about 1.3 million Australian dollars in those days).[17]

It is interesting to speculate whether Heller really was intending to donate the painting to the National Gallery of Art or if he was using the opportunity of a central place in a major exhibition to increase the currency of *Blue Poles*. This practice had become such a common ploy by art dealers, that museums have decided not to accept for exhibition art works owned by dealers.[18] In 1974, Dodge joined the staff of the Australian National Gallery and shortly thereafter, in 1975, as Senior Research Officer, prepared the report that facilitated the acquisition of the Ambum Stone.

PRIMITIVE: "ORIGINAL AS OPPOSED TO DERIVATIVE"

The search for the Ambum Stone is replete with irony. This narrative started with the challenge faced by the author when the National Gallery of Australia was reluctant to release information pertaining to the provenance and acquisition of the Ambum Stone, as "such information cannot be made readily available to the public on request." Information policies changed at the gallery and in the same issue of *artonview* that describes the conservation of the Ambum Stone, the gallery published a four-page article titled "In Search of Lucian Freud"?[19] That article details the acquisition and purchase of a painting by a contemporary artist, the type of information that had never been published with respect to the Ambum Stone. Biographies of artists belonging to the Western art tradition are often published, as the gallery does with Aboriginal artists. However, less sensitive institutions may not be equally concerned with the authors of "tribal art."

An exceptional piece of creativity such as the Ambum Stone deserves the same acclaim and documented history as does the *Book of Kells*, *Blue Poles*, and Lucian Freud's three-year-old derivative work *After Cezanne*. It is this acknowledgment of creativity and beauty for the art of Papua New Guinea that Goldman was seeking in the 1960s and the gallery sought in 1970s.

Curators have acknowledged the need to personalize ethnographic art and thereby give recognition to individual artists and their works. Such work as Adrian Gerbrands's epic study[20] of the art of the Asmat of the south coast of Irian Jaya (West Papua) sought to accord the same honors to the village carver as is so readily given to Western artists. More recently, his former student Dirk Smidt has prepared an exhibition for the Rijksmuseum voor Volkenkunde in Leiden that features tradition and innovation in the art of the Kamoro of the southwest coast of Indonesian West Papua, with a focus on the artists and the context of the preparation of the art work.[21]

WORTH: "RELATIVE VALUE OF A THING IN RESPECT OF ITS QUALITIES"

Recall the response of Bryan Cranstone of the British Museum as an anthropologist to Philip Goldman, that the Ambum Stone's value was diminished, as the archaeological context was not fully known. Also, the example given by Claire L. Lyons of the different stances taken by gallery curators and by archaeologists over the "Antique Platter of Gold," where the gallery curators supported the dealer and the museum while archaeologists opposed the dealer and supported Italy in its efforts toward restitution. More recently, it was reported:

> In October last year, an agreement signed by 18 of the world's leading museums defended the concept of the "universal museum" containing objects from different cultures around the world. The agreement made it clear that calls for restitution or repatriation should be resisted. The declaration was greeted with outrage by a number of countries and cultural groups.[22]

EVENT: "AN INCIDENCE"

Two recent events, one in the highlands and the other in Port Moresby, have a particular relevance to the story of the Ambum Stone. In May 2002, the *Post-Courier*, a leading newspaper of Papua New Guinea, reported:

> An Engan tribe was rebuffed yesterday in its attempts to get a billion-kina judgment from a judge. All hope is not lost, however. Justice Timothy Hinchliffe, sitting in Mount Hagen, dismissed an application by the tribe to have the judge rule in favour by default on the billion kina claim. But he left the door open by giving the defendants, the National Museum and Art Gallery, 14 days to file to defend the tribe's claim. The Judge was asked to declare that the plaintiff, Michael Mangal Tukuliya, for and on behalf of the Kunalini tribe of Anditali village in the Kompiam/Ambum district of Enga, be granted a default judgment.[23]

This incidence refers to the alleged loan of an object, similar in appearance to the Ambum Stone, to a curator of the museum. The stone was destroyed when it was returned via a government police station that was burned down in a local skirmish. The judge referred to the case as a very important and large claim. The second event is the "Notice of Theft" by the Pacific Arts Association:

> On May 19, 2003 the Papua New Guinea National Museum and Art Gallery lost a number of important artifacts from its galleries, due to a break-in into the Museum at night. The thieves forced their way into the building, emptied an important showcase in the Life and Land Gallery (Prehistory), and smashed show cases containing body ornaments in the Independence gallery.
>
> At least 14 stolen artifacts (possibly 5 more, including a replica) were taken, amongst them the "stone bird pestle" collected by Denys Faithful from the Nere people of West Laigap, between Strickland and Porgera, Enga Province as well as 13 other prehistoric objects, virtually the entire museum's collection of carved stone objects.[24]

In 1974, when Douglas Newton wrote his prophetic words forecasting that "this would undoubtedly stimulate the search for more such things, consequently wrecking of potential sites, smuggling, and all other bad things," he and the gallery could not have been aware that some thirty years later those predictions would come true in such a confronting fashion as a robbery of the national museum.

EGOISM: "TO ONE'S OWN INTEREST"

Perhaps the Ambum Stone more than anything else is a chronicle of egos and how association with the object has served to strengthen individuals. In the distant prehistoric past, possibly 3,500 years ago, the object was carved, most likely not as an individual act but in a way that reinforced social patterns; personal, gender, and group relations; and identities, as is the case today when the people of the highlands make their looped-net bags. Maureen Mckenzie's[25] *Androgynous Objects: String Bags and Gender in Central New Guinea* is a superb presentation of the manufacture and cultural role that looped-net string bags play in the highlands of Papua New Guinea. At sometime, perhaps the Ambum Stone was exchanged either directly for other valuables or entered in to the ubiquitous system of creating a debt between groups such that an interdependent relationship is maintained over the social landscape and between generations. Most likely the object moved between different communities and no doubt was valued by each group that possessed it. Just what intrinsic quality was uppermost in the minds of the creator and the possessors is difficult to know, but certainly it would have been charged with cultural significance. Then it was buried or cached, perhaps to keep it safe.

The Enga clansmen who controlled the spirits and recharged the power of the Ambum Stone during the cult ceremonies would have gained prestige within their group. But what about the boys who said they took it from the clan ceremonial grounds? What did they get out of it other than twenty or more shillings? One wonders if they ascribe their people's recent misfortunes through war and sickness to the loss of the protective power of the Ambum Stone. And what about the brother who has a damaged face from an exploding shotgun? Misfortune and death are not things that just happen by chance in the highlands. Rival clansmen acting in concert with supernatural forces are said to bring about malevolent happenings.

For a short time, the Wabag trade store manager had an object somebody else wanted, as did the unidentified person said by Goldman to have exported the carved stone and sold it to him.

Goldman, from the perspective of a former anthropology student of New Guinea art, wanted to know what he had, and in the early 1960s he provided everything that he knew, save the map of the find spot, to the editor of the *Journal of Polynesian Studies*. To his disappointment he received no meaningful responses. Mind you, at that time, the anthropology of the highlands was poorly known and its prehistory was completely opaque. Goldman, to his credit, sought information from a wide range of experts. He is regarded as one of the new, 1960s, generation of African and Oceanic art dealers. Jeremy MacClancy in a fascinating account, "A Natural Curiosity: The British Market in Primitive Art," writes:

> They were men of repute, each with his own gallery. Together with other established gallery owners who exhibited primitive art, they gave confidence to buyers and lent stability to the market. It is with them that the close dealer-client relationship started to become the most common way of selling expensive items.[26]

The art market is highly competitive and image is what the dealer seeks in offering top-quality pieces and receiving record prices. In the 1960s, investments in "tribal" art rose to such heights that, according to MacClancy, all but the richest collectors were priced out of the market. This brought about a shift from established art to an expansion of the "primitive" art market. Most of the dealers did not leave Britain, and in MacClancy's words, Philip Goldman's repeated tours of Papua New Guinea were exceptional.

Enter, in the 1970s, the Australian National Gallery. It was a late arrival in the art-collection game and sought an international collection. The National Gallery wanted the Ambum Stone, saw its aesthetic value, and finally purchased it. Its communication with the Papua New Guinea National Museum and Art Gallery was incomplete. In retrospect, apparently the museum did not know that the gallery had in fact purchased the piece until some years after the transaction was completed. The Australian National Gallery's timing may have been poor; it is likely that it purchased the Ambum Stone at the top of the market, just as the bubble burst. Since the mid-1970s the market has became "soft or skittish."[27] But it got a masterpiece!

LINGAM: "A PHALLUS-SHAPED OBJECT WORSHIPED AMONG THE HINDUS"

To sweeten the price pill, on 13 May 1977, after two years of negotiating, Goldman wrote to Mollison:

> Further to your visit and our conversation I enclose photographs of 3 Lingam stones which are in my possession. I would be prepared to donate a Lingam of your choice to the National Gallery since I am unable to effect any change in price for Ambum stone.[28]

The offer of the lingam stone may have given the gallery the added stimulus it sought, as Newton at that time was still hesitant to state that the Ambum Stone was worth anywhere near what Goldman was asking. That this offer of the phallus-shaped artifact was accepted is confirmed by telegram stating:

> Grateful if as matter of urgency you would collect from Goldman . . . one Ambum stone and one lingum [sic] stone stop.[29]

The movement of the sale to Switzerland took the Australian National Gallery by surprise. In 2008, when I asked Philip

Goldman about the sale he said that at the time he was recovering from an accident and cannot remember why it took place in Switzerland. There is no reason to imply that there was anything untoward in this but one of his many business transactions.

Today alarm bells would have rung. For, as Neil Brodie states:

> Even if it can be demonstrated unequivocally that an antiquity was taken illegally from its country of origin, if it was subsequently bought in good faith in a country such as Switzerland it will no longer be regarded in law as stolen.[30]

This is indeed, as Polly Wiessner says, a sad story. Researching the history of the Ambum Stone has led me down paths that I did not necessarily wish to pursue, but there you have it. But not really, as there is more to come in the epilogue to this story.

NOTES

1. Other examples are those registered in the Queensland Museum collections as E-4200 Mortar-stone and E-4201-2 Mortar-stone.

2. Beate Tworek-Matuszkiewicz. 2001. "The Ambum Stone." *artonview* 26: 58–59.

3. Norman Palmer in a panel discussion at the National Gallery of Australia, Canberra, on 17 July 2001.

4. The ICOM Code of Professional Ethics was adopted unanimously at the Fifteenth General Assembly of ICOM in Buenos Aires on 4 November 1986 and amended by the Twentieth General Assembly of ICOM, meeting in Barcelona on 6 July 2001.

5. ICOM Code of Professional Ethics, 2001.

6. Neil Brodie, Jenny Doole, and Peter Watson. 2000. *Stealing History: The Illicit Trade in Cultural Material*. Report for the Muse-

ums Association and ICOM-UK. MacDonald Institute for Archaeological Research, Cambridge, 3.

7. Brodie, Doole, and Watson, *Stealing History*, 6.

8. Timothy Webb. 2002. "Appropriating the Stones: The 'Elgin Marbles' and English National Taste." In Elazar Barkan and Ronald Bush (eds.), *Claiming the Stones, Naming the Bones*. The Getty Research Institute, Los Angeles, 51–96.

9. Claire Lyons. 2002. "Objects and Identities: Claiming and Reclaiming the Past." In Elazar Barkan and Ronald Bush (eds.), *Claiming the Stones, Naming the Bones*. The Getty Research Institute, Los Angeles, 116–37.

10. See Elizabeth Simpson. 1977. *The Spoils of War: World War II and Its Aftermath—the Loss, Reappearance and Recovery of Cultural Property*. Harry N. Abrams Inc., New York; Elazar Barkan. 2000. *The Guilt of Nations: Restitution and Negotiating Historical Injustices*. W.W. Norton, New York; and Elazar Barkan. 2002. "Amending Historical Injustices: The Restitution of Cultural Property—an Overview." In Elazar Barkan and Ronald Bush (eds.), *Claiming the Stones, Naming the Bones*. The Getty Research Institute, Los Angeles, 16–46.

11. *The Independent*. 2002. "Museums Face New Clamour to Return 'Plunder.'" *Canberra Times*, 1 April, 8.

12. Museums Association. 2002. *Code of Ethics for Museums: Ethical Principles for All Who Work for or Govern Museums in the UK*. Museums Association, London, 16.

13. Georgina Safe and Susan McCulloch. 2002. "Gallery Brushes Off 'Nazi Plunder' Threat." *Weekend Australian*, 20–29 December, 4.

14. Sasha Grishin. 2003. "A Collection of Masterpieces." In Pauline Green (ed.), *Building the Collections*. National Gallery of Australia, Canberra, 216 (footnote reads Douglas Newton, letter to Mollison, 19 November 1974, ibid).

15. Grishin, "A Collection of Masterpieces," 226.

16. Martin Bailey. 2004. "What Happened to the Maharajah of Indore's Brancusi Birds?" *The Art Newspaper*, 45 (March): 12–13.

17. Alan Dodge. 2003. "Brave New World." In Pauline Green (ed.), *Building the Collections*. National Gallery of Australia, Canberra, 47–58.

18. Jeremy MacClancy. 1997. "A Natural Curiosity: The British Market in Primitive Art." *Res. Anthropology and Aesthetics*, 15 (Spring): 163–76; and refer also to Murray Satov. 1997. "Catalogues, Collectors, Curators: The Tribal Art Market and Anthropology." In Jeremy MacClancy (ed.), *Contesting Art: Art, Politics and Identity in the Modern World*. Berg Publishers, Oxford, 219.

19. Brian Kennedy. 2001. "In Search of Lucian Freud." *artonview* 26: 28–31.

20. Adrian A. Gerbrands. 1967. *Wow-Ipits, Eight Asmat Woodcarvers of New Guinea*. Mouton & Co, The Hague.

21. Dirk Smidt (ed.). 2003. *Kamoro Art: Tradition and Innovation in a New Guinea Culture*. KIT Publishers, Amsterdam and Rijksmuseum voor Volkenkunde, Leiden.

22. From Museums Association website www.museumsassociation.org (accessed on 2 October 2003).

23. *Post-Courier*, 2 May 2002.

24. Pacific Arts Association. 2003. "Notice of Theft." 15 October; and Pamela Swadling. 2003. Contribution to "Appraising and Documenting the Theft of Prehistoric Stone Artifacts from PNG National Museum on 19 May 2003." Department of Archaeology and Natural History, The Australian National University.

25. Maureen Mckenzie. 1991. *Androgynous Objects: String Bags and Gender in Central New Guinea*. Harwood Academic Publishers, Melbourne.

26. MacClancy, "A Natural Curiosity."

27. MacClancy, "A Natural Curiosity."

28. Document 59/104 FOI.

29. Document 78/126 FOI.

30. Brodie, Doole, and Watson, *Stealing History*, Introduction.

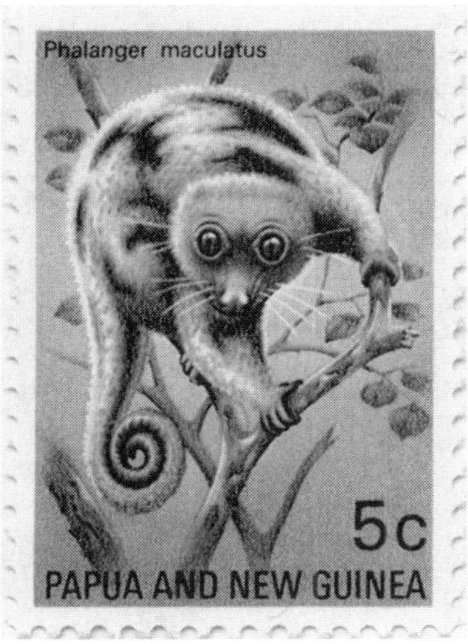

Epilogue

Complexities of the Enga *tee* and the Melpa *moka* economic exchange systems, politically uniting large sectors of the highlands, are well beyond the comprehension of any single participant. Valuables are accumulated over years across a distant and varied landscape; clans vie for authority and honor through the display and giving of valuables. As Ongka, the renowned Kawelka "big man" from the Mt. Hagen area of the highlands observed, the *moka* is like a large snake moving through the grass. You see only parts of the serpent, for it is too large to see it all at one time.[1] Then the snake emerges from the grass and its full extent can be seen. The story of the Ambum Stone is much like the snake in the grass, parts can be seen and have been discussed in the past, but never has there been an attempt to recount the entire story. The twists and turns of the Ambum Stone story have taken us through the millennium and around the globe. Regrettably there remained a gap that I could not fill, no matter how much testimony was acquired or how many people I contacted. How was the stone moved from a trade store in Wabag—because Philip Goldman was definite that he did not buy it from Ron Ingles—to be offered for sale to Goldman in London?

As I was writing the story of the Ambum Stone and discussing it with colleagues, the question inevitably asked of me was, should it be returned to the Papua New Guinea National Museum and Art Gallery? Since it had never been owned by the museum, and technically speaking was the property of an Enga clan but in the possession of the National Gallery of Australia, the resolution of this question seemed to raise intractable challenges. I suggest that the Ambum Stone was:

- taken from a clan ceremonial ground by two young brothers
- allegedly acquired by a trade store operator
- transferred to an unidentified individual in contravention of the legislation that restricted the transfer of carved stones
- exported from Papua New Guinea by in unidentified individual
- sold at a substantial price by an art dealer, Philip Goldman, to the Australian National Gallery
- purchased by the Australian National Gallery following correspondence with the Papua New Guinea Museum and Art Gallery

It would seem that there was both a violation of individual/group property rights as well as possible infringements of the law of the Territory of Papua New Guinea. Also, there is the untested status of the artifact relative to the Australian customs regulations that "gives the Australian Customs Service the authority to intercept, seize and return items of national cultural significance if requested by the PNG authorities."[2]

LET THERE BE LIGHT: "ILLUMINATED"

Clemency Chase Coggins has given considerable thought over a long period to the illicit traffic in art. Quoting the work of Paul Bator, Coggins emphasizes that

> it is his observation that the art world operates in secret. The art world requires concealment at every level to protect sources, to protect buyers, to protect itself. . . .
>
> If all such transactions were public (and honest) there might be no illicit market. . . . I submit that the highest value, both before and above national or international concerns about cultural property, is the truth about the object itself. More important than the law. More important than property rights. Just the facts—as close as possible to the whole truth that remains.[3]

ECOLOGY: "INSTITUTIONS AND THEIR RESULTING INTERDEPENDENCE"

When discussing the international trade in cultural property, Merryman's concept of a "kind of ecology" is useful and powerful:

> Empirically, cultural property centrally includes the sorts of things that dealers deal in, collectors collect, and museums acquire and display; principally works of art, antiquities, and ethnographic objects. They are the foci of a social subsystem we can call "the cultural property world," which is populated by artists, collectors, dealers and auction houses, museums and their professionals, art historians, archaeologists and ethnographers, and source nation cultural officials, among others. There people and institutions form a kind of ecology; whatever significantly affects one actor affects the others.[4]

Key components of this "cultural ecology" are objects within social systems where all players are interdependent. Let us focus for a moment on dependence theory within social systems. Anthropologists look at dependence as being generated by a stratification of society, with the flow of wealth from the periphery toward the center and an ascendancy of an aristocracy. There are obvious benefits and hence a desire among individuals to belong or to be part of the center. And there is rivalry within a bounded world where trade or acquisition, perhaps more than possession, creates a landscape of dependence. An individual can possess an object, but it takes more than one person to trade. Galleries are not only places that display wealth in the terms of objects of art but also attest to the almost divine nature of the traders. A thirst for artifacts by collecting institutions and the prestige and power acquired by directors and curators when acquiring significant art works and the need by critics to belong to the collecting culture is undoubtedly one of the major forces shaping the illicit cultural property market.[5] This relationship of dependence can be described in ecological terms as the lungs or the engines of the cultural property world. Given the interdependence of the institutions and the key players, there would then seem to be no correcting force except for the at times overly zealous archaeologists whom we shall return to later in this epilogue.

My review of the global situation advances the notion that the kind of behavior that feeds on the "ecology of tainted collections," that is, the environmental niche between what is legal and what is illegal, while being most regrettable, certainly is to be anticipated. Combine gains to be accrued by the transport through space and time of objects and our common human urge to possess, coupled with our innate greed and the difficulty of prosecuting transgressors, and there is sufficient fertile ground for conflicts of interest and exposures of human fallibilities to be frequent and universal. The all-important dimension of pecuniary value brings us face-to-face with one of the many entanglements that must be considered.

Here is the rub. Artifacts are valued by academic disciplines and cultural institutions in markedly different ways. Archaeologist might value an artifact for the information that it carries about customs that can no longer be observed.[6] Of particular interest to archaeologists is a detailed description of the context in which the object was found or was used. The ethnographer values it for the information that the object can tell us about the customs and practices of a living community. The same object, if regarded as having artistic qualities, may be valued by the art connoisseur for its aesthetic properties. If it is comparatively rare and becomes a highly prized work of art, substantial economic value will be ascribed to it by an art dealer. Obviously the archaeologist and the ethnographer want to know as much as possible about its earlier context and the process of its acquisition. However, such information, in some circumstances, could prove to be embarrassing to individuals and institutions if there was subterfuge during the acquisition process and perfidy or a loss of faith between the parties engaged in its trade. Transporting the object from its place in an ethnographic community where it may have been purchased for tens of dollars to an international metropolis could increase its value a thousandfold. If we introduce a time factor where the object was collected a century ago, the value could increase to hundreds of thousands of dollars. Gabriela Petkova speaks of a 2,000 percent profit from treasure hunting in Bulgaria.[7] It appears as if few if any countries are immune from the activity of looters.

Merryman is not the only author to consider the culture of collecting. "To understand the forgery problem, one must understand the forgery culture" is the opening sentence of *The Lie*

Became Great: The Forgery of Ancient Near Eastern Cultures. Muscarella develops this notion further:

> The forgery culture is stratified and multi-faceted. It has a kinship system, a hierarchical structure, systems of gift exchange, laws, a coded language, judges and juries (usually the same), a police force. Its inhabitants include professors, curators, scientists, museum officials and trustees, dealers, smugglers, auction house employees, collectors and forgers. An imperial culture, it colonizes other, more legitimate cultures, drawing into its realm scholars, students, and the general public.
>
> Individuals function in this capacity willingly or as fellow travelers (because of prestige, power, and financial support granted), some out of a fear (i.e. of losing one's job or someone's affection and support); others are more innocent or ignorant, not realizing they perform important tasks that help the culture to thrive.[8]

The core of the book is an illustrated identification of more than 1,250 artifacts in the collections of great museums of the world that Muscarella asserts are fakes. If proven to be true, this is a sad testimony to institutional incompetence, particularly in one instance where the entire contents of the museum is questioned.[9] Archaeologists are just as concerned as are art historians with the monumental scale of the trade in fake and tainted objects. There are instances where entire prehistoric cultures are represented by materials that have no true provenance and could well be the product of a modern workshop. Christopher Reed notes:

> Over the centuries when demand for a certain sort of artwork out-stripped supply, the forgers go to work. When ancient Romans conceived that owning an original Classic Greek

> sculpture was a step up in the good life, the supply of genuine pieces quickly vanished and Roman craftsmen churned out Greek statuary until the poet Horace could exclaim in the first century B.C.: "He who knows a thousand works of art, knows a thousand frauds."[10]

RECIPROCITY: "GIVING AND TAKING"

Kuk archaeological site is being considered for World Heritage listing as one of the earliest manifestations of a natural landscape modified for agricultural purposes. Archaeologists, under the direction of Jack Golson of The Australian National University, studied the multiple agricultural phases of the highlands valley site dating to as early as 9,000 years ago. As the fieldwork reached its conclusion, 700 acres of partially drained swampland continued to be operated as a government experimental tea plantation until it was closed in 1990. The land reverted to the provincial government and all effective management ceased. Local tribesmen resettled the property and planted gardens and coffee trees. Lack of government control over the potential World Heritage landscape has stalled the heritage listing process. John Muke and officers from the National Museum have attempted to overcome the impasse by speaking with elders from the clans of the Kawelka and Jika that are competing to occupy the abandoned station. Interesting perspectives on the ownership of the intellectual property produced from the archaeological excavations have emerged during those discussions.

Highlanders' view of the relationship between the outsiders and themselves is complex, ever-changing, and instructive. Kuk is associated with the notable Kawelka tribesman Ongka. Muke sought his opinion of the personal relationship between Western archaeologists and their local "colleagues." Ongka, who has been the leading character in ethnographic movies and a close associate of the anthropologist Andrew Strathern, states:

> They have used me and made so much money out of me and now, you come here to protect the things that will make others become famous in future. You also come to sell my ideas and things. What have you given back to me?[11]

Muke concludes that

> Ongka's perspective is that his intellectual creativity represents an investment in the future, like a seed. If it is successful, and the tree that grows from his seed bears fruit, then those who have benefited from the fruit will be indebted to him as the source person.[12]

Ownership of knowledge, that which makes an organizer of sacred events and a manager of the economic landscape a "big man," has considerable value to the Kawelka. Reciprocity and the long-term maintenance of important interpersonal ties are the all-important attributes that are foremost in Ongka's thoughts and the hallmarks of personal relationships throughout Papua New Guinea.

In the minds of the highlanders, the ownership of the Ambum Stone by the National Gallery of Australia gives to its possessors power and wealth. They, the Enga, in turn receive nothing in exchange for losing possession of the "bones of the ancestors." Galleries and museums may claim that they have made a culture universally known and respected throughout the art world and that an antiquity like the Ambum Stone is of universal cultural value as suggested by the Papua New Guinea ambassador to the United States:

> The Jolika Collection will continue to exhibit the values, artistic expressions and craftsmanship of our creative ances-

> tors. Our ancestors were not simply specimens that we can regulate to the anthropological past: rather, our traditional people were—and are (though their living creativity is seen as works of art)—creative humans who left behind, for present and future generations to enjoy, an array of unique works of art, sculptures, masks and even the remains of their tribal leaders. The substantial contributions of the Friede family in supporting PNG in preserving our cultural history through their extensive collection—and the efforts of the de Young Museum in promoting and ensuring that America appreciates PNG's art and culture—are certainly admirable.[13]

But, and this is a big but, highlanders seek tangible signs of the all-important and all-pervasive custom of reciprocity. A few public collecting institutions have managed to have a vibrant connection with the peoples who provided the materials for their collections. Jim Specht of the Australian Museum in Sydney is perhaps the most respected person to undertake the repatriation of ethnographic specimens to national institutions and local cultural centers. In 1977, the Australian Museum returned seventeen objects to the Papua New Guinea National Museum to fill gaps in its collection. Prott and O'Keefe write:

> Compensation in any event, need not be money. Papua New Guinea and the Solomon Islands "compensated" the Australian Museum, in a truly Melanesian way, by gifts of artifacts, which the Museum accepted as culturally and scientifically satisfying, thus resulting in balanced reciprocity, assessed, it should be noted, not on a monetary basis.[14]

Paul Taçon expands upon the efforts of Specht:

> Over the last twenty years the Australian Museum has come to be recognized internationally as a world leader in the return

> of cultural property to its country of origin. Important items have been returned to Papua New Guinea, the Solomon Islands, Vanuatu, New Zealand, Canada and India.
>
> The leadership of Specht, Head of the Department of Anthropology, made the difference to the Australian Museum's role in returning cultural property. His involvement in UNESCO committees in the 1980s, which drew up guidelines that refined our approach to issues of return, and his longer involvement with the cultural centres in the Pacific, led to trusting relationships being developed.[15]

Long-term maintenance of trusting relationships is the key to successful repatriation. An attempt by the National Museum of the Solomon Islands to repatriate artifacts acquired by Raymond Firth and housed in the Australian Museum in Sydney faltered most likely because "it lacked a social context." Bonshek, in her review of this case, states:

> I highlight the implication for museums, that not all collections are contested sites in which ethnographic and political authority is challenged. On the contrary I suggest that, with regard to the 1928–1929 Firth collection, the museum is a site holding objects which mediate specific social relationships. This collection is important because it embodies the relationships of the Tikopia people with Raymond Firth.[16]

Obviously the relationship of the people of Tikopia with the Firth collection will change as each new generation establishes its own set of distinctive cultural values. There might come a day when possession of the collection becomes a social-values issue and restitution is brought up for reconsideration.

Considerable resources have been allocated by the National Museum of the American Indian, a branch of the Smithsonian Institution in Washington, to connecting with and meeting the social and spiritual needs of First Peoples throughout the Americas. The Native American Graves Protection and Repatriation Act (NAG-PRA) has fostered dialogue between federal land and collections managers, and tribal councils. Systems have developed where there are tribal historic preservation offices and procedures have been put into place to ensure that sensitive information is confidential and that there is no misappropriation of intellectual property.

ADVOCATE: "ONE WHO PLEADS"

When anthropologists and archaeologists seek to redress injustices, and there is no recourse to law, they may seek social justice through acting as an advocate;[17] in part to combat ethnocentrism

Box Epilogue. 1

REPATRIATION BY THE NMAI: "RETURN TO COUNTRY OF BIRTH"

Repatriation is the process whereby specific kinds of American Indian cultural items held in the National Museum of the American Indian are returned to lineal descendants and culturally affiliated Indian tribes, Alaska Native clans or villages, and Native Hawaiian organizations. Human remains, funerary objects, sacred objects, and objects of cultural patrimony are all materials that may be considered for repatriation.

> Repatriation at NMAI is a uniquely proactive and collaborative process. The Repatriation Office conducts its research independently from other Smithsonian repatriation programs and has a separate advisory committee.[1]

1 From www.nmai.si.edu/subpage.cfm?subpage=collaboration&second=repatriation (accessed on 20 March 2007).

(tendency of viewing our own culture as being superior to that of others and not ascribing validity to others' beliefs and behaviors). Generally, anthropologists are neither trained to be advocates nor are they necessarily experienced with legal systems. One of the most prolonged and notable efforts to assist imperiled tribes is that of Napoleon A. Chagnon. He first made contact with the Yanomamö and started to study their kinship and social system in 1964, when to some extent they were protected by their isolation. Dwelling in the Amazon rainforest on the border between Brazil and Venezuela, Yanomamö lands are being taken away from them and their culture destroyed. Chagnon has shifted his focus from a purely anthropological perspective to one that puts forward the detrimental genocidal policies of governments that have failed to protect their indigenous peoples.[18]

Chagnon's plea for the plight of the Yanomamö is not an act of academic or political opportunism. But anthropological advocacy can be clouded by attempts to achieve social justice, and advocates must seek to maintain scientific objectivity. At no time over the past five years, did I consider the story of the Ambum Stone as a vehicle that would return the artifact to its highlands home.

PURITY: "FREEDOM FROM MORAL CORRUPTION"

The Jolika collection of Papua New Guinea artifacts, acquired during the lifetime of John Friede, and exhibited in 2006 at the de Young Museum in San Francisco, is an example of where the age of the ethnographic specimens serves an indicator of their purity as Oceanic art.[19] One of the criticisms of the exhibition is that it severely separates the ethnographic past from the present and is not at all concerned with hybrid works of art. Margaret Mackenzie in a review of the exhibition writes:

> When contemporary PNG artists visit from overseas, typically they face the expectation, already familiar from tourists, that they perpetuate "pickled" versions of their traditions. Experimentation with hybrid forms and new media can be limited by the pressures in the host country for artists to remain representative of their own national backgrounds rather than to venture into current experimental art spaces where they are visiting. The active contemporary art scene of Papua New Guinea receives no recognition in the de Young display or catalogue. Friede's focus on antiquity and his lack of interest in contemporary works can enshrine a primitivism that dismisses peoples of today as inferior inheritors of a glorified past in a disdained present. Perceptions of unchanging timelessness separate them through an exoticism, an orientalism, of distance and difference, from those who live in industrialized sophisticated cities. This perspective obliterates awareness of the globalizing connections that link everyone to current, human, commonality.[20]

To the anthropologists, art that portrays a transition from precontact to post-Western influence helps to understand the acculturation process and choices that peoples make during a period of marked change. A comparative study offers insights into changing values during the process of modernization. Implicit in the de Young exhibition is a cruel denial that the contemporary artists of Papua New Guinea, those that draw their inspirations from traditional art and employ Western media such as silk screen graphic prints, are of any value. As a contrast to this approach, the National Gallery of Australia and the Papua New Guinea National Museum and Art Gallery have successfully collaborated on a major exhibition of Papua New Guinea prints spanning the period from the 1960s into the twenty-first century.[21]

But, there is one clearly modern piece illustrated in the catalog of the Jolika collection (and it is one of my favorites); unfortunately it was not on display. Decorated in comic-book fashion with a magnificent picture of the Phantom emblazoned with the words "*man no savy dai*"—"man who does not know how to die"—this western highlands shield is dated to the 1960s.[22] Unfortunately the artist is not recorded, but with some inquiry we might be able to find out more about the highland artist that chose to depict the comic book figure of the Phantom on a war shield.

As do ethnographic objects, archaeological artifacts—remember that the Ambum Stone is both—become inflated in value as they are moved from their place of origin to metropolitan centers. An artifact revealed by a backhoe in a field in Italy garners the tomb robber hundreds of dollars; thousands of dollars is paid to the middleman; hundreds of thousands if not millions are paid by the art connoisseur or gallery curator to add the artifact to their collection. Peter Watson and Cecilia Todeschini discuss in detail the economics of the illicit trade in artifacts in *The Medici Conspiracy*.[23] They refer to the investigation of a London antiquities dealer that revealed that the dealer's stock was stored in thirty-five warehouses and had a listed value of £125 million. In another instance, four frescos that once decorated a tomb in an ancient Greek city south of Naples were purchased for $75,000 and donated to the Getty Museum in Los Angeles. The frescos were valued at $2,500,000 for taxation purposes, netting the donor a substantial taxation relief.[24] Not only were the frescos likely to have been removed illegally from the tomb, but all information relating to the context and provenance also would have been destroyed.

The Papua New Guinea National Museum has suffered major setbacks, in particular the robbery in May 2003 of its carved-stone collection. Between fourteen and twenty stone objects, and one replica, were stolen.[25] Among these stone masterpieces were unique objects such as stone mortars and pestles carved in the shape of bird figures, many of which had been illustrated in publications by Douglas Newton and Pamela Swadling. The loss was publicized (for example on The Pacific Arts Association website), along with drawings of some of the objects. None of the objects has been recovered. Such problems were forecast by Les Groube when he spoke of the difficulty of creating a national vision among some 900 ethnic groups.[26] For those "enlightened Westerners" who worked diligently in the 1960s and 1970s to create a better kind of postcolonial society in Papua New Guinea, the outcome some three decades later leaves us empty. The reader may wonder why there is no reference to material in the files of the Papua New Guinea National Museum and Art Gallery. Frankly, it is because the record-keeping system of the museum and lines of communication have collapsed.

Do not for one brief moment assume that I am advocating the return of the Ambum Stone to the National Museum. The National Gallery of Australia has had the stone on display for thirty years. And remember that the last carved stone object that was returned to a highlands community at their insistence was burned in the local police station when it was assaulted during tribal "troubles." At this time, it is not advisable to travel into the district where the Ambum Stone once resided, even though that place is relatively close to the main administrative center of Wabag, the capital of the Enga Province. Wiessner's many comments on the draft manuscript were followed a few days later by correspondence that may hold the key to unlocking this seemingly hopelessly entangled situation:

> Dear Brian, Seeing all those cockatoos was one of the great pluses of my visit to ANU—can't believe they exist in the wild. . . . It is I who must send appreciation to you for the work you have done and for the in depth understanding you

> have brought to the traffic of sacred objects. This is extremely important work. . . . After my recent visit to Enga, I hope to rebuild the cultural centre with a research component and set up exhibits that will take topics like warfare, youth, the role of women, etc and trace them through time up to today and see if they can come up with some of their own solutions as the Enga have for generations. There is such a huge problem with youth in Enga who are unaware of tradition, history, educated in a system that does not teach them to value their culture and yet does not prepare more than a few for life in another world. One can just feel the frustration seething and the result is the current rampant fighting with high-powered weapons. The Enga are keen on this enterprise and Akii's son is now doing some of the work—he is excellent. So now I am embarking on the project of raising funds.[27]

But where do we go from here? Enga leaders are worlds apart from the art connoisseurs of the National Gallery of Australia; or are they? The answer to the challenge, I believe, lies with the traditional Enga way of dealing with disputes. Management gurus speak of achieving a win-win situation where both aggrieved parties appear to benefit. Quite frankly, one should not try for resolution but for best-practice heritage management and an ongoing feel-good–feel-good outcome. But how does one reach a position in the Ambum Stone dispute such that everyone feels good? As we have seen with the Enga, winning is not what is sought after in competitions such as war and ceremonial distributions. The objective is to achieve an outcome that benefits as much as possible all of the contending parties and their allies. Glamour, face, and prestige are to be retained and enhanced. There is a financial and human-investment price to pay, but that cost is a necessary factor to becoming, as well as maintaining, one's position as a "big man" or manager.

After all, in the words of the Melpa "big man" Ongka, it is not what you have but what you give away that counts. It is by giving that one becomes a "big man" and humbles their opposition. As we have seen, "big men" influence the course of events favorably in the interest of their clan's people and far-flung trade partners through persuasive oratory skills, a familiarity with the traditional past of their group, specific knowledge of recent events, and rewards to the leading men of associated clans.

Who acquired the Ambum Stone in Wabag and exported it and sold it to Goldman in London? This link in the chain of ownership was not confirmed until almost five years after I started my research and at the very moment when the manuscript was being prepared to send to the publisher. It was Pamela Swadling who noticed a reference in the notes of Graeme Pretty, a former curator of the South Australian Museum and collector for the Commonwealth Art Advisory Board, to carved stone artifacts in the collections of the Queensland Museum. Pretty's notes have the stone bowls being collected in 1965, but the Queensland Museum catalog has them listed as 1955–1964.[28] The Queensland Museum acquired the Wabag stone artifacts from Keith Buxton. Was it Keith Buxton who exported the Ambum Stone from Papua New Guinea perhaps along with the objects now at the Queensland Museum that he just might have obtained an export permit for some four decades ago and sold it to Philip Goldman? Or, is this just one of those odd coincidences? Buxton was on the list of contacts, but he died before I could talk with him. In his book, *Papua New Guinea: The Golden Years* (for all too many of us) he indicates that he was in Wabag in the early 1960s and that he later came to deal in artifacts. The catalog of the Queensland Museum lists a substantial quantity of artifacts as being acquired from Keith Buxton, including "two carved stone bowls from—cave—Enga—Wabag."[29]

Can we know for certain that Buxton sold the Ambum Stone to Goldman? The easiest way was to ask Philip Goldman, and that is what I did! After I had received the information from the Queensland Museum about their acquisition from Buxton of carved stone objects from Enga, I sought to find Buxton through the "Una Voce" website that tracks former Papua New Guinea public servants. There I found his obituary written by his daughter. I sent an e-mail to Philip Goldman advising of important new information and that I would like to talk to him about it. Off I went to complete what every university lecturer seems to spend the most of their time doing—photocopying.

When I returned to my office, there was an answering machine message from Philip Goldman. Philip reiterated that he had nothing new to add, that he had told me everything that he could recall. A second e-mail with a copy of Keith Buxton's obituary attached was sent to Goldman, and I went off to do some more photocopying. Upon returning to my office, I found a second message from Goldman with his phone number as well as a statement that his memory had been jogged and that indeed he had purchased the Ambum Stone from Keith Buxton. It is conceivable, as I have pointed out strange things happened in Papua New Guinea, that Buxton received an export permit for the "Wabag cave" artifacts and after providing the collection to the Queensland Museum sought to recoup his expenses through the sale of a single object, the Ambum Stone. Goldman recognized that he had purchased a masterpiece. He took it to Bryan Cranstone at the British Museum in an attempt to obtain any information on this kind of object. Philip recounts that Cranstone was not interested, as the Ambum Stone did not have an archaeological provenance, and offered him only ten pounds more than he had paid for it. But the British Museum did make exceptionally fine resin-based and correctly weighted copies. Goldman had the stone photographed by the best ethnographic photographer available to him, Werner Forman, then sought the help of the anthropological community to determine just what he had. However, the role of the Ambum Stone in Enga society was not to emerge in full until thirty years later when Wiessner and Tumu published their study *Historical Vines*.

Remember, for the Kawelka, status is gained not by how much you have but by what you give away. In Ongka's words, "Now that I have given you these things, I have won. . . . I have knocked you down by giving so much."[30]

REALITY: "ACTUAL TRUTH OR FACT"

Who Owns Objects? brings us back to a harsh and bleak reality. In 2004 a seminar and workshop was held at Oxford with nine papers presenting markedly different viewpoints with gloomy perspectives. If the papers are at all representative of the opinions of the diversity of professionals involved with the trade in artifacts, then there is little hope of reconciliation. Neil Brodie leads off with "Smoke and Mirrors." Brodie has published extensively and received an award from the European Archaeological Association for *Stealing History: The Illicit Trade in Cultural Material* jointly authored with J. Doole and P. Watson, and it is reasonable to assume that his writing represent viewpoints that are widely held within the archaeological community.[31] He concludes:

> In the introduction to this paper I claimed that the conditions necessary for an open public debate over the antiquities trade do not currently exist. I hope to have shown it is because antiquities dealers are biased reporters whose testimony cannot

be trusted to be objective, and because some museum staff are withholding what might be useful information about their relevant practice.[32]

George Ortiz, an international collector of considerable stature, follows Brodie with an article based upon fifty years of collecting:

> I must ask those politically correct scholars and fundamentalist archaeologists: Who will be interested in your preoccupations? What institutions, foundations, individuals or bureaucrats will want to fund or support those who either fight them or bring them no prestige or votes?[33]

His article refers to the poor condition of artifacts in collecting institutions:

> Three hundred bundles of precious Paracas textiles are in storage in the archaeological museum in Pueblo Libre without proper conservation.[34]

Ortiz's argument is straightforward: Our collecting institutions cannot care for the vast corpus of objects that constitute the heritage of nations. He writes that archaeologists excavate sites and then do not care for the findings and in many cases do not care for the sites or publish their reports. There is no doubt that the Ambum Stone was well looked after once it was in the hands of Philip Goldman and that it was broken while on loan to a museum. Had the Ambum Stone been on display at the National Museum and Art Gallery of Papua New Guinea, it would have been stolen along with the other carved-stone masterpieces.

John Boardman, retired professor of classical archaeology and art at Oxford, presents a position in opposition to that of Colin Renfrew. Boardman states that he long sensed that there was something wrong about the course of legislation for the control of antiquities, and its effects on scholarship and public museums, not just collectors.

> It is easy to be moved by pictures of robbed sites, monuments and museums; they represent a tragic loss. . . . The complainers are simply not living in the same real world as the rest of us, and the high-minded attitude, in which many philistine governments acquiesce because it seems correct, is both harming scholarship and attacking a very natural human interest in collecting, by individuals or museums.[35]

Boardman is concerned that antiquities made out of gold or silver will simply be melted down to realize their precious metal value if they cannot be legally traded. Kampmann writes that the United Kingdom legislation that permits the registration of findings is far better than the situation that obtains in her native Germany even though there is a tradition that dates back to the time of the emperor Hadrian "who decreed that treasures found in the ground should be split between the finder and the land owner."[36]

"Repatriation and its Discontents: The Glasgow Experience," the last article in *Who Owns Objects?* is by Mark O'Neill. O'Neil narrates an account of the repatriation of a ghost shirt that was said to have been removed from the body of a warrior killed at Wounded Knee.[37] Comments in the visitor's book were strongly in favor of the return of the ghost shirt.

Progress is being made according to Peter Watson, in part through pressure to deal effectively with the vast quantities of art objects that are stolen every year and the paintings, sculptures, drawings, antiquities, and rare books that surface after having been "separated" from their Jewish owners during the Second World War. Fewer objects are being identified by the Art Loss Register as stolen (from a peak of 8,000 in 1992). The market is becoming better informed and wary of objects without a record of ownership or requisite export permits. Although optimistic that progress is being made, Watson remains skeptical, as he is convinced that galleries may only provide information that serves to enhance the value of an object.[38]

UNIDROIT is an international effort toward harmonizing national laws. Lyndel Prott writes that it has not achieved uniform law, yet the 1995 Convention on Stolen and Illegally Exported Cultural Objects has had an impact. Prott states that progress has been made with as little interference as is possible with the legal art trade:

> The Convention has not achieved uniform law, but it has achieved minimum uniform rules. The experience in recent years has been that national courts increasingly seek to harmonise their interpretation of key concepts in accordance with the aims and purposes of an international treaty. This is increasingly evident in the case-law collected by UNIDROIT on other harmonizing Conventions.[39]

Another factor is entering the complex equation, and that is the reluctance of institutions to loan objects that might be displayed along with tainted objects. A recent example is the threatened withdrawal by the Greek government of nineteen works destined for an exhibition of the work of the Greek sculp-

Box Epilogue. 2

ART LOSS REGISTER

The website www.artloss.com is a database of items that have been registered as lost or stolen. Individuals and institutions are encouraged to register art works in a pre-loss database to facilitate the cracking down on art crime.

tor Praxiteles at the Louvre. The Louvre stated that it had no choice but to withdraw its request for a loan of the five-foot-tall sculpture of Apollo, believed to be the sun god, that was acquired in 2004 by the Cleveland Museum from a firm "accused of business improprieties in the past." The Greek government suggests that the Apollo figure may have been looted but that it did not wish to have its actions interpreted by the Louvre as a threat.[40]

We seem to be back where we started, with the words of H. L. Mencken: "For every complex problem, there is a solution that is simple, neat, and wrong."

What I have argued for is that for each notable instance of tainted art or purloined ethnographic material there is a unique and highly complex story to be revealed.[41] We should start exactly where Clemency Coggins said that we should, with the truth and with openness, as much as it may be uncomfortable for us to admit our foibles and shortcomings as archaeologists, and as connoisseurs.

NOTES

1. Ernest Vincze, Charlie Nairn, Andrew Strathern, and Pattie Winter, *Ongka"s Big Moka*, (video recording), Granada Television International, London.

2. Commonwealth of Australia. 1956. *Customs (Prohibited Imports) Regulations*, Schedule 3, Item 9A.

3. Clemency Chase Coggins. 1995. "A Licit International Trade in Ancient Art: Let There Be Light." *International Journal of Cultural Property* 1(4): 63; and Coggins reference to Paul M. Bator. 1981/1982. *The International Trade in Art*. University of Chicago Press, Chicago & London, 84–86.

4. John Henry Merryman. 1998. Book review of Jeanette Greenfield, *The Return of Cultural Treasures. International Journal of Cultural Property* 7(1): 283–84.

5. Merryman, book review of *The Return of Cultural Treasures*, 283–84.

6. Refer to Neil Brodie, Morag M. Kersel, Christina Luke, and Kathryn Walker Tubb. 2006. *Archaeology, Cultural Heritage, and the Antiquities Trade*. University Press of Florida, Gainesville.

7. Gabriela Petkova. 2004. "How to Get a 2,000% Profit from Selling an Object." *International Journal of Heritage Studies* 10(4): 361–67.

8. Oscar White Muscarella. 2000. *The Lie Became Great: The Forgery of Ancient Near Eastern Cultures*. STYX Publications, Groningen, 1.

9. Peter Watson. 2000. "How Forgeries Corrupt Our Top Museums." *New Statesman* 13(637): 14–15.

10. Christopher Reed. 2004. "Wrong!" *Harvard Magazine*, September/October 44 quoted by Ronald D. Spencer. 2005. "The Expert and the Object." In Kate Fitz Gibbon (ed.), *Who Owns the Past: Cultural Policy, Cultural Property and the Law*. Rutgers University Press, New Brunswick and London, 160.

11. John D. Muke. 2000. "Ownership of Ideas and Things: A Case Study of the Politics of the Kuk Prehistoric Site." In Kathy Wimp and Mark Busse (eds.), *Protection of Intellectual, Biological and Cultural Property in Papua New Guinea*. Asia Pacific Press, ANU, Canberra and Conservation Melanesia Inc., Port Moresby, 96.

12. Muke, "Ownership of Ideas and Things," 101.

13. Evan J. Paki to John E. Buchannan, Jr. Letter of 21 April 2006.

14. Lindel V. Prott and P. J. O'Keefe. 1989. *Law and the Cultural Heritage*, Volume 3, *Movement*. Professional Books Limited, Oxford, 898; and J. Specht. 1979. "The Australian Museum and the Return of Artifacts to Pacific Island Countries." *Museum* 31(1): 28–31.

15. Paul Taçon, Jack Golson, Kirk Huffman, and Des Griffin. 2004.

"Jim Specht's Brilliant Career: A Tribute." In Val Attenbrow and Richard Fullagar (eds.), *A Pacific Odyssey: Archaeology and Anthropology in the Western Pacific. Papers in Honour of Jim Specht.* Records of the Australian Museum, Supplement 29, Australian Museum, Sydney.

16. Elizabeth Bonshek. 2004. "Ownership and a Peripatetic Collection: Raymond Firth's Collection from Tikopia, Solomon Islands." In Val Attenbrow and Richard Fullagar (eds.), *A Pacific Odyssey: Archaeology and Anthropology in the Western Pacific. Papers in Honour of Jim Specht.* Records of the Australian Museum, Supplement 29, Australian Museum, Sydney, 43.

17. Philip Conrad Kottak. 2005. *Mirror for Humanity: A Concise Introduction to Cultural Anthropology*. McGraw Hill, New York, 6–8.

18. Napoleon A. Chagnon. 1992. *Yanomamö: The Last Days of Eden*. Harcourt Brace Jovanovich, Publishers, San Diego.

19. John Friede et al. 2005. *New Guinea Art Masterpieces from the Jolika Collection of Marcia and John Friede* (2 vols.). Fine Arts Museums of San Francisco in Association with 5 Continents Editions, Milan, Italy.

20. Margaret Mackenzie. 2007. "Jolika Collection of New Guinea Art, de Young Museum, San Francisco, California, Opened October 2005." Book and Media Reviews. *The Contemporary Pacific* 19(1): 347.

21. Melanie Eastburn. 2006. *Papua New Guinea Prints*. National Gallery of Australia, Canberra (Director's Foreword).

22. Friede, *New Guinea Art Masterpieces from the Jolika Collection of Marcia and John Friede*, 2:190.

23. Peter Watson and Cecilia Todeschini. 2006. *The Medici Conspiracy: The Illicit Journey of Looted Antiquities from Italy's Tomb Raiders to the World's Greatest Museums*. Public Affairs, New York.

24. Watson and Todeschini, *The Medici Conspiracy*, 177.

25. The Pacific Arts Association, 9 August 2003 from http://pacificarts.org/theft.html (accessed on 18 October 2003).

26. Les Groube. 1985. "The Ownership of Diversity: The Problem of Establishing a National History in a Land of Nine Hundred

Ethnic Groups." In Isable McBryde (ed.), *Who Owns the Past?* Oxford University Press, Oxford, 49–73.

27. Polly Wiessner to Brian Egloff. Letter of 21 November 2004.

28. Carved stone artifacts from Papua New Guinea have long fascinated archaeologists. Graeme Pretty was one of the early archaeologists to compile an inventory. See G. L. Pretty. 1965. "Two Stone Pestles from Western Papua and Their Relationship to Prehistoric Pestles and Mortars from New Guinea." *Records of the South Australian Museum* 12:119–30. Also refer to R. Bulmer and S. Bulmer. 1962. "Figurines and Other Stones of Power among the Kyaka of Central New Guinea." *Journal of the Polynesian Society* 71:192–208.

29. Olivia Robinson, senior curator at Queensland Museum, provided me with a list of the eighty artifacts acquired from Keith Buxton.

30. From http://home.earthlink.net/~mrance/CommColl/CultAnth/ongkasummary.html (accessed on 31 January 2007).

31. Brodie's article takes the place of the paper presented at the workshop by Colin Renfrew.

32. Neil Brodie. 2006. "Smoke and Mirrors." In Eleanor Robson, Luke Treadwell, and Chris Gosden (eds.), *Who Owns Objects? The Ethics and Politics of Collecting Cultural Artefacts*. Oxbow Books, Oxford, 11.

33. George Ortiz. 2006. "Overview and Assessment after Fifty Years of Collecting in a Changing World." In Eleanor Robson, Luke Treadwell, and Chris Gosden (eds.), *Who Owns Objects? The Ethics and Politics of Collecting Cultural Artefacts*. Oxbow Books, Oxford, 30.

34. Ortiz, "Overview and Assessment after Fifty Years of Collecting in a Changing World," 24. Ortiz is referring to the 1928 excavations of Julio Tello. Tello was mentioned in chapter 4 of this volume with respect to having been the excavator and illustrator of the Paracas textile in the collection of the National Gallery of Australia.

35. John Boardman. 2006. "Archaeologist, Collectors, and Museums." In Eleanor Robson, Luke Treadwell, and Chris Gosden (eds.), *Who Owns Objects? The Ethics and Politics of Collecting Cultural*

Artefacts. Oxbow Books, Oxford, 33 and 37. Note that the selection of the photograph on the cover of *Who Owns Objects?* perhaps reveals the bias of the editors in that it depicts an archaeological site in Iraq being looted.

36. Ursula Kampmann. 2006. "Who Owns Objects? A View from the Coin Trade." In Eleanor Robson, Luke Treadwell, and Chris Gosden (eds.), *Who Owns Objects? The Ethics and Politics of Collecting Cultural Artefacts*. Oxbow Books, Oxford, 67, 69.

37. Mark O'Neil. 2006. "Repatriation and Its Discontents: The Glasgow Experience." In Eleanor Robson, Luke Treadwell, and Chris Gosden (eds.), *Who Owns Objects? The Ethics and Politics of Collecting Cultural Artefacts*. Oxbow Books, Oxford, 105–28.

38. Peter Watson. 2001. "If It's Art, It Must Be Fake." *New Statesman* 14(653): 23–24.

39. Lyndel V. Prott. 1997. *Commentary on the UNIDROIT Convention*. Institute of Art and Law, Leicester, 87.

40. Steven Litt. 2007. "Omission: Apollo—Why Cleveland's Prized New Praxiteles Is Not in a Show of the Classical Sculptor's Work at the Louvre." *ARTNews* April: 62.

41. The same case-by-case determination is advocated for the repatriation of Paleo-Indian remains by Heather J. H. Edgar, Edward A. Jolie, Joseph F. Powell, and Joe E. Watkins. 2007. "Contextual Issues in Paleoindian Repatriation: Spirit Cave Man as a Case Study." *Journal of Social Archaeology* 7(1): 101–21.

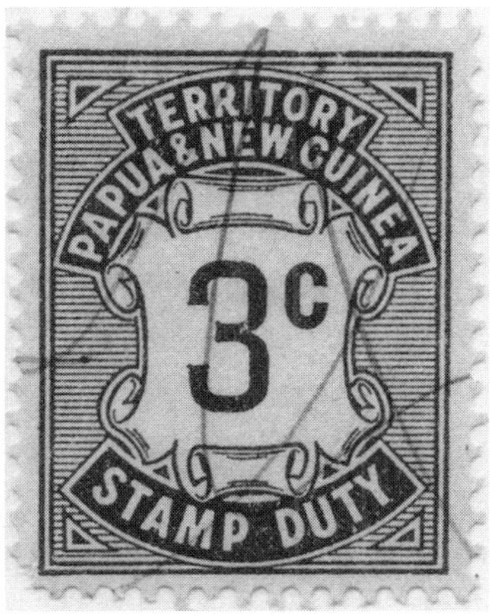

Bibliography

Anon. 1965. "A Remarkable Stone Figure from the New Guinea Highlands." *Journal of the Polynesian Society* 74:76–77.

Appiah, Kwame Anthony. 1997. "Cosmopolitan Patriots." *Critical Inquiry*, 23(3): 617–39.

Australian National Gallery. 1978. *The Genesis of a Gallery, Part 2: A Touring Exhibition from the Collection of the Australian National Gallery*. Commonwealth Government Printer, Canberra.

Awekotuku, Ngahuia Te. 2002. "More Than Skin Deep: *Ta Moko* Today." In Elazar Barkan and Ronald Bush (eds.), *Claiming the Stones, Naming the Bones*. The Getty Research Institute, Los Angeles, 243–54.

Bailey, Martin. 2004. "What Happened to the Maharajah of Indore's Brancusi Birds?" *The Art Newspaper* 45(March): 12–13.

Ballard, Chris. 1994. "The Centre Cannot Hold: Trade Networks and Sacred Geography in the Papua New Guinea Highlands." *Archaeology in Oceania* 29: 130–48.

———. 1995. *Death of a Great Land: Ritual, History and Subsistence Revolution in the Southern Highlands of Papua New*

Guinea. Unpublished doctoral thesis. The Australian National University.

Barkan, Elazar. 2000. *The Guilt of Nations: Restitution and Negotiating Historical Injustices*. W.W. Norton, New York.

———. 2002. "Amending Historical Injustices: The Restitution of Cultural Property—an Overview." In Elazar Barkan and Ronald Bush (eds.), *Claiming the Stones, Naming the Bones*. The Getty Research Institute, Los Angeles, 16–46.

Barkan, Elazar, and Ronald Bush (eds.). 2002. *Claiming the Stones, Naming the Bones: Cultural Property and the Negotiation of National and Ethnic Identity*. The Getty Research Institute, Los Angeles.

Bator, Paul M. 1981/1982. *The International Trade in Art*. University of Chicago Press, Chicago & London.

Bayliss-Smith, Tim, and Jack Golson. 1992. "A Colocasian Revolution in the New Guinea Highlands? Insights from Phase 4 at Kuk." *Archaeology in Oceania* 27: 1–21.

Bjerre, Jens. 1964. *Savage New Guinea*. M. Joseph, London.

Boardman, John. 2006. "Archaeologist, Collectors, and Museums." In Eleanor Robson, Luke Treadwell, and Chris Gosden (eds.), *Who Owns Objects? The Ethics and Politics of Collecting Cultural Artefacts*. Oxbow Books, Oxford, 33–46.

Bonshek, Elizabeth. 2004. "Ownership and a Peripatetic Collection: Raymond Firth's Collection from Tokopia, Solomon Islands." In Val Attenbrow and Richard Fullagar (eds.), *A Pacific Odyssey: Archaeology and Anthropology in the Western Pacific. Papers in Honour of Jim Specht*. Records of the Australian Museum, Supplement 29, Australian Museum, Sydney, 37–45.

Brodie, Neil. 2006. "Smoke and Mirrors." In Eleanor Robson, Luke Treadwell, and Chris Gosden (eds.), *Who Owns Objects? The Ethics and Politics of Collecting Cultural Artefacts*. Oxbow Books, Oxford, 1–14.

Brodie, Neil, Jenny Doole, and Peter Watson. 2000. *Stealing History: The Illicit Trade in Cultural Material*. Report for the Museums Association and ICOM-UK. MacDonald Institute for Archaeological Research, Cambridge.

Brodie, Neil, Jennifer Doole, and Colin Renfrew (eds.). 2001. *Trade in Illicit Antiquities: The Destruction of the World's Archaeological Heritage*. McDonald Institute Monographs, Cambridge.

Brodie, Neil, and Kathryn Walker Tubb (eds.). 2002. *Illicit Antiquities: The Theft of Culture and the Extinction of Archaeology*. Routledge, London.

Brodie, Neil, Morag M. Kersel, Christina Luke, and Kathryn Walker Tubb. 2006. *Archaeology, Cultural Heritage, and the Antiquities Trade*. University Press of Florida, Gainesville.

Bulmer, R. and S. Bulmer. 1962. "Figurines and Other Stones of Power among the Kyaka of Central New Guinea." *Journal of the Polynesian Society* 71:192–208.

Bulmer, Susan. 1969. "New Guinea's Laws Concerning National Cultural Property." *Man in New Guinea* 1(3): 2–4.

Burke, Kelly, and Peter Gotting. 2000. "Artefact Smashed While on Loan." *Sydney Morning Herald*, 11 May, 3.

———. 2000. Precious Artefact Broken by French Was Already a Bust. *Sydney Morning Herald*, 12 May, 3.

Busse, Mark. 2000. "The National Cultural Property (Preservation) Act." In Kathy Wimp and Mark Busse (eds.), *Protection of Intellectual, Biological and Cultural Property in Papua New Guinea*. Pacific Area Press, The Australian National University and Conservation Melanesia, Inc., Port Moresby, 81–95.

Buxton, Keith. 2002. *Papua New Guinea: The Golden Years*. Keith Buxton, Maryborough, Queensland.

Canberra Times. 2001. "Gallery's $7.4m Bargain Nudes." 30 April, 1.

Caruana, Wally. 2003. "The Collection of Indigenous Australian Art: Beginnings and Some Highlights." In Pauline Green (ed.), *Building the Collections*. National Gallery of Australia, Canberra, 193–209.

Chagnon, Napoleon A. 1992. *Yanomamö: The Last Days of Eden*. Harcourt Brace Jovanovich, Publishers, San Diego.

Chippendale, Christopher, and David W. J. Gill. 2000. "Material Consequences of Contemporary Classical Collecting." *American Journal of Archaeology* 104: 463–511.

Clark, W. C. 1971. *Place and People: An Ecology of a New Guinean Community*. University of California Press, Berkeley.

Coggins, Clemency Chase. 1995. "A Licit International Trade in Ancient Art: Let There Be Light." *International Journal of Cultural Property* 1(4): 61–79.

Colley, Sarah. 2002. *Uncovering Australia: Archaeology, Indigenous People and the Public*. Allen & Unwin, Crows Nest, NSW.

Commonwealth of Australia, Senate Legislative Committee. 2000–2001. Environment, Communication, Information Technology and the Arts, Answer to Questions on Notice, Supplementary Budget Estimates, Thursday, 30 November 2000, ECITA 296-3001, Hansard, 30/11/00, question 128, page no. 212.

Connolly, Bob, Robin Anderson, and Richard Oxenburgh. 1984. *First Contact* (video recording). Arundel Productions, Glebe, New South Wales.

Connolly, Bob, and Robin Anderson. 1987. *First Contact: New Guinea's Highlanders Encounter the Outside World*. Penguin Group, New York.

Craig, Barry. 1990. "The Return of Ethnographic Material to Papua New Guinea." *Bulletin of the Conference of Museum Anthropologists '89*, 23: 73–87.

———. 1996. *Samting belong tumbuna: The Collection, Documentation and Preservation of the Material Cultural Heritage of Papua New Guinea*. Unpublished doctoral thesis, Flinders University of South Australia.

Craig, Barry and David Hyndman (eds.). 1990. *Children of Afek: Tradition and Change among the Mountain-Ok of Central New Guinea*. Oceania Monograph 40.

Crawford, A. L. 1977. *The National Cultural Council: Its Aims and Functions; with Guidelines for Establishing and Operating Cultural Centres within Papua New Guinea*. National Cultural Council, Port Moresby.

Craxton, John, and Peter Warren. 2004. "A Neocycladic Harpist?" In Neil Brodie and Catherine Hills (eds.), *Material Engagements: Studies in Honour of Colin Renfrew*. McDonald Institute Monographs, Cambridge, 109–13.

Crim, Jeremiah. 2003. "Scholar Accuses Museums of Looting." *The Daily Pennsylvanian*, 22 October, www.dailypennsylvanian.com.

Cuervo-Cazurra, Alvaro, and Ruth V. Aguilera. 2003. "The Worldwide Diffusion of Codes of Good Governance." In Anna Grandori (ed.), *Corporate Governance and Firm Organization: Microfoundations and Structural Forms*. Oxford University Press, Oxford, 318–48.

Dalton, Rex. 2006. "Guinea Experts Cry Foul on Tribal Exhibits." *Nature* 440(6 April): 722–23.

Denbow, James R. 1984. "Prehistoric Herders and Foragers of the Kalahari: The Evidence for 1500 Years of Interaction." In Carmel Schrire (ed.), *Past and Present in Hunter Gatherer Studies*. Academic Press, Orlando, Florida, 175–93.

Department of Posts and Telegraph. 1970. *Early History—New National Heritage Stamp Issue*. Territory of Papua New Guinea.

Dodge, Alan. 2003. "Brave New World." In Pauline Green (ed.), *Building the Collections*. National Gallery of Australia, Canberra, 47–58.

du Cros, Hillary. 2002. *Much More Than Stones and Bones*. Melbourne University Press, Melbourne.

Dunn, Amanda. 2001. "How *Blue Poles* Polarised Australia." *The Age*, 25 January, Green Guide, 14.

Eastburn, Melanie. 2006. *Papua New Guinea Prints*. National Gallery of Australia, Canberra.

Edgar, Heather J. H., Edward A. Jolie, Joseph F. Powell, and Joe E. Watkins. 2007. "Contextual Issues in Paleoindian Repatriation: Spirit Cave Man as a Case Study." *Journal of Social Archaeology* 7(1): 101–21.

Egloff, Brian. 1978. "The *Kula* before Malinowski: A Changing Configuration." In J. Specht and J. P. White (eds.), *Trade and Exchange in Melanesia*. Special issue, *Mankind* 11: 429–35.

———. 1979. *Recent Prehistory in Papua*. Research School of Pacific Studies, The Australian National University (Terra Australis, 4).

Egloff, Brian, and Gava Aura (eds.). 1977. *Pottery of Papua New Guinea: The National Collection*. Papua New Guinea National Museum and Art Gallery, Port Moresby.

Egloff, B., and J. Egloff. 1978. *The Prehistory of Papua New Guinea*. Trustees, National Museum and Art Gallery, Boroko.

Egloff, Brian, Nicolas Peterson, and Sue Wesson. 2005. *Biamanga and Gulaga: Aboriginal Cultural Association with Biamanga and Gulaga National Parks*. Office of the Registrar, Aboriginal Land Rights Act 1983, Surry Hills, New South Wales.

Ellis, W. F. 1965. "Comments on The Papua New Guinea Public Museum and Art Gallery with Proposal for Future Development." *Annual Report of the Trustees of the Papua New Guinea Museum and Art Gallery, 1963–1964*, Port Moresby, 19–32.

Farrington, I., and H. C. Parrott. 1989. "The Paracas Textile Held by the Australian National Gallery, Canberra, Australia: An Examination of the Case for Its Restitution to the Government of Peru." Unpublished manuscript.

Feil, Daryl K. 1984. *Ways of Exchange: The Enga Tee of Papua New Guinea*. University of Queensland Press, St. Lucia.

Fforde, Cressida. 2004. *Collecting the Dead: Archaeology and the Reburial Issue*. Duckworth, London.

Fforde, C., J. Hubert, and P. Turnbull (eds.). 2002. *The Dead and Their Possessions*. Routledge, London.

Fitz Gibbon, Kate. 2005. "The Elgin Marbles: A Summary." In Kate Fitz Gibbon (ed.), *Who Owns the Past: Cultural Policy, Cultural Property and the Law*, Rutgers University Press, New Brunswick, NJ, and London.

Friede, John, et al. 2005. *New Guinea Art Masterpieces from the Jolika Collection of Marcia and John Friede* (2 vols.). Fine Arts Museums of San Francisco in Association with 5 Continents Editions, Milan, Italy.

G. H. 2003–2004. "The Trouble with Puggle." *Nature Australia* Summer: 82–83.

Gammage, Bill. 1998. *The Sky Travellers: Journeys in New Guinea 1938–1939*. The Miegunyah Press of Melbourne University Press, Melbourne.

Ganslmayr, H., H. Landais, G. Lewis, P. Makambila, P. N. Perrot, J. W. Pre, and J. Vistel. 1979. "Study on the Principles, Conditions and Means for the Restitution or Return of Cultural Property in View of Reconstituting Dispersed Heritages." *Museum* 31(1): 62–66.

Gardner, Helen. 2000. "Gathering for God: George Brown and the Christian Economy in the Collection of Artefacts." In Michael O'Hanlon and Robert L. Welsch (eds.), *Hunting the Gatherers: Ethnographic Collectors, Agents and Agency in Melanesia, 1870s–1930s*. Berghahn Books, New York and Oxford, 35–54.

Gash, Noel, and June Whittaker. 1975. *A Pictorial History of New Guinea*. The Jackaranda Press, Milton, Queensland.

Gathercole, Peter, and David Lowenthal. 1990/1994. *The Politics of the Past*. Routledge, New York.

Gerbrands, Adrian A. 1967. *Wow-Ipits: Eight Asmat Woodcarvers of New Guinea*. Mouton & Co, The Hague.

Gerstenblith, Patty. 2002. "Cultural Significance and the Kennewick Skeleton: Some Thoughts on the Resolution of Cultural Heritage Disputes." In Elazar Barkan and Ronald Bush (eds.), *Claiming the Stones, Naming the Bones*. The Getty Research Institute, Los Angeles, 162–97.

Gibbs, Philip J. 1978. "The *Kepele* Ritual of the Western Highlands of Papua New Guinea." *Anthropos* 73: 434–48.

Golson, Jack. 2000. "A Stone Bowl Fragment from the Early Middle Holocene of the Upper Wahgi Valley, Western Highlands Province, Papua New Guinea." *Australian Archaeologist: Collected Papers in Honour of Jim Allen*. Coombs Academic Publishing, The Australian National University, 231–48.

Gosden, Chris, and Chantal Knowles. 2001. *Collecting Colonialism: Material Culture and Colonial Change*. Berg, Oxford and New York.

Gray, Ann. 2003. "Truly National." In Pauline Green (ed.), *Building the Collections*. National Gallery of Australia, Canberra, 73–115.

Greenfield, Jeanette. 1989/1996. *The Return of Cultural Treasures*. Cambridge University Press, Cambridge.

Grishin, Sasha. 2003. "A Collection of Masterpieces." In Pauline Green (ed.), *Building the Collections*. National Gallery of Australia, Canberra, 211–23.

Groube, Les. 1985. "The Ownership of Diversity: The Problem of Establishing a National History in a Land of Nine Hundred Ethnic Groups." In Isable McBryde (ed.), *Who Owns the Past?* Oxford University Press, Oxford, 49–73.

Haddon, Alfred C. 1901–1935. *Reports of the Cambridge Anthropological Expedition to Torres Straits*. The University Press, Cambridge.

Hoffman, Barbara T. (ed.). 2006. *Art and Cultural Heritage: Law, Policy and Practice*. Cambridge University Press, Cambridge.

Hubert, Jane. 1989. "A Proper Place for the Dead: A Critical Review of the 'Reburial Issue.'" In R. Layton (ed.), *Conflict in the Archaeology of Living Traditions*. Routledge, London, 131–66.

Iamo, Wari, and Jacob Simet. 1998. "Cultural Diversity and Identity in Papua New Guinea: A Second Look." In Virginia R. Domínguez and David Y. H. Wu (eds.), *From Beijing to Port Moresby: The Politics of National Identity in Cultural Policies*. Gordon and Breach, Amsterdam, 189–204.

The Independent. 2002. "Museums Face New Clamour to Return 'Plunder.'" *Canberra Times*, 1 April, 8.

International Museums Office. 1940. *Manual on the Technique of Archaeological Excavations*. International Institute of Intellectual Co-operation, Paris.

Jentsch, T., and R. Doetsch. 1986. *Keman, Eine Siedlung im Hochland von Papua-Neuguinea: Bestandsaufnahme und Untersuchung des kulturellen Wandels*. Dietrich Reimer Verlag, Berlin.

Kaiku, Resonga. 1980. "Restoration of National Cultural Property: The Case of Papua New Guinea." In Robert Edwards and Jenny Stewart (eds.), *Preserving Indigenous Cultures: A New Role for Museums*. Australian Government Publishing Service, Canberra, 175–83.

Kampmann, Ursula. 2006. "Who Owns Objects? A View from the Coin Trade." In Eleanor Robson, Luke Treadwell, and Chris Gosden (eds.), *Who Owns Objects? The Ethics and Politics of Collecting Cultural Artefacts*. Oxbow Books, Oxford, 61–76.

Kennedy, Brian. 2001. "In Search of Lucian Freud." *artonview* 26: 28–31.

Kottak, Phillip Conrad. 2005. *Mirror for Humanity: A Concise Introduction to Cultural Anthropology*. McGraw Hill, New York.

Lindstrom, Lamont. 1998. "*Pasin Tumbuna*: Culture and Nationalism in Papua New Guinea." In Virginia R. Domínguez and David Y. H. Wu (eds.), *From Beijing to Port Moresby: The Politics of National Identity in Cultural Policies*. Gordon and Breach, Amsterdam, 141–88.

Litt, Steven. 2007. "Omission: Apollo: Why Cleveland's Prized New Praxiteles Is Not in a Show of the Classical Sculptor's Work at the Louvre." *ARTNews* April: 62.

Long, John, Michael Archer, Timothy Flannery, and Suzanne Hand. 2002. *Prehistoric Mammals of Australia and New Guinea: One Hundred Million Years of Evolution*. The Johns Hopkins University Press, Baltimore and London.

Lyons, Claire L. 2002. "Objects and Identities: Claiming and Reclaiming the Past." In Elazar Barkan and Ronald Bush (eds.), *Claiming the Stones, Naming the Bones*. The Getty Research Institute, Los Angeles, 116–37.

MacClancy, Jeremy. 1997. "A Natural Curiosity: The British Market in Primitive Art." *Res. Anthropology and Aesthetics* 15 (Spring): 163–76.

Machlin, Milt. 2000. *The Search for Michael Rockefeller*. Akadine Press, Pleasantville, New York.

Mackenzie, Margaret. 2007. "Jolika Collection of New Guinea Art, de Young Museum, San Francisco, California, Opened October 2005." Book and Media Reviews. *The Contemporary Pacific* 19(1): 345–51.

Malinowski, Bronislaw. 1922. *Argonauts of the Western Pacific*. Routledge, London.

McBryde, Isabel. 1985. Introduction. In Isabel McBryde (ed.), *Who Owns the Past?* Oxford University Press, Oxford, 1–10.

Mckenzie, Maureen. 1991. *Androgynous Objects: String Bags and Gender in Central New Guinea.* Harwood Academic Publishers, Melbourne.

Meggitt, Mervyn. 1956. "The Valleys of the Upper Wage and Lai Rivers, Western Highlands, New Guinea." *Oceania* 27: 90–135.

———. 1958. "The Enga of the New Guinea Highlands." *Oceania* 28: 253–330.

———. 1967. "Patterns of Leadership among the Mae Enga of New Guinea." *Anthropological Forum* 2: 20–35.

———. 1977. *Blood Is Their Argument: Warfare among the Mae Enga Tribesmen of the New Guinea Highlands.* Mayfield Publishing Company, Palo Alto, CA.

Menzies, J. I. 1987. "Reflections on the Ambun [*sic*] Stone." *Science in New Guinea* 13(2): 170–73.

Merryman, John Henry. 1998. Book review of Jeanette Greenfield, *The Return of Cultural Treasures.* In *International Journal of Cultural Property* 7(1): 283–84.

Messenger, Phyllis Mauch. 1991. *The Ethics of Collecting Cultural Property: Whose Culture? Whose Property?* University of New Mexico Press, Albuquerque.

Miklouho-Maclay, Nikolai Nikolaevich. 1975. *New Guinea Diaries, 1871–1883.* Kristan Press, Madang.

Muke, John D. 2000. "Ownership of Ideas and Things: A Case Study of the Politics of the Kuk Prehistoric Site." In Kathy Wimp and Mark Busse (eds.), *Protection of Intellectual, Biological and Cultural Property in Papua New Guinea.* Asia Pacific Press, ANU, Canberra and Conservation Melanesia Inc., Port Moresby, 96–115.

Musa, Helen. 2000. "Foetal 'Echidna' Repairs Complete." *Canberra Times*, 21 September, 3.

———.2000. "No Blarney, Gallery Chief May Be Left Holding the Gnomes." *Canberra Times*, 12 August, C4.

———. 2001. "PNG Artefact Found to Be 3500y Old." *Canberra Times*, 1 May, 3.

Muscarella, Oscar White. 2000. *The Lie Became Great: The Forgery of Ancient Near Eastern Cultures*. STYX Publications, Groningen.

Museums Association. 2002. *Code of Ethics for Museums: Ethical Principles for All Who Work for or Govern Museums in the UK*. Museums Association, London.

Newton, Douglas. 1974. "Pre-historic Stone Carvings and Their Relationship to the Ethnographical Art of New Guinea." Paper presented at a symposium, The Art of Oceania, McMaster University, 22 August 1974.

———. 1978. (author given as D.N. no title). In *Genesis of a Gallery, Part 2: A Touring Exhibition from the Collection of the Australian National Gallery*. Australian National Gallery, Canberra, 26–27.

———. 1979. "Prehistoric and Recent Art Styles in Papua New Guinea." In S. M. Mead (ed.), *Exploring the Visual Art of Oceania*. University of Hawaii Press, Honolulu, 32–57.

Nicolas, Alain. 2000. *L'art des Papous et des Austronésiens de Nouvelle-Guinée*. Scala, Marseille.

O'Hanlon, Michael, and Robert L. Welsch (eds.). *Hunting the Gatherers: Ethnographic Collectors, Agents and Agency in Melanesia, 1870s–1930s*. Berghahn Books, New York and Oxford.

O'Keefe, Patrick J. 1977. *Trade in Antiquities: Reducing Destruction and Theft*. Unesco Publishing, Paris and Archetype Publications, London.

O'Neil, Mark. 2006. "Repatriation and Its Discontents: The Glasgow Experience." In Eleanor Robson, Luke Treadwell, and Chris Gosden (eds.), *Who Owns Objects? The Ethics and Politics of Collecting Cultural Artefacts*. Oxbow Books, Oxford, 105–28.

Ortiz, George. 2006. "Overview and Assessment after Fifty Years of Collecting in a Changing World." In Eleanor Robson, Luke Treadwell, and Chris Gosden (eds.), *Who Owns Objects? The Ethics and Politics of Collecting Cultural Artefacts*. Oxbow Books, Oxford, 15–32.

Owsley, Douglas W., and Richard L. Jantz. 2002. "Kennewick Man: A Kin? Too Distant." In Elazar Barkan and Ronald Bush (eds.),

Claiming the Stones, Naming the Bones. The Getty Research Institute, Los Angeles, 141–61.

Papua New Guinea Museum. 1965. *Catalogue of Artefacts in the Papua New Guinea Museum (with details of data required for specimens in the future)*. Acting Government Printer, Port Moresby.

Papua New Guinea Museum. 1966. *Preliminary Catalogue Archaeological Monuments in the Territory of Papua New Guinea*. Government Printer, Port Moresby.

Papua New Guinea Museum. 1974. *Guide to the Preservation of National Cultural Property in Papua New Guinea and Guide to the Collecting of Artefacts for the Papua New Guinea Museum*. Papua New Guinea Museum Leaflet, Port Moresby.

Parrott, Helen. 1990. "The Restitution of a Paracas Textile to Peru: The Australian International View." *Bulletin of the Conference of Museum Anthropologists '89*, 23: 88–96.

Peters, Ann H. 2004. "Textile Theft in Inca, Peru: A Threat to Heritage and Its Conservation." From www.elcomercioperu.com.pe/EdicionImpresa/Html/2004-10-15/impNacional0206946.html (accessed on 12 December 2006).

Petkova, Gabriela. 2004. "How to Get a 2,000% Profit from Selling an Object." *International Journal of Heritage Studies* 10(4): 361–67.

Pretty, G. L. 1965. "Two Stone Pestles from Western Papua and Their Relationship to Prehistoric Pestles and Mortars from New Guinea." *Records of the South Australian Museum* 12:119–30.

Prott, Lyndel V. 1997. *Commentary on the UNIDROIT Convention*. Institute of Art and Law, Leicester, 87.

Prott, Lindel V., and P. J. O'Keefe. 1989. *Law and the Cultural Heritage*, Volume 3: *Movement*. Professional Books Limited, Oxford.

Quinnell, Michael. 2000. "Before It Has Become To Late." In Michael O'Hanlon and Robert L. Welsch (eds.). *Hunting the Gatherers: Ethnographic Collectors, Agents and Agency in Melanesia, 1870s–1930s*. Berghahn Books, New York and Oxford, 81–102.

Rappport, Roy A. 1968. *Pigs for the Ancestors: Ritual in the Ecology of a New Guinea People*. Yale University, New Haven.

Reed, Christopher. 2004. "Wrong!" *Harvard Magazine*, September/October, 44, quoted by Ronald D. Spencer. 2005. "The Expert and the Object." In Kate Fitz Gibbon (ed.), *Who Owns the Past: Cultural Policy, Cultural Property and the Law*, Rutgers University Press, New Brunswick, NJ, and London, 160.

Renfrew, Colin. 2000. *Loot, Legitimacy and Ownership: The Ethical Crisis in Archaeology*. Duckworth, London.

———. 2001. Forward. In Neil Brodie, Jennifer Doyle, and Colin Renfrew (eds.), *Trade in Illicit Antiquities: The Destruction of the World's Archaeological Heritage*. MacDonald Institute for Archaeological Research, Cambridge, xi–xii.

Robson, Eleanor, Luke Treadwell, and Chris Gosden (eds.). 2006. *Who Owns Objects? The Ethics and Politics of Collecting Cultural Artefacts*. Oxbow Books, Oxford.

Rowell, Hilary. 1998/2002. "A History of PNG Records." In Peter Nagle (ed.), *Papua New Guinea Records 1883–1942*. National Archives of Australia, Appendix 4.

Safe, Georgina, and Susan McCulloch. 2002. "Gallery Brushes Off 'Nazi Plunder' Threat." *The Weekend Australian*, 20–29 December, 4.

Satov, Murray. 1997. "Catalogues, Collectors, Curators: The Tribal Art Market and Anthropology." In Jeremy MacClancy (ed.), *Contesting Art: Art, Politics and Identity in the Modern World*. Berg Publishers, Oxford, 215–41.

Schiefelin, Edward L., and Robert Crittenden. 1991. *Like People You See in a Dream: First Contact in Six Papua Societies*. Stanford University Press, Stanford.

Shelton, Anthony. 1997. Book review of Jeanette Greenfield, *The Return of Cultural Property [sic]*. In *International Journal of Heritage Studies* 3(2): 126–28.

Sillitoe, Paul. 1983. *Roots of the Earth: Crops in the Highlands of Papua New Guinea*. New South Wales University Press Limited, Kensington.

Simpson, Elizabeth. 1977. *The Spoils of War: World War II and Its Aftermath—the Loss, Reappearance and Recovery of Cultural Property*. Harry N. Abrams Inc., New York.

Smidt, Dirk. 1975. *The Seized Collections of the Papua New Guinea Museum*. Creative Arts Centre and Papua New Guinea Museum, Port Moresby.

———. 1977. "The National Museum and Art Gallery of Papua New Guinea, Port Moresby." *Museum* 29(4): 226–39.

Smidt, Dirk. (ed.). 2003. *Kamoro Art: Tradition and Innovation in a New Guinea Culture*. KIT Publishers, Amsterdam and Rijksmuseum voor Volkenkunde, Leiden.

Smith, Laura Jane. 2004. *Archaeological Theory and the Politics of Cultural Heritage*. Routledge, London and New York.

Snodgrass, Anthony. 2004. "The Parthenon Marbles as an Archaeological Issue." In Neil Brodie and Catherine Hills (eds.), *Material Engagements: Studies in Honour of Colin Renfrew*. McDonald Institute Monographs, Cambridge, 115–24.

Solomon, Jill, and Aris Solomon. 2004. *Corporate Governance and Accountability*. John Wiley & Sons, Ltd., Chichester.

Somare, Michael Thomas. 1975. *Sana: An Autobiography of Michael Somare*. Niugini Press, Port Moresby.

Specht, J. 1979. "The Australian Museum and the Return of Artefacts to Pacific Island Countries." *Museum* 31(1): 28–31.

Spreier, Scott W., Mary H. Fontaine, and Ruth L. Malloy. 2006. "Leadership Run Amok: The Destructive Potential of Overachievers." *Harvard Business Review*, June: 72–82.

Stead, I. M. 1998/2000. *The Salisbury Hoard*. Stroud, Tempus.

Steinbauer, Fredrich. 1969. *Neo-Melanesian Dictionary*. Kristen Press, Madang.

Stratford, Neil. 1997. *The Lewis Chessmen and the Enigma of the Hoard*. The British Museum Press, London.

Strathern, Andrew (ed.). 1979. *Ongka: A Self-account by a New Guinea Big-man*. St. Martin's Press, New York.

Swadling, Pamela. 1996. *Plumes from Paradise: Trade Cycles in Outer Southeast Asia and Their Impact on New Guinea and Nearby Islands until 1920*. Papua New Guinea National Museum, Boroko, in association with Robert Brown & Associates (Qld.) Pty. Ltd.

———. 2003. "Contribution to Appraising and Documenting the Theft of Prehistoric Stone Artifacts from PNG National Museum on 19 May 2003." Department of Archaeology and Natural History, The Australian National University, Canberra.

Swadling, P., and R. Hide. 2005. "Changing Landscape and Social Interaction: Looking at Agricultural History from a Sepik-Ramu Perspective." In Andrew Pawley, Robert Attenborough, Jack Golson, and Robin Hide (eds.), *Papuan Pasts Cultural, Linguistic and Biological Diversity of Papuan-speaking Peoples*. Pacific Linguistics, Canberra, 289–327.

Swadling, Pamela, et al. 1981/1986. *Papua New Guinea's Prehistory*. Papua New Guinea National Museum and Art Gallery in association with Gordon and Gotch, Boroko, Papua New Guinea.

Swadling, Pamela, Polly Wiessner, and Akii Tumu. N.d. "Prehistoric Stone Artefacts from Enga and the Implications of Links between the Highlands, Lowlands and Islands for Early Agriculture in Papua New Guinea." Unpublished manuscript.

Taçon, Paul, Jack Golson, Kirk Huffman, and Des Griffin. 2004. "Jim Specht's Brilliant Career: A Tribute." In Val Attenbrow and Richard Fullagar (eds.), *A Pacific Odyssey: Archaeology and Anthropology in the Western Pacific. Papers in Honour of Jim Specht*. Records of the Australian Museum, Supplement 29, Australian Museum, Sydney, 1–8.

Thomas, Nicholas. 1991. *Entangled Objects: Exchange, Material Culture, and Colonialism in the Pacific*. Harvard University Press, Cambridge.

The Trustees. 1974. *Guide to the Collections*. Papua New Guinea Public Museum and Art Gallery, Port Moresby.

Tubb, Kathryn W. (ed.). 1995. *Antiques Trade or Betrayed: Legal, Ethical and Conservation Issues*. Archetype Publications, London.

Tubb, Kathryn Walker, and Neil Brodie. 2001. "From Museum to Mantelpiece: The Antiquities Trade in the United Kingdom." In Robert Layton, Peter G. Stone, and Julian Thomas (eds.), *Destruction and Conservation of Cultural Property*. Routledge, London and New York, 102–16.

Tumu, A., E. Minion, A. Kayaks, and P. Wiessner. 1989. *A View of Enga Culture*. Kristen Press, Madang.

Tworek-Matuszkiewicz, Beata. 2001. "The Ambum Stone." *artonview* 26: 58–59.

United Nations Educational, Scientific and Cultural Organization. 1970. Convention on the Means of Prohibiting and Preventing the Illicit Import, Export and Transfer of Ownership of Cultural Property. UNESCO, Paris.

Vincze, Ernest, Charlie Nairn, Andrew Strathern, and Pattie Winter. *Ongka's Big Moka* (video recording). Granada Television International, London.

Waddell, Eric. 1972. *The Mound Builders: Agricultural Practices, Environment, and Society in the Central Highlands of New Guinea*. University of Washington Press, Seattle.

Wardell, Allen. 1994. *Island Ancestors: Oceanic Art from the Masco Collection*. University of Washington Press in Association with the Detroit Institute of Arts, Seattle and Detroit.

Watkins, Joe. 2000. *Indigenous Archaeology: American Indian Values and Scientific Practice*. AltaMira Press. Walnut Creek, CA.

Watson, James B. 1967. "Horticultural Traditions in the Eastern New Guinea Highlands." *Oceania* 38(2): 81–89.

———. 1977. "Pigs, Fodder, and the Jones Effect in Postipomoean New Guinea." *Ethnology* 16: 57–70.

———. 2000. "How Forgeries Corrupt Our Top Museums." *New Statesman* 13(637): 14–15.

Watson, Peter. 2001. "If It's Art, It Must Be Fake." *New Statesman* 14(653): 23–24.

Watson, Peter, and Cecilia Todeschini. 2006. *The Medici Conspiracy: The Illicit Journey of Looted Antiquities from Italy's Tomb Raiders to the World's Greatest Museums*. Public Affairs, New York.

Webb, Timothy. 2002. "Appropriating the Stones: The 'Elgin Marbles' and English National Taste." In Elazar Barkan and Ronald Bush (eds.), *Claiming the Stones, Naming the Bones*. The Getty Research Institute, Los Angeles, 51–96.

Welsch, Robert. 2000. "One Time, One Place, Three Collections: Colonial Processes and the Shaping of Some Museum Collections from German New Guinea." In Michael O'Hanlon and Robert L. Welsch (eds.), *Hunting the Gatherers: Ethnographic Collectors, Agents and Agency in Melanesia, 1870s–1930s*. Berghahm Books, New York, 155–79.

———. 2005. "One Symphony from Many Voices: Collectors, Collecting Activities, and the Culture of Collecting since 1870." In John Friede et al. New Guinea Art Masterpieces from the Jolika Collection of Marcia and John Friede (2 vols.). Fine Arts Museums of San Francisco in Association with 5 Continents Editions, Milan, Italy, 2:8–29.

Wiessner, Polly. 2002. "The Impact of Egalitarian Institutions on Warfare among the Enga: An Ethnohistorical Perspective." Paper prepared for the project: War and Society from an Archaeological and Social Anthropological Perspective, Seminar on Warfare in the South Pacific: Strategies, Histories and Politics, Moesgaard Museum, University of Aahaus, Denmark.

———. 2002. "Egalitarian Structures and the Institutionalisation of Inequality among the Enga." *Current Anthropology* 43(2): 233–69.

Wiessner, Polly, and Akii Tumu. 1998. *Historical Vines: Enga Networks of Exchange, Ritual, and Warfare in Papua New Guinea*. Smithsonian Institution Press, Washington, DC, and London.

Wilson, David. 1985. "Return and Restitution: A Museum Perspective." In Isabel McBryde (ed.), *Who Owns the Past*. Oxford University Press, Oxford, 99–106.

Index

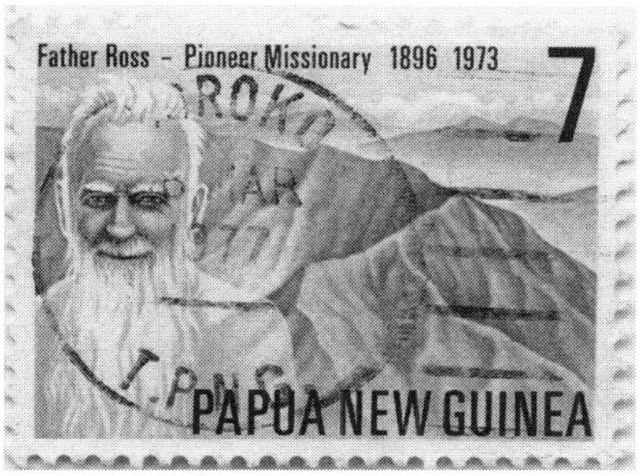

Personalities and Agents

Many individuals have contributed to the story of the Ambum Stone. Some of them I have met, others I communicated with over the telephone or corresponded with via e-mail or Queen's post, and others are lifelong friends. Included in the list of personalities are people that I did not have direct contact with but whose unpublished material influenced the course of the research. It is not surprising that there is a strong feeling of shared experience among those individuals who lived for part of their lives in Papua New Guinea. Their willingness to share information and search out old notes is seemingly boundless. Perhaps this comes from the indelible mark that is placed upon one's self after having spent time in "PNG."

Father H. Aufenanger, in 1965, replied to Goldman's request for information on the Ambum Stone. Aufenanger wrote to Goldman that he understood that Yampu village was the current site of the leper station and mentioned the name of Father Verwilt as being familiar with the place.

Chris Ballard studies the rituals and subsistence base of the southern highlanders as well as the history of European exploration of New Guinea. Chris shared with me his photographs of Ambum-like stones at Tari.

Jens Bjerre, author of *Savage New Guinea*, is an adventurer and photographer who worked in the highlands and elsewhere in the world (not retired at eighty years).

Paul Brennan worked as a linguist with Lutheran missionaries at Wabag during the 1970s and founded the Wabag cultural collection and museum. He has had a long-standing interest in the Ambum Stone. Paul is living in Hawaii.

L. D. Brongersma of the Rijksmuseum van Natuurlijke Historie wrote to Philip Goldman on 3 June 1965 in reply to Goldman's request for information on the Ambum Stone. He passed on a suggestion by Dr. R. M. Husson, curator of mammals at Rijksmuseum van Natuurlijke Historie, that the stone is carved in the form of a fruit bat (*Cynopterus* spp).

Ralph Bulmer was an anthropologist who worked in the highlands during the early 1960s. In the late 1960s he became professor of anthropology at the fledgling University of Papua New Guinea. It was in a copy of his letter to Paul Brennan of 10 November 1978 that I noticed that he had mentioned that Jens Bjerre and Denys Faithful would have been in the Ambum Valley at the time of the sale of the Ambum Stone (recently deceased).

Keith Buxton was a medical assistant in Papua New Guinea in the 1960s and then entered the travel industry and also dealt in artifacts. Keith's obituary by his daughter Michelle is on the "Una Voce"—www.pngaa.net (accessed on 15 May 2007).

Wally Caruana as a curator at the National Gallery of Australia is quoted by the *Canberra Times*. He is a specialist in Aboriginal art (retired).

John Coleman is a former patrol officer who once owned the Wabag trade store. He was a successful businessman in Mt. Hagen and retired to live in Queensland.

Barry Craig is an ethnologist with extensive experience in the western highlands of Papua New Guinea, including the collecting of artifacts for the Commonwealth Art Advisory Board. More recently he was a curator of the Papua New Guinea National Museum and Art Gallery and is now at the South Australian Museum. In his doctoral thesis he documents aspects of the illegal artifact trade in Papua New Guinea.

Robert Deane as assistant director of Administrative and Technical Services at the Australian National Gallery, spoke to Geoffrey Mosuwadoga (director of the Papua New Guinea Public Museum and Art Gallery) in December 1975 about the Ambum Stone during Mosuwadoga's visit to the Australian National Gallery. This was prior to the purchase of the Ambum Stone by the gallery (retired).

Alan Dodge, on 27 October 1975 as senior research officer, prepared the curator's report as a prelude to the Australian National Gallery purchasing the Ambum Stone. This report and the director's recommendation are included as an appendix to the minutes of the Council, Australian National Gallery. At the time that Dodge prepared the report, the Gallery had received the first letter from Mosuwadoga (on behalf of the president of the trustees, Michael Somare) advising the gallery to proceed with the purchase; two months later a second letter, this one from Mosuwadoga, was received advising the Gallery that the Papua New Guinea National Museum and Art Gallery wished to be involved in the purchase (director, Art Gallery of Western Australian).

Denys Faithful as a patrol officer was active in the western highlands during the early 1960s when he collected artifacts for the museum (retired in Queensland).

Ian Farrington is an archaeologist at The Australian National University who specializes in the prehistory of Peru. He was active in investigating the Paracas textile once held by the National Gallery of Australia that was returned to Peru.

Martin Fowler is the architect who designed the Papua New Guinea National Museum and Art Gallery building (now living in Melbourne).

Bill Gammage was a lecturer at the University of Papua New Guinea, then a professor of history at the University of Adelaide and The Australian National University. Bill put me in contact with former government medical and administrative officers. His award-winning book *The Sky Travellers: Journeys in New Guinea 1938–1939* provides valuable insights into the relationships between the highlanders and the members of the Australian expedition that explored the cultural landscape of the Ambum River valley (retired).

Philip Goldman purchased the Ambum Stone in 1962–1963 and brought it into prominence through publication in the *Journal of the Polynesian Society*. After lengthy negotiations, he sold the Ambum Stone to the Australian National Gallery in 1977. Philip highly valued the Ambum Stone, shared his interests with me, continually sought further information on its ethnographic context. He was disappointed that at the time little was known about such objects. He is retired and is living in the United Kingdom.

Jack Golson is emeritus professor of archaeology at The Australian National University and an authority on the foundations of prehistoric agriculture in the highlands. It was his discovery and dating of the archaeological context of a fragment of a prehistoric carved stone bowl from his excavations at Kuk that provided the 5,000-year-old date for the fragment.

Ben Heller is best known as an artifact collector and dealer who sold *Blue Poles*, a painting by Jackson Pollock, to the Australian National Gallery for a profit on the order of $1 million (deceased).

Robin Hide is an anthropologist at The Australian National University with research experience in the highlands.

Hartmut Holtzknecht is well informed on the history of the Lutheran missionaries of New Guinea (his family being the third generation to experience the territory), and now is a researcher at The Australian National University.

Captain Frank Hurley was a larger-than-life explorer and photographer with Mawson's 1911 expedition to Antarctica and also served with the Australian Imperial Forces in France in 1917 and in the Middle East in 1918. He explored and collected in the Gulf of Papua in the 1920s and locked horns with Sir Hubert Murray over the export of artifacts (deceased).

Ron Ingles was the operator of the Wabag trade store in the early 1960s and is believed to have been the original purchaser of the Ambum Stone. I searched, but was unable to find him.

B. E. W. Kelson, as secretary, Commonwealth Art Advisory Board, in March of 1972 drafted correspondence to Philip Goldman that led to the acquisition by the gallery of the Ambum Stone.

Kendi brothers circa 1962 claim to have removed the Ambum Stone from the village ceremonial ground where it had been secreted by their father. They met with Polly Wiessner in October of 2001 and discussed their actions. The brothers told Polly that they had sold the artifact to the operator of the Wabag trade store, recalling his name as Ron Ingles.

Brian Kennedy was director of the National Gallery of Australia at the time of my investigation into the provenance and purchase two decades earlier of the Ambum Stone.

Father Tony Krajic is a retired highland missionary now residing at the home of his order in Illinois. My correspondence to him was unanswered.

Rod Lacey has written a history of Papua New Guinea. Rod provided information on the activities of missionaries and government officers (lives in Ballarat).

Beverly Lawrence was the spouse of the operator of the Wabag trade store in the mid-1960s. She recalls that Ron Ingles had a lockup for artifacts under the house. Beverly has retired and lives with her husband at Byron Bay.

Valda Leehy as secretary of the Interim Council of the Australian National Gallery drafted correspondence that was sent to the Papua New Guinea National Museum and Art Gallery that facilitated the purchase of the Ambum Stone.

Sir William MacGregor was instrumental in the acquisition for the Australian government of a substantial collection of artifacts that during the war years was sent to Australian museums for safe keeping (deceased).

Roy Mackay was preparatory in charge of the Papua New Guinea Museum. Roy contributed substantially to the development of the museum, particularly the natural history collections and was active in enforcing the export controls (retired).

Sir Alan Mann was a judge in the territories and played a major role in the founding of the Papua New Guinea Museum in the 1960s (deceased).

Robyn Maxwell lectures at The Australian National University and is a curator at the National Gallery of Australia. Robyn was referred to by the *Canberra Times,* on 12 September 2000, as a spokesperson for the gallery. She is a specialist in Southern Asian textiles.

Mervyn Meggitt conducted anthropological research in the 1950s and 1960s with the Mae Enga (recently deceased).

James Mollison was the inaugural director of the Australian National Gallery at the time of the purchase of the Ambum Stone.

Geoffrey Mosuwadoga, an artist from the Trobriand Island, was the director of the Papua New Guinea Museum and Art Gallery at the time of the purchase by the Australian National Gallery of the Ambum Stone (deceased).

Sir Hubert Murray, as a judge and administrator of Papua, was instrumental in the drafting of the 1913 antiquities legislation, and most likely it was his authority that fostered the development in the 1920s of the plans for a museum to be constructed in Port Moresby. Sir Hubert seized ethnographic material collected by Hurley (deceased).

Helen Musa is the arts editor of the *Canberra Times* who sought answers to the breaking of the Ambum Stone when it was on loan to the Marseilles Musée D'Arts Africains, Océaniens, Amérindiens.

Douglas Newton was an authority on the art of Papua New Guinea, curator of the Museum of Primitive Art, New York, and advisor to the Australian National Gallery. Douglas corresponded freely with me. He initially advised against the purchase of the Ambum Stone (recently deceased).

Helen Parrott, with Ian Farrington, coauthored a report on the Paracas textile that was held by the National Gallery of Australia and repatriated to Peru.

John Santolin is the Freedom of Information officer at the National Gallery of Australia; he compiled the documents that were supplied to me.

Dirk Smidt was assistant director and director of the Papua New Guinea National Museum and Art Gallery and added to the collections through rigorous enforcement of the export controls, purchase from dealers, and collecting expeditions. Dirk is a curator at the Rijksmuseum voor Volkenkunde, Leiden.

Sir Michael Somare was a schoolteacher then the president of the Board of Trustees of the Papua New Guinea Museum and Art Gallery. He has served as the chief minister and as a prime minister. Sir Michael gave his unqualified support to the enforcement of the artifact export controls.

James Specht, as a curator of anthropology at the Australian Museum in Sydney, maintained a close relationship with the Papua New Guinea Public Museum and Art Gallery. Jim provided me with papers documenting the Murray-Hurley controversy of the 1920s. He is retired but has a continuing association with the Australian Museum, Sydney.

Michel Strauss is the London art expert who provided a second opinion on the value of the Ambum Stone. He agreed with Newton that it was exceptional and stated that "it could be worthwhile paying over the odds for it, such as $50,000 or $60,000."

Glenn Summerhayes was an archaeologist at The Australian National University active in Papua New Guinea. He provided photographs of the carved stone from Tukisenda that is similar in appearance to the Ambum Stone. Glen is now a professor of archaeology at the University of Otago, Dunedin.

Pamela Swadling was a curator of the Papua New Guinea National Museum and Art Gallery and is the foremost authority on prehistoric carved stone artifacts. Pamela is a visiting fellow at The Australian National University.

Bill Tomasetti was a retired Papua New Guinea government officer who provided information on other ex-government officers (recently deceased).

Akii Tumu is the coauthor of *Historical Vines*, and director of the Enga Museum at Wabag in the highlands of Papua New Guinea.

Beata Tworek-Matuszkiewicz is the conservator at the National Gallery of Australia who undertook conservation of the Ambum Stone.

Chris J. Vass, a former government officer in the Western Highlands, provided me with the names of missionaries and government officials that were active in the Ambum Valley during the 1960s.

Father Joe Verwilt replied to my request for information. Father Joe worked from January 1960 to June 1966 in the Ambum area and had no knowledge of the Ambum Stone. His colleague Father Gerard Bus, who was in the Wabag area from 1948, knew nothing of the stone other than having seen it on a postage stamp. He is retired in Belgium.

Paul Wholt was a linguist with the Lutheran missions in the Wabag area and lives in the United States.

Polly Wiessner is the coauthor of *Historical Vines*, the definitive study of Enga rituals and cult objects. As a member of the anthropology faculty at the University of Utah, Polly supported the investigations with fieldwork. She was the joint author of the preliminary paper presented at the "Papua New Guinea Then and Now" symposium held at the University of Sydney.

Norm Wilson started his career in Papua New Guinea as a patrol officer and became a trustee of the Papua New Guinea Public Museum and Art Gallery. Norm facilitated the research by providing contact information for former government officers (scholar and retired).

Christina Wright, as the administrative officer at the Papua New Guinea National Museum and Art Gallery during the 1960s through to the 1980s, was the mainstay of its operations. She retired and enrolled as a postgraduate student at Charles Sturt University, Bathurst, where she completed a master's thesis on the history of the Papua New Guinea National Museum and Art Gallery (recently deceased).

Bishop Doug Young is situated in the Highlands as the bishop of the Roman Catholic Society of the Divine Word. He assisted me with addresses for missionaries who had once been active in the Ambum Valley.

About the Author

Brian Egloff holds a PhD in prehistory from the Australian National University as well as an MA from the University of North Carolina and a BSc from the University of Wisconsin-Milwaukee. He is an adjunct associate professor of cultural heritage studies at the University of Canberra and president of the ICOMOS International Committee for Archaeological Heritage Management. His first major work was with Joffre Coe and Bennie Keel when he undertook the historical archaeology component of the National Science Foundation funded study of the cultural and ecological base of the Cherokee nation. This was followed by doctoral research on the recent prehistory of eastern Papua. He has served as an assistant to the director, Papua New Guinea National Museum and Art Gallery (1971–1978), he was the director of the Port Arthur Conservation and Development Project (1981–1987), and he co-managed, with Benita Johnson, the Tam Ting Caves Conservation Project in the Lao PDR (1993–1997). Over the past thirty years he has published reports, monographs, and books dealing with Aboriginal land rights in southeastern Australia. In 2007, as a visiting scholar at the Getty Conservation Institute, he drafted international guidelines for archaeological heritage management.